APRIL 2017

South China Sea Lawfare:

Post-Arbitration Policy Options and Future Prospects

Edited by *Fu-Kuo Liu*, *Keyuan Zou*, *Shicun Wu*, and *Jonathan Spangler*

South China Sea Think Tank
南海智庫

Taiwan Center for Security Studies
臺灣安全研究中心

This report is the result of a collaborative effort by an international team of authors. The content of the report does not necessarily reflect the views of the individual authors, the editors, their respective institutions, or the governments involved in the South China Sea maritime territorial disputes.

Citation:
Fu-Kuo Liu, Keyuan Zou, Shicun Wu, and Jonathan Spangler (eds.), *South China Sea Lawfare: Post-Arbitration Policy Options and Future Prospects*, Taipei: South China Sea Think Tank / Taiwan Center for Security Studies, April 20, 2017.

Citation for individual chapters:
Author Name, "Chapter Title," in Fu-Kuo Liu, Keyuan Zou, Shicun Wu, and Jonathan Spangler (eds.), *South China Sea Lawfare: Post-Arbitration Policy Options and Future Prospects*, Taipei: South China Sea Think Tank / Taiwan Center for Security Studies, April 20, 2017.

South China Sea Think Tank
Asia-Pacific Policy Research Association
Fl. 10, No. 221, Sec. 4, Zhongxiao East Rd.
Daan District, Taipei City
Taiwan (ROC) 10690
+886 927 727 325
research@scstt.org

Taiwan Center for Security Studies
No. 64, Wanshou Rd.
Wenshan District, Taipei City
Taiwan (ROC) 11666
+886 2 8237 7213
tcsstw.org@gmail.com

Cover photo:
ROC Coast Guard humanitarian rescue drill near Itu Aba (Taiping) Island on November 29, 2016 (ROC Coast Guard)

NTD 300 / USD 10 / RMB 70 (print)
ISBN 978-986-92828-2-6 (print)
ISBN 978-986-92828-3-3 (ebook/pdf)

Contents

TCSS

Taiwan Center for Security Studies (TCSS) serves as a platform for research and dialogue between international experts on issues of East Asian security and cross-strait relations. It is affiliated with National Chengchi University in Taipei, Taiwan.

mcsstw.org

SOUTH CHINA SEA THINK TANK 南海智庫

South China Sea Think Tank (SCSTT) is an independent, non-profit organization that promotes dialogue, research, and education on South China Sea issues. It does not take any institutional position on the disputes. SCSTT is part of the Asia-Pacific Policy Research Association (APPRA).

scstt.org

Executive Summary

On July 12, 2016, the Tribunal in the South China Sea arbitration case issued its Award, officially bringing closure to the arbitral proceedings initiated by the Philippines against China in early 2013. In the Award, the Tribunal's conclusions overwhelmingly supported the Philippines' positions regarding almost all of the fifteen submissions in its Memorial.[1] The Tribunal also rejected or opted not to take into account the vast majority of China's positions as elaborated through official statements and was similarly not persuaded by arguments issued or evi-

The Award has significant implications for the South China Sea maritime territorial disputes, which remain one of the most potent and complex issues affecting stability and security in the Asia-Pacific region and beyond.

dence presented by Taiwan.

The Award, especially due to relevant countries' policy responses and the enduring controversy over its content, has significant implications for the South China Sea maritime territorial disputes, which remain one of the most potent and complex issues affecting stability and security in the Asia-Pacific region and beyond. In the post-arbitration context, rival claimants and major stakeholders have been forced to recalibrate their rhet-

---

1 See "Table 1: Summary of the Philippines' Submissions and Tribunal's Awards" in the introduction to this report.

oric, strategies, and policies in order to safeguard their interests and rights in the maritime area while maintaining an image internationally that is conducive to achieving these aims.

This report, entitled *South China Sea Lawfare: Post-Arbitration Policy Options and Future Prospects*, builds upon the success of the first *South China Sea Lawfare* report that was published in early 2016.[2] By bringing together an international team of experts writing on the different approaches of each claimant and stakeholder, it aims to serve as a more inclusive reference on post-arbitration South China Sea policy issues than the many other analyses published in the aftermath of the Award.

In Part I: Introduction, the report begins by giving a brief overview of the arbitral proceedings in historical perspective and summarizing the legal positions of the parties involved and the Tribunal's conclusions as described in its

> Bringing together an international team of experts writing on the different approaches of each claimant and stakeholder, it aims to serve as a more inclusive reference on post-arbitration South China Sea policy issues than the many other analyses published in the aftermath of the Award.

---

2 On January 29, 2016, the first South China Sea Lawfare report was published by the South China Sea Think Tank and the Taiwan Center for Security Studies. Fourteen authors from ten countries contributed to the publication, for which research began immediately following the release of the Award on Jurisdiction and Admissibility on October 29, 2015, in the Philippines v. China arbitration case. The report can be downloaded from http://scstt.org/reports/2016/525/.

two awards. In Part II: Rival Claimants and Part III: Major Stakeholders, the chapters focus on (1) the specific policy approaches of each country or actor; (2) the implications of the Award for each; (3) the legal, diplomatic, and security policy options available to them; and (4) their future prospects in the post-arbitration context of the South China Sea. In Part IV: Conclusion, the report explores the implications of the Award for international maritime law and the future of maritime territorial disputes. By encouraging and compiling a diversity of views on the South China Sea, the editors hope that this report will serve over the coming years as a resource for policymakers, a foundation for future research, and an example of constructive international collaboration in the midst of the disputes.

By encouraging and compiling a diversity of views on the South China Sea, the editors hope that this report will serve as a resource for policymakers, a foundation for future research, and an example of constructive international collaboration in the midst of the disputes.

Part I:
Introduction

South China Sea Policy Options in the Post-Arbitration Context

Jonathan Spangler

Abstract

The arbitration case and the Tribunal's conclusions as outlined in the Award have major legal, diplomatic, and security implications for rival claimants and major stakeholders in the South China Sea. As a result, states and other actors must consider their relevant policy options and proceed accordingly. This chapter begins by providing a condensed historical overview of the arbitral proceedings, which are summarized by dividing the timeline into the pre-arbitration context, the Philippines' initiation and China's response, the Award on Jurisdiction and Admissibility of October 2015, and the Award of July 2016 on the merits and remaining issues in the arbitration case. It then considers the implications of the Award and the related common policy options available to multiple claimants and stakeholders. Legally, these implications and policy options relate to the status of features, sovereignty issues, maritime rights and entitlements, and obligations in maritime spaces. Diplomatically, they involve recalibrating diplomatic relations and preferences regarding the means of dispute settlement. In terms of security, they include legal justification for military operations, emboldened securitization efforts, and opportunities for confidence-building and cooperation. In considering these issues, the chapter aims not to provide an exhaustive account of all relevant implications and policy options but to serve as a foundation for the chapters that follow as well as future research and policy discussions on the South China Sea maritime territorial disputes.

Introduction

Over the past year, many in-depth historical accounts and comprehensive analyses of the arbitral proceedings and actors' responses to the arbitration case have been published. Among these, there is *South China Sea Lawfare: Legal Perspectives and International Responses to the Philippines v. China Arbitration Case*, the predecessor to this report, also jointly published by the South China Sea Think Tank and Taiwan Center for Security Studies. Released in January

2016, three months after the Award on Jurisdiction and Admissibility was issued by the Tribunal, that report included contributions from sixteen scholars who were collectively tasked with providing detailed analyses of the perspectives of ten rival claimants or major stakeholders in the South China Sea maritime territorial disputes.

In this report, we have encouraged our team of authors to minimize discussions of the background of the arbitral proceedings in order to focus specifically on the present and future of the South China Sea disputes in the post-arbitration context.

To serve as a basic foundation for readers, this chapter first provides a very brief timeline of the arbitral proceedings.[1] It then offers a bird's-eye view of the legal, diplomatic, and security implications of the Award and policy options for rival claimants and major stakeholders moving forward as discussed in much greater detail in the chapters that follow.

> China and the Philippines have exchanged views on the maritime disputes since the 1970s in various diplomatic fora.

Philippines v. China in a Nutshell

Regardless of one's views on the Philippines v. China arbitration case itself, there is a general consensus among government officials, researchers, and non-academic observers that the arbitral proceedings have borne major impacts on the South China Sea maritime territorial disputes. Although the details of the proceedings, different actors' legal perspectives, and relevant responses are complex and beyond the scope of this brief introduction, the issue can be roughly summarized by dividing the timeline into the pre-arbitration context, the Philippines' initiation and China's response, the Award on Jurisdiction and Admissibility of October 2015, and the Award of July 2016 on the merits and remaining issues in the arbitration case.

Pre-Arbitration Context

In the decades prior to the arbitration case, the South China Sea witnessed various rounds of bilateral and multilateral negotiations regarding dispute settlement. All the while, the history of the maritime area has been punctu-

---

1   For a more detailed historical overview, please refer to the introduction of the previous report. See Jonathan Spangler and Olga Daksueva, "Philippines v. China Arbitration Case: Background, Legal Perspectives, and International Responses," in Fu-Kuo Liu and Jonathan Spangler (eds.), *South China Sea Lawfare: Legal Perspectives and International Responses to the Philippines v. China Arbitration Case*, January 29, 2016, pp. 17–37.

ated by armed clashes, occupations by force and without, and heated political rhetoric mostly involving reassertions of sovereignty or accusations of illegal actions by rival claimants. China and the Philippines have exchanged views on the maritime disputes since the 1970s in various diplomatic fora. Bilateral efforts resulted in multiple statements and agreements, including the Joint Statement between the People's Republic of China and the Republic of the Philippines concerning Consultations on the South China Sea and on Other Areas of Cooperation in 1995, the Joint Statement of the China-Philippines Experts Group Meeting on Confidence-Building Measures in 1999, the Joint Statement between the Government of the People's Republic of China and the Government of the Republic of the Philippines on the Framework of Bilateral Cooperation in the Twenty-First Century in 2000, and a joint press statement following the third China-Philippines Experts' Group Meeting on Confidence-Building Measures in 2001.[2] In 2002, the Declaration on the Conduct of Parties in the South China Sea (DOC) was signed between member states of the Association of Southeast Asian Nations (ASEAN) and China. After that, negotiations within ASEAN on adopting a legally binding Code of Conduct in the South China Sea (COC) continued, eventually resulting in a draft agreement being accepted in 2012 and preliminary discussions with China but with no substantive agreement having yet been reached.

> The history of the maritime area has been punctuated by armed clashes, occupations by force and without, and heated political rhetoric mostly involving reassertions of sovereignty or accusations of illegal actions by rival claimants.

Initiation and Response

On January 22, 2013, the Philippines formally initiated arbitral proceedings against China under Article 287 and Annex VII of the United Nations Convention on the Law of the Sea (UNCLOS). On February 19, 2013, China, via a Note Verbale, rejected and returned the Philippines' Notification and Statement of Claim initiating the proceedings, stated that it would neither accept nor participate in the arbitration, and provided reasoning to support its position.

---

2   Jonathan Spangler and Olga Daksueva, "Philippines v. China Arbitration Case: Background, Legal Perspectives, and International Responses," in Fu-Kuo Liu and Jonathan Spangler (eds.), *South China Sea Lawfare: Legal Perspectives and International Responses to the Philippines v. China Arbitration Case*, January 29, 2016, pp. 17–37.

Philippines' Submissions

The Philippines, in its Memorial presented to the Tribunal on March 30, 2014, requested that the Tribunal issue an Award regarding fifteen submissions related to the status and legal entitlements of certain features in the South China Sea, the conduct of states and other actors in the disputed areas, and the legal legitimacy of China's historical claims. These are summarized in Table 1. In its testimony during the arbitral proceedings, the Philippines also requested that the Tribunal address other key issues beyond the scope of its fifteen Submissions, including the legal status of features in the Spratly Islands.

Award on Jurisdiction and Admissibility

Following a hearing in July 2015 and several months of deliberations, the Tribunal issued its Award on Jurisdiction and Admissibility on October 29, 2015. In this preliminary award, the arbitrators concluded that they had jurisdiction regarding seven of the Philippines' Submissions, reserved consideration on another seven, and requested clarification about one. (See Table 1.) China responded with a foreign ministry statement that declared that the Award "is null and void, and has no binding effect on China," criticized the Philippine government for its "political provocation under the cloak of law," and reiterated its previous position of non-acceptance and non-participation.

Award on Merits and Remaining Issues

From November 24–30, 2015, the Tribunal held the Hearing on the Merits and Remaining Issues of Jurisdiction and Admissibility, in which it heard the Philippines' arguments related to the arbitration case. On July 12, 2016, the Arbitral Tribunal issued its Award. The Philippines' submissions and additional claims, the Tribunal's conclusions contained in its Award on Jurisdiction and Admissibility, and its conclusions made in the Award are summarized in Table 1 below.

> China responded with a foreign ministry statement that declared that the Award "is null and void, and has no binding effect on China," criticized the Philippine government for its "political provocation under the cloak of law," and reiterated its previous position of non-acceptance and non-participation.

Implications and Policy Options

The profound implications for states and actors involved in the South China Sea disputes come not only from the content of the Award itself but also from the responses and actions of others in the post-arbitration context. For analytical purposes, the implications and relevant policy options are roughly categorized in this chapter and throughout the report as relating to legal, diplomatic, and security issues. Needless to say, these issues are tightly intertwined, and there is much overlap and interaction between these loose categorizations. Nevertheless, they are useful in achieving the aim of more clearly illustrating the key issues that are at stake. Many implications and policy options are shared in part by different states, regional groupings, and other actors. At the same time, due to the unique contexts in which each of them operates, there are also other implications and policy options specific to certain claimants or stakeholders, but these will be addressed in full in subsequent chapters.

the legal implications resulting from the conclusions outlined in the Award demand that rival claimants and major stakeholders consider their relevant policy options and proceed accordingly.

Status of Features

The Tribunal's conclusions about the legal status of features have major implications for maritime delimitation in the South China Sea. For both those whose legal positions have been backed up by the arbitrators and those whose national interests have been negatively impacted, key decisions must be made as a result. In particular, countries have been forced to express support for the Award, reject it and provide sufficient justification for doing so, or find a safe middle ground based on partial acceptance and/or ambiguity. Although it is yet to be seen, the reality is that even those that have explicitly expressed support for the Award would likely no longer agree with it in its entirety if the Tribunal's conclusions were used in the future in a way that was detrimental to those countries' own national interests.

> Countries have been forced to express support for the Award, reject it and provide sufficient justification for doing so, or find a safe middle ground based on partial acceptance and/or ambiguity.

> The Award made implicit legal conclusions about sovereignty.

Legal Implications

The Tribunal's interpretations of international maritime law, particularly those affecting the legal status of features, sovereignty issues, maritime rights and entitlements, and obligations in maritime spaces have effectively redrawn the legal landscape of the South China Sea. In turn,

In other words, even explicit and apparently full support today may only translate to partial support in the future. History shows that countries are often unlikely to participate in compulsory international arbitration mechanisms when the outcome would clearly prove detrimental to their interests.

	Philippines' Submission or Additional Claim March 30, 2014; November 30, 2015	Tribunal's Position in Award on Jurisdiction and Admissibility October 29, 2015	Tribunal's Position in Final Award July 12, 2016
1	China's maritime entitlements in the South China Sea, like those of the Philippines, may not extend beyond those permitted by [UNCLOS].	Reserved consideration	UNCLOS "defines the scope of maritime entitlements in the South China Sea, which may not extend beyond the limits imposed therein." (X, 1203, B, 1)
2	China's claims to sovereign rights and jurisdiction, and to "historic rights", with respect to the maritime areas of the South China Sea encompassed by the so-called "nine-dash line" are contrary to the Convention and without lawful effect to the extent that they exceed the geographic and substantive limits of China's maritime entitlements under UNCLOS.	Reserved consideration	China's claims regarding "historic rights, or other sovereign rights or jurisdiction, [within] the 'nine-dash line' are contrary to [UNCLOS and have no] lawful effect [where] they exceed the geographic and substantive limits of China's maritime entitlements under [UNCLOS]". UNCLOS "superseded any historic rights, or other sovereign rights or jurisdiction, in excess of the limits imposed therein." (X, 1203, B, 2)
3	Scarborough Shoal generates no entitlement to an exclusive economic zone or continental shelf.	Had jurisdiction	Scarborough Shoal is a rock without EEZ or continental shelf entitlements. (X, 1203, B, 6) It is entitled to territorial waters.
4	Mischief Reef, Second Thomas Shoal and Subi Reef are low-tide elevations that do not generate entitlement to a territorial sea, exclusive economic zone or continental shelf, and are not features that are capable of appropriation by occupation or otherwise.	Had jurisdiction	Mischief Reef and Second Thomas Shoal are low-tide elevations without territorial sea, EEZ, or continental shelf entitlements. They are not "capable of appropriation." (X, 1203, B, 4) Subi Reef is a low-tide elevation without territorial sea, EEZ, or continental shelf entitlements. It is not "capable of appropriation, but may be used as the baseline for measuring the breadth of the territorial sea of high-tide features situated at a distance not exceeding the breadth of the territorial sea." (X, 1203, B, 5) It is within the 12-nm territorial waters of Sandy Cay, which is a high-tide feature. (X, 1203, B, 3, d)
5	Mischief Reef and Second Thomas Shoal are part of the exclusive economic zone and continental shelf of the Philippines.	Reserved consideration	Mischief Reef and Second Thomas Shoal are low-tide elevations without territorial sea, EEZ, or continental shelf entitlements, and "there are no overlapping [EEZ or continental shelf] entitlements … in the areas." (X, 1203, B, 4)
6	Gaven Reef and McKennan Reef (including Hughes Reef) are low-tide elevations that do not generate entitlement to a territorial sea, exclusive economic zone or continental shelf, but their low-water line may be used to determine the baseline from which the breadth of the territorial sea of Namyit and Sin Cowe, respectively, is measured.	Had jurisdiction	Gaven Reef (South) and Hughes Reef are low-tide elevations without territorial sea, EEZ, or continental shelf entitlements. They are not "capable of appropriation, but may be used as the baseline for measuring the breadth of the territorial sea of high-tide features situated at a distance not exceeding the breadth of the territorial sea." (X, 1203, B, 5) Gaven Reef (South) is within the 12-nm territorial waters of Gaven Reef (North) and Namyit Island, which are high-tide features. (X, 1203, B, 3, e) Hughes Reef is within the 12-nm territorial waters of McKennan Reef and Sin Cowe Island, which are high-tide features. (X, 1203, B, 3, f)
7	Johnson Reef, Cuarteron Reef and Fiery Cross Reef generate no entitlement to an exclusive economic zone or continental shelf.	Had jurisdiction	Johnson Reef, Cuarteron Reef and Fiery Cross Reef are rocks without EEZ or continental shelf entitlements. (X, 1203, B, 6) They are entitled to territorial waters.

	Philippines' Submission or Additional Claim March 30, 2014; November 30, 2015	Tribunal's Position in Award on Jurisdiction and Admissibility October 29, 2015	Tribunal's Position in Final Award July 12, 2016
8	China has unlawfully interfered with the enjoyment and exercise of the sovereign rights of the Philippines with respect to the living and non-living resources of its exclusive economic zone and continental shelf.	Reserved consideration	China "breached its obligations under Article 56" regarding "the Philippines' sovereign rights over the living resources of its exclusive economic zone" by implementing its 2012 South China Sea fishing moratorium and not making "exception for areas of the South China Sea falling within the exclusive economic zone of the Philippines [or] limiting the moratorium to Chinese flagged vessels." (X, 1203, B, 9)
9	China has unlawfully failed to prevent its nationals and vessels from exploiting the living resources in the exclusive economic zone of the Philippines.	Reserved consideration	China "breached its obligations under Article 58(3)" by not preventing "fishing by Chinese flagged vessels" at Mischief Reef and Second Thomas Shoal, which are within the Philippines' EEZ, in May 2013. (X, 1203, B, 11)
10	China has unlawfully prevented Philippine fishermen from pursuing their livelihoods by interfering with traditional fishing activities at Scarborough Shoal.	Had jurisdiction	China has, since May 2012, "unlawfully prevented fishermen from the Philippines from engaging in traditional fishing at Scarborough Shoal," which "has been a traditional fishing ground for fishermen of many nationalities." (X, 1203, B, 11)
11	China has violated its obligations under the Convention to protect and preserve the marine environment at Scarborough Shoal and Second Thomas Shoal.	Had jurisdiction	China "breached its obligations under Articles 192 and 194(5)" because it "was aware of, tolerated, protected, and failed to prevent" environmentally destructive activities by fishermen from Chinese flagged vessels, who "have engaged in the harvesting of endangered species on a significant scale[and] the harvesting of giant clams in a manner that is severely destructive of the coral reef ecosystem" in the South China Sea. (X, 1203, B, 12)
12	China's occupation and construction activities on Mischief Reef (a) violate the provisions of the Convention concerning artificial islands, installations and structures; (b) violate China's duties to protect and preserve the marine environment under the Convention; and (c) constitute unlawful acts of attempted appropriation in violation of the Convention.	Reserved consideration	China "breached its obligations under Articles 123, 192, 194(1), 194(5), 197, and 206" because its land reclamation and construction have "caused severe, irreparable harm to the coral reef ecosystem" without cooperating, coordinating, or communicating environmental impact assessments with other countries. (X, 1203, B, 13) China "breached Articles 60 and 80" through its "construction of artificial islands, installations, and structures at Mischief Reef without the authorisation of the Philippines" because the feature is a low-tide elevation not capable of appropriation within the Philippines' EEZ. (X, 1203, B, 14)
13	China has breached its obligations under the Convention by operating its law enforcement vessels in a dangerous manner causing serious risk of collision to Philippine vessels navigating in the vicinity of Scarborough Shoal.	Had jurisdiction	China "breached its obligations under Article 94" and "violated Rules 2, 6, 7, 8, 15, and 16 of the Convention on the International Regulations for Preventing Collisions at Sea, 1972" by causing "serious risk of collision and danger to Philippine ships and personnel" through the "operation of its law enforcement vessels" on April 28 and May 26, 2012. (X, 1203, B, 15)

	Philippines' Submission or Additional Claim March 30, 2014; November 30, 2015	Tribunal's Position in Award on Jurisdiction and Admissibility October 29, 2015	Tribunal's Position in Final Award July 12, 2016
14	Since the commencement of this arbitration in January 2013, China has unlawfully aggravated and extended the dispute by, among other things: (a) interfering with the Philippines' rights of navigation in the waters at, and adjacent to, Second Thomas Shoal; (b) preventing the rotation and resupply of Philippine personnel stationed at Second Thomas Shoal; and (c) endangering the health and well-being of Philippine personnel stationed at Second Thomas Shoal.	Reserved consideration	China has aggravated the disputes over "the status of maritime features in the Spratly Islands" as well as those about the countries' "respective rights and entitlements" and "the protection and preservation of the marine environment" at Mischief Reef. (X, 1203, B, 16) China has enlarged the disputes over "the protection and preservation of the marine environment to Cuarteron Reef, Fiery Cross Reef, Gaven Reef (North), Johnson Reef, Hughes Reef, and Subi Reef." (X, 1203, B, 16)
15	Original: China shall desist from further unlawful claims and activities. Amended: China shall respect the rights and freedoms of the Philippines under the Convention, shall comply with its duties under the Convention, including those relevant to the protection and preservation of the marine environment in the South China Sea, and shall exercise its rights and freedoms in the South China Sea with due regard to those of the Philippines under the Convention.	Requested clarification	China should have abstained from activities with "a prejudicial effect [on] the execution of the decisions to be given" and activities that "might aggravate or extend the dispute during" the arbitral proceedings. (X, 1203, B, 16)
	Additional Issues		
1	Itu Aba (Taiping) Island is a rock, not an island, under Article 121(1) and 121(3) of UNCLOS. (Itu Aba Island is occupied by Taiwan and is the largest feature in the Spratly Islands.)		Itu Aba (Taiping) Island is a rock without EEZ or continental shelf entitlements because "no maritime feature claimed by China within 200 nautical miles of Mischief Reef or Second Thomas Shoal constitutes a fully entitled island." (X, 1203, A, 2, a)
2	Thitu Island is a rock, not an island, under Article 121(1) and 121(3) of UNCLOS. (Thitu Island is occupied by the Philippines and is the second-largest feature in the Spratly Islands.)		Thitu Island is a rock without EEZ or continental shelf entitlements because "no maritime feature claimed by China within 200 nautical miles of Mischief Reef or Second Thomas Shoal constitutes a fully entitled island." (X, 1203, A, 2, a)

	Philippines' Submission or Additional Claim March 30, 2014; November 30, 2015	Tribunal's Position in Award on Jurisdiction and Admissibility October 29, 2015	Tribunal's Position in Final Award July 12, 2016
3	West York Island is a rock, not an island, under Article 121(1) and 121(3) of UNCLOS. (West York Island is occupied by the Philippines and is the third-largest feature in the Spratly Islands.)		West York Island is a rock without EEZ or continental shelf entitlements because "no maritime feature claimed by China within 200 nautical miles of Mischief Reef or Second Thomas Shoal constitutes a fully entitled island." (X, 1203, A, 2, a)

Table 1 Summary of the Philippines' Submissions and Tribunal's Awards

Sovereignty Issues

Although the Tribunal, China, and the Philippines all separately recognized in official statements that the Tribunal did not have jurisdiction over sovereignty issues, discussions of other issues in the Award made implicit legal conclusions about sovereignty. For example, the arbitrators (1) interpreted the legal status of features (i.e., the 'rocks' or 'islands' question) in the Spratly Islands and Scarborough Shoal, (2) recognized the Philippines' 200-nautical-mile exclusive economic zone (EEZ) extending from its coastlines, (3) concluded that China's nine-dash line claims are not in ac-

> Aside from the immediate reputational damage done to Beijing for supporting such activities now deemed to be illegal under international law, these conclusions may have important ripple effects as other countries may think twice about the potential legal repercussions of their own activities at sea.

cordance with international law to the extent that they represent claims to rights or entitlements in excess of those accorded by the United Nations Convention on the Law of the Sea (UNCLOS), and (4) determined that Philippine fishermen enjoy historical fishing rights in the vicinity of the Scarborough Shoal. Taken individually, each of these could be understood as not necessarily representing decisions on sovereignty issues. However, given the interconnected nature of the issues, their combined effect could undoubtedly have a profound impact on issues of sovereignty.

This is a conundrum that governments and international legal scholars are still in the process of grappling with. For states and other actors, how to address the issue, if at all, will necessarily factor into the formulation of their South China Sea policy approaches in the future.

Maritime Rights and Entitlements

As mentioned above, the Tribunal made conclusions related to the legal status of features under UNCLOS, the Philippines' EEZ, and China's nine-dash line. As a result, the Award has major implications for maritime rights and entitlements. Moreover, these implications are not necessarily limited to the South China Sea because decisions made in past international arbitration cases often serve as precedents for those in future cases. As the sovereignty claims and entitlements of all rival claimants are affected either directly or indirectly by the Award (most notably, the conclusion that no features in the Spratly Islands or Scarborough Shoal are EEZ-entitled), these countries will all need to factor the new reality into their South China Sea policy approaches, whether they recognize the legal effect of the Award or not. Moreover, non-claimant stakeholders such as Australia, India, Japan, and the US must also consider their revised policy options for military, commercial, and other operations in the South China Sea.

Obligations in Maritime Spaces

Another key issue that the Tribunal considered in its Award was Chinese activities on maritime features and the actions of Chinese or China-flagged vessels in relevant maritime areas. The arbitrators concluded that China had breached its obligations under UNCLOS by (1) engaging in artificial island creation and infrastructural development on features within the Philippines' EEZ, (2) allowing environmentally destructive living resource extraction operations to take place, and (3) interfering in Filipinos' lawful fishing activities. Aside from the immediate reputational damage done to Beijing for supporting such activities now deemed to be illegal under international law, these conclusions may have important ripple effects as other countries may think twice about the potential legal repercussions of their own activities at sea.

Diplomatic Implications

In addition to legal issues, the Award and subsequent responses in the post-arbitration context present important diplomatic implications and interpreted by observers as weak or otherwise toned-down for fear of disrupting relations with Beijing. Therefore, these soft statements demonstrate not so much that those actors oppose the Tribunal's conclusions but that China's influential role in the global economic system and political order is a paramount consideration for them. The extent to which these cautious approaches aimed at maintaining the diplomatic status quo will continue to be so widespread remains to be

> Rival claimants and major stakeholders have had to recalibrate their bilateral and multilateral diplomatic relations to suit the post-arbitration context.

relevant policy options. These relate to the recalibration of diplomatic relations between countries and other actors and preferences regarding means of dispute management.

Recalibrating Relations

Because of the legal impacts of the Award on the status of features, sovereignty issues, maritime rights and entitlements, and obligations in maritime spaces, rival claimants and major stakeholders have had to recalibrate their bilateral and multilateral diplomatic relations to suit the post-arbitration context.

In terms of relevant policy options, a major aspect of efforts to recalibrate diplomatic relations has been for states and other actors to determine how vocal to be in their support for or opposition to the Award and whether or not – and, if so, how – to criticize and respond to the actions of other actors. On the whole, most have opted for diplomatic caution and ambiguity regarding issues perceived as sensitive. At the time of writing, only seven countries had publicly expressed support for the Award and called upon the parties to abide by the Tribunal's conclusions as outlined within. Many others have demonstrated a high level of diplomatic caution by issuing vague and ambiguously or indirectly worded statements. In many cases, these have been

seen, and the issue will likely depend on the international community's ongoing assessment of Chinese actions in the region.

Means of Dispute Management

Following the Award, many actors have been emboldened in expressing their pre-existing preferences regarding means of dispute management. There are a range of possible options for managing or settling territorial disputes, including through bilateral and multilateral diplomatic negotiations and consultations, negotiations within regional groupings, third-party mediation, and international arbitration. Each of the claimants and stakeholders in the South China Sea has their own preferences on the issue. The Philippines' unexpected unilateral initiation of arbitral proceedings against China was the first of its kind in the South China Sea and a first for China. Once the arbitral proceedings had been initiated, they effectively pushed aside other available means of dispute management until the case had concluded. Now, in the post-arbitration context, rival claimants and major stakeholders can again more meaningfully advocate their preferences, and each must consider which dispute management policy options best serve their interests and those of the region.

Security Implications

Although the Award only directly addressed a small subset of security issues that exist in the South China Sea (i.e., regarding Chinese law enforcement activities), it does have several broader security implications. These relate to legal justifications for law enforcement and military operations, the emboldening of countries in their regional securitization efforts, and emerging opportunities for confidence-building and cooperation.

Legal Justifications for Law Enforcement and Military Operations

Because the Tribunal sought to determine in its Award the legal status of features in the Spratly Islands and Scarborough Shoal (i.e., as "rocks" without EEZ entitlements under UNCLOS), confirmed the Philippines' EEZ entitlements, and concluded that China's nine-dash line claims are not in accordance with international law where they represent claims to rights or entitlements in excess of those accorded by UNCLOS, a new, albeit incomplete, clarity has emerged regarding maritime delimitation – at least from the perspectives of actors supportive of the arbitration case. For countries conducting military or law enforcement operations in the South China Sea, the content of the Award may offer legal justifications for such activities. Based on the Tribunal's conclusions, for example, littoral states will be able to use the Award to justify law enforcement operations targeting illegal fishing activities within EEZs as drawn from the coastlines without having to consider the possibility of EEZ-entitled islands in the Spratly Islands affecting these maritime boundaries. Moreover, other countries, including non-claimants, will be able to more conveniently provide legal justification for freedom of navigation (FON) operations with less concern for any potential legal effect of China's nine-dash line claim.

> For countries conducting military or law enforcement operations in the South China Sea, the content of the Award may offer legal justifications for such activities.

Emboldened Securitization Efforts

One further implication of the possible legal justifications for law enforcement and military operations noted above is that the Award may embolden countries in their securitization efforts. Increased law enforcement and naval presence in maritime areas compounded with an increased confidence in the legality of relevant activities could, in turn, lead to an increased risk of incidents at sea. Countries will have to carefully consider the geographic scope, objectives, and transparency of their activities when formulating relevant policy.

Opportunities for Confidence-Building and Cooperation

On the other hand, the "legal clarity with caveats" that the arbitration case has provided may present some opportunities for confidence-building and cooperation on security issues. Vast maritime expenses were addressed in the Award to different extents and with varying conclusions. In some of those maritime areas, rival claimants may find points of agreement, which could serve as foundations for negotiations that later develop into confidence-building measures and security cooperation. In particular, there may be substantial diplomatic space for cooperation on maritime law enforcement and non-traditional security issues such as piracy and drug trafficking.

Conclusion

As outlined above, the Award has major legal, diplomatic, and security implications for rival claimants and major stakeholders in the South China Sea. As a result, states and other actors must consider their relevant policy options and proceed accordingly. Legally, these implications and policy options relate to the status of features, sovereignty issues, maritime rights and entitlements, and obligations in maritime spaces. Diplomatically, they involve recalibrating diplomatic relations and preferences regarding the means of dispute settlement. In terms of security, they include legal justification for mil-

> In some maritime areas, rival claimants may find points of agreement, which could serve as foundations for negotiations that later develop into confidence-building measures and security cooperation.

itary operations, emboldened securitization efforts, and opportunities for confidence-building and cooperation. The issues considered include only those that are common to multiple claimants and stakeholders. To be sure, there are also many crucial country- or actor-specific implications and policy options to be addressed in the post-arbitration context of the South China Sea maritime territorial disputes. It is these issues and more that are discussed in greater detail in the chapters that follow.

Jonathan Spangler is the Director of the South China Sea Think Tank. His research focuses on Asia-Pacific regional security, maritime territorial disputes, and cross-strait relations. His publications, projects, and contact information can be found at jspangler.org.

Part II:
Rival Claimants

Post-Arbitration South China Sea:

China's Legal Policy Options and Future Prospects

Nong Hong

Abstract

With the Award being released on July 12, 2016, the South China Sea arbitration case, lasing for more than three years, has come to an end. The Tribunal concluded in its thoroughly one-sided Award that many of China's maritime claims in the South China Sea were contrary to the United Nations Convention on the Law of the Sea (UNCLOS) and that actions supported by the Chinese government had thereby violated the Philippines' sovereign rights and freedoms. In general, China's legal policy approach to territorial disputes is based on its preference for negotiation and/or consultation directly with the other party, and its position of non-participation in and non-acceptance of the South China Sea arbitration case and its awards has been coherent. The end of the proceedings does not mean the end of the disputes between the two countries and within the region. However, it does have important legal and political implications for China and other states. First of all, it has had detrimental impacts on China's sovereignty claims and related entitlements. Second, the Arbitral Tribunal expanded its jurisdiction and ignored the legitimate and reasonable claims of the coastal states. Third, this unpleasant result helped the Chinese government justify its position of non-participation and non-acceptance as this ruling has severely harmed China's national interests. Fourth, it raises doubts about the role of UNCLOS in maritime dispute settlement. This has legal implications not just for China but for international law more broadly. Finally, the Award does not lead to the settlement of the maritime disputes between the contracting states of UNCLOS in the South China Sea. That said, the arbitration case has motivated China and ASEAN to speed up negotiations on a Code of Conduct. It has also created an opportunity for both China and the Philippines, which have openly expressed their willingness to engage in bilateral negotiations. These developments also raise important questions about the role that extra-regional actors should play in the disputes. The South China Sea has a complicated past and an uncertain future, but cooperation among nations could stabilize the region and bring tranquility to this important sea.

Introduction

With the Award released on July 12, 2016, by the Arbitral Tribunal established under Annex VII of the United Nations Convention on the Law of the Sea (UNCLOS), the South China Sea arbitration case, lasing for more than three years, has come to an end. Unlike similar cases that resulted in more balanced conclusions regarding maritime disputes between two claimants, the Award is considered an overwhelming win for the Philippines.

China's position of non-participation and non-acceptance can be clearly explained by its legal culture and state practice regarding international dispute settlement. Its strong opposition to the arbitration case has been clearly analyzed in its Position Paper on December 7, 2014, which deeply questioned the jurisdiction of the Arbitral Tribunal and admissibility of the case.[1] A careful review of the Award on merits and remaining issues of jurisdiction and admissibility has verified China's skepticism that the South China Sea arbitration case is not purely an attempt to resort to an international judiciary in order to resolve the maritime disputes. Instead, it is a political game of international law.

China is now facing tremendous pressure from some members of the international community, especially the United States and Japan, calling for a full implementation of the Award. China's position of non-participation and non-acceptance has won overwhelming support from its people, particularly since the Award was issued on July 12, 2016. This unpleasant result helped the Chinese government justify its position of non-participation and non-acceptance as the Tribunal's conclusions severely harm China's national interests. For some Chinese international law scholars that believed that participation would have given China a better chance to present its legal argument and evidence, the Award eliminated their confidence and belief that international law, especially UNCLOS, could have a constructive and positive role in settling the maritime disputes in the South China Sea. Hence, China is unlikely to recognize or comply with the Award.

Facing a dilemma arising from the Award, China, the Philippines, and other claimant states must recalibrate

China's position of non-participation and non-acceptance can be clearly explained by its legal culture and state practice regarding international dispute settlement.

---

1   "Position Paper of the Government of the People's Republic of China on the Matter of Jurisdiction in the South China Sea Arbitration Initiated by the Republic of the Philippines," Ministry of Foreign Affairs, People's Republic of China, December 7, 2014, <http://www.fmprc.gov.cn/mfa_eng/zxxx_662805/t1217147.shtml>.

their policy approaches and reconsider their available policy options. This paper analyses China's approach to international law and third party compulsory dispute settlement mechanisms and its positions and legal bases for these positions in the South China Sea arbitration case. It then explores the legal implications arising from the Award and also the further implications for international law, including UNCLOS and Article 298 in particular. The paper suggests that between China and the Philippines, only direct negotiations based on mutual respect will be constructive and able to rebuild lost confidence. The discussions on exploring other regional and local remedies that have emerged among China and other claimant states and ASEAN and should continue. Moreover, fostering regional functional cooperation based on the principles of Article 123 of UNCLOS should be enhanced, and other stakeholders in the South China Sea will have to play a more constructive role in contributing to the peace and stability of the region.

> China has always advocated bilateral negotiations as the most practical means of dispute settlement between states. In practice, China has resolved several of its bilateral disputes with other countries through negotiation and consultation.

Legal Policy Approach

China's legal policy approach to territorial disputes has involved emphasizing its preference for bilateral negotiations and consultations, exclusion of compulsory arbitration for dispute settlement, and non-participation in the Philippines' unilaterally initiated arbitration case and non-acceptance of the resulting awards.

Preference for Bilateral Negotiations

Ways of peaceful dispute settlement include good office[2], mediation, consultation, negotiation, arbitration, courts, and so on. In most cases, China prefers direct negotiation and/or consultation with the other party. This orientation mostly originates from and owes itself to Chinese culture and history. China has always advocated bilateral negotiations as the most practical means of dispute settlement between states. In practice, China has resolved several of its bilateral disputes with other countries through negotiation and consultation, such as border and

---

2   Typically, these are low-key actions by a third party to bring opposing parties to dialogue or negotiation. Good offices may include informal consultations to facilitate communication; offers of transportation, security, or venues; or fact-finding. The third party may suggest ways of negotiations and achieving a settlement but usually stops short of participating in negotiations.

dual nationality disputes, among other issues. As far as the judiciary is concerned, China's attitude is very conservative. Thus far, no dispute between China and any other state had ever been brought before the International Court of Justice (ICJ) or other international tribunals, so the South China Sea arbitration case is an exception in this regard. During the Sino-India border conflict in 1962, China refused India's proposal to submit the dispute to international arbitration by stating that the "Sino-India border dispute is an important matter concerning the sovereignty of the two countries, and the vast size of more than 100,000

> During the Sino-India border conflict in 1962, China refused India's proposal to submit the dispute to international arbitration

square kilometres of territories. It is self-evident that it can only be resolved through direct bilateral negotiations. It is never possible to seek a settlement from any form of international arbitration."[3] However, after the 1980s, it changed its policy by consenting to arbitration in treaties that it ratified to, but confined this only to economic, trade, scientific, transport, environmental, and health areas.[4] Some conventions require the contracting states to accept compulsory judicial dispute settlement procedures. For instance, UNCLOS makes it obligatory for its state parties to select at least one of the compulsory procedures: the ICJ, International Tribunal for the Law of the Sea (ITLOS), arbitration, or special arbitration. Upon ratification of the convention, China did not state which mechanism it had accepted. Therefore, it was deemed to accept the mechanism of arbitration.[5]

Exclusion of Compulsory Arbitration for Dispute Settlement

Meanwhile, China's perception of the role of international courts in dispute settlement is also passive. In treaties in which it is a party, China has usually made a reservation about the clause of judicial settlement by the ICJ. On September 5, 1972, China declared that it did not recognize the statement of the former Chinese government on Acceptance of the Compulsory Jurisdiction of the ICJ. In fact, it refused to settle any dispute with other countries through the ICJ. On the other hand, as a UN Security Council member, it has nominated judges of Chinese nationality to the ICJ as well as to other international courts, such as ITLOS. Since these courts are composed mainly of judges from the West, developing countries, including China, are doubtful about the impartiality and justice the international judiciary can maintain.[6] As for UNCLOS, China declared on September 7, 2006, under Article 298 the exclusion of certain disputes (such as those concerning maritime delimitation in territorial disputes or military use of the ocean) with other countries from the jurisdiction of the international judiciary or arbitration.[7] As one Chinese scholar points out, there is slim chance that China would change its attitude towards third-party dispute settlement forums in the near future with regard to its dispute in the South China Sea.[8]

Nevertheless, some other international legal scholars in China started to bring to the table the issue of third-party compulsory dispute settlement forums. At the "Symposium on China's Energy Security and the South China Sea" held in China in December 2004, for example, Jia Yu explained the reasons why China felt reluctant to go to an international court to address its disputes with other countries, especially regarding sovereignty claims and maritime jurisdiction. Unlike the assumptions of some western scholars,

---

3   Gao Yanping, "International Dispute Settlement," in Wang Tieya (ed.), *International Law*, Beijing: Law Press, 1995, pp. 611–612. [Chinese]

4   Zou Keyuan, *China-ASEAN Relations and International Law*, Oxford: Chandos Publishing, 2009, p. 31.

5   UNCLOS, Article 297(3).

6   Zou, *China-ASEAN Relations and International Law*, 2009, p. 32.

7   "China's Declaration in Accordance with Article 298 of UNLOCS," September 7, 2006.

8   Interview with Dr. Wu Shicun.

China's hesitation does not come from a lack of evidence for its sovereignty claims in the cases of the East China Sea and South China Sea. In fact, as the former ITLOS Judge Chan Ho Park pointed out, compared with Vietnam and other South China Sea countries, China has more historic evidence to show its jurisdiction in the South China Sea.[9] Jia Yu argued that China's reluctance to accept a third party settlement forum comes from, first of all, the lack of experience in international litigation, and secondly, the lack of expertise in the international law field with regard to dispute

China Sea under "abundant historical and legal grounds."[12] He blamed the dispute on the Philippines' "illegal occupation of some of the Chinese islets and atolls of the Spratly Islands" and claimed that China had been "consistently working towards resolving the disputes through dialogue and negotiations to defend Sino-Philippine relations and regional peace and stability."[13]

On February 19, 2013, China officially refused to participate in the proceedings.[14] In addition, China accused the Philippines of making factually flawed accusations and of violating the Declara-

> The political culture of China and many Asian countries, which emphasizes a belief in good neighbourly relations, will be jeopardized if the differences have to be resolved by third-party involvement.

settlement.[10] Apart from the reasons given by Jia Yu, the political culture of China and many Asian countries, which emphasizes a belief in good neighbourly relations, will be jeopardized if the differences have to be resolved by third-party involvement and is therefore a psychological obstacle to using third-party mechanisms.

Non-Participation and Non-Acceptance

China's position on the South China Sea Arbitration case, namely non-participation and non-acceptance, has been coherent. On January 23, 2013, the day after the Philippines filed its Notification and Statement of Claim,[11] the Chinese Foreign Ministry spokesman stated that China has "indisputable sovereignty" over the South

tion on the Conduct of Parties in the South China Sea (DOC).[15] Chinese Foreign Ministry spokesman Hong Lei mentioned the consensus that China and ASEAN member states reached when they signed the DOC in November 2002 that disputes should be solved through talks between the na-

---

9   Interview with Judge Chan Ho Park in Shanghai, 2005.

10   Jia Yu, Presentation at the "Energy Security and the South China Sea" Conference, Haikou, 2004.

11   "Notification of Statement and Claim," Notification, No. 13-0211, Department of Foreign Affairs, Republic of the Philippines, January 22, 2013, <http://www.philippineembassy-usa.org/uploads/pdfs/embassy/2013/2013-0122-Notification%20and%20Statement%20of%20Claim%20on%20West%20Philippine%20Sea.pdf>.

12   "China reiterates islands claim after Philippine UN move", BBC, January 23, 2013, <http://www.bbc.co.uk/news/world-asia-21163507>.

13   "China reiterates islands claim after Philippine UN move", BBC, January 23, 2013, <http://www.bbc.co.uk/news/world-asia-21163507>.

14   "China rejects Philippines' arbitral request", China Daily, February 19, 2013, <http://www.chinadaily.com.cn/china/2013-02/19/content_16238133.htm>.

15   Article 5 states that "[t]he Parties undertake to exercise self-restraint in the conduct of activities that would complicate or escalate disputes and affect peace and stability including, among others, refraining from action of inhabiting on the presently uninhabited islands, reefs, shoals, cays, and other features and to handle their differences in a constructive manner." See "Declaration on the Conduct of Parties in the South China Sea," Foreign Ministers of ASEAN and People's Republic of China, November 4, 2002, <http://cil.nus.edu.sg/rp/pdf/2002%20Declaration%20on%20the%20Conduct%20of%20Parties%20in%20the%20South%20China%20Sea-pdf.pdf>.

tions directly involved.[16]

China considers the act of initiating arbitral proceedings unfriendly and damaging to Sino-Philippine relations. China complained that "the Philippine side had failed to notify the Chinese side, not to mention seeking China's consent, before it actually initiated the arbitration."[17] There are several reasons why China rejected the arbitral proceedings, including (1) China has been consistent in its position on resolving the disputes between Beijing and Manila through bilateral negotiations; (2) under international law, China has the right to turn down the request from the Philippines for arbitral proceedings to

The Award can be understood in terms of the direct legal implications for China and the further implications for international law, especially the role of UNCLOS in settling or managing maritime disputes.

take place because it has made a declaration under Article 298 of UNCLOS; and (3) the act of filing the arbitration case poses an obstacle for the two countries in developing friendly relations.

In addition, China also questioned whether the Arbitral Tribunal had jurisdiction over the case. Although the Philippines did specifical-ly discuss the territorial issue in its Notification and Statement of Claim, it is impossible to discuss most of its claims without first clarifying Chinese and Philippine sovereignty over island features in the South China Sea. For example, the majority of the Philippines' claims assume that China only has territorial sovereignty over a few "rocks," such as Chigua Jiao (Johnson Reef), Huayang Jiao (Cuarteron Reef) and Yongshu Jiao (Fiery Cross Reef) in the Nansha (Spratly) Islands,[18] while intentionally ignoring the fact that China has claimed sovereignty over the entire Nansha (Spratly) Islands. Hence, China maintains that the Philippines' claims are essentially maritime delimitation claims that involve questions of territorial sovereignty. Such questions, however, are excluded from UNCLOS arbitration under Article 298. Thus, China believes that its rejection of the arbitration has a solid basis in international law.

Legal Implications of the Award

The Award can be understood in terms of the direct legal implications for China and the further implications for international law, especially the role of UNCLOS in settling or managing maritime disputes. For China, these legal implications include detrimental impacts on sovereignty claims and related entitlements in the South China Sea, illegalization of certain Chinese activities, improved grounds for justifying its non-participation in and non-acceptance of the arbitral proceedings, increased doubts about the use of international law for dispute settlement, and reinforcement of the view that other stakeholders' legal perspectives and actions do not contribute to regional peace and stability.

First, the Award suggests that China's history-based claims within the nine-dash line do not

16   Hong Lei, "Foreign Ministry Spokesperson Hong Lei's Regular Press Conference on October 28, 2014," Ministry of Foreign Affairs, People's Republic of China, October 28, 2014, <http://www.fmprc.gov.cn/mfa_eng/xwfw_665399/s2510_665401/t1204813.shtml>; Hong Lei, "Foreign Ministry Spokesperson Hong Lei's Regular Press Conference on November 23, 2015," Ministry of Foreign Affairs, People's Republic of China, November 23, 2015, <http://www.fmprc.gov.cn/mfa_eng/xwfw_665399/s2510_665401/t1317589.shtml>.

17   Sun Xiangyang, "Press Conference By Chinese Embassy On Philippines' Submission of a Memorial to the Arbitral Tribunal on disputes of the South China Sea with China," Embassy of the People's Republic of China in the Republic of the Philippines, April 1, 2014, <http://ph.china-embassy.org/eng/xwfb/t1143166.htm>.

18   "Notification of Statement and Claim," Notification, No. 13-0211, Department of Foreign Affairs, Republic of the Philippines, January 22, 2013, pp. 12–13, <http://www.philippineembassy-usa.org/uploads/pdfs/embassy/2013/2013-0122-Notification%20and%20Statement%20of%20Claim%20on%20West%20Philippine%20Sea.pdf>.

include a claim to "historic title," which bear the characteristics of sovereignty and would be excluded from the Tribunal's jurisdiction by China's declaration in 2006 based on Article 298 of UNCLOS. Rather, China's claim is one of "historic rights," which the Tribunal judged to be an exclusive claim of sovereign rights and jurisdiction in the exclusive economic zone (EEZ) of the Philippines. The Tribunal concluded that China's claims were contrary to UNCLOS and without lawful effect wherein they exceeded the geographic and substantive limits of China's maritime entitlements under the Convention. This finding has

tures in the Scarborough Shoal or Spratly Islands of the South China Sea are capable of sustaining human habitation or economic life of their own.[20] As such, none of the land features in the South China Sea meets the definition of an "island" under Article 121 of UNCLOS. In other words, there is no entitlement to an EEZ or continental shelf generated by any land feature claimed by China in the Scarborough Shoal or Spratly Islands. One of the most significant elements of the ruling was its finding that Itu Aba (Taiping) Island, the largest feature in the Spratly group, currently occupied by Taipei, is not an "island" but is in-

> The Arbitral Tribunal threw out decades of jurisprudential caution by directly addressing the distinction between "islands" and "rocks" and added an arbitrary "historical use" test in the case of features that are difficult to define.

two major flaws. The Tribunal interpreted the nine-dash line as a line of "historic rights" even though China has never made a public statement about the legal meaning of this line. Second, supposing that the nine-dash line was regarded by China as a line of "historic rights," the Tribunal took a different and contradictory stance for China and the Philippines. It did agree that Manila is entitled to reach beyond the text of the Convention to enjoy non-exclusively exercised traditional fishing rights in the territorial sea of the Scarborough Shoal, which was part of the body of general international law preserved by UNCLOS. However, the Tribunal denied China's historic rights in foreign EEZs, and its reasoning was unsatisfactory. Its limitation of artisanal fishing rights to territorial seas rather than other exclusive maritime zones constituted an arbitrary narrowing of the jurisprudence created in Eritrea v Yemen.[19]

Second, the Award provides that no land fea-

stead merely a "rock". As pointed out by Sourahb Gupta, the Arbitral Tribunal threw out decades of jurisprudential caution by directly addressing the distinction between "islands" and "rocks" and added an arbitrary "historical use" test in the case of features that are difficult to define. The Tribunal's interpretation bears little resemblance to the spirit of Article 121 which was deliberately ambiguous in its wording.[21]

This finding on Article 121(3) had tremendous implications with regard to jurisdictional questions related to a range of activities conducted by China in the South China Sea, including fishing, marine scientific research, reclamation, and law enforcement. Mischief Reef is regarded by the Tribunal as a low-tide elevation and hence cannot be deemed to be sovereign territory, unlike a 'rock' or an 'island', as per UNCLOS. Further, because Mischief Reef has now been judged as residing on the undisputed continental shelf of

---

19   In Eritrea v. Yemen, the ICJ had reached beyond the Western legal tradition to imaginatively rule that such rights accrue as a sort of "servitude internationale" (i.e., a non-possessory right or interest in access and resources) in waters that were hitherto the "high seas" within a semi-enclosed sea but have since become part of a coastal state's EEZ.

20   "The Tribunal Renders Its Award," Press Release, Permanent Court of Arbitration, July 12, 2016, <http://www.pcacases.com/web/sendAttach/1801>.

21   Sourahb Gupta, "No Restraint: Judicial Activism in the South China Sea Arbitration Ruling," *ICAS Bulletin*, August 31, 2016, <http://chinaus-icas.org/wp-content/uploads/2016/08/ICAS-Bulletin-August-31-2016.pdf>.

the Philippines, China has no possible sovereign rights or jurisdiction that could extend over the sea area of Mischief Reef. This poses a major challenge for China in justifying its reclamation and facility construction activities in Mischief Reef.

All the other land reclamation and artificial island-building has been within China's legal rights. They are built on 'rocks' which are considered to be sovereign territory. However, the Award also suggests that China's land reclamation activities have caused harm to the coral reef ecosystem and thereby, in violation of its international treaty obligations,[22] damaged the marine environment.[23] Given the provisions of international law, including UNCLOS, with respect to the protection and preservation of the marine environment, it becomes a critical issue whether China has fulfilled its obligations. China's official statement from the Ministry of Foreign Affairs suggested China has conducted environmental impact assessments (EIAs) and that it is continuing to monitor the impact of its reclamation activities. It seems necessary for China to make the EIAs public and acknowledge its duty to cooperate with potentially affected states.[24] Giving warning of the islands' presence and appropriate publicity as to their depth, positions, and dimensions should also be encouraged. As China defends its land reclamation as improving China's capacity to deliver maritime public services, China needs to show evidence that it is using the reclaimed features and infrastructure for maintaining maritime safety and security, offering support for search and rescue operations, scientific research, and other civilian uses.

> China needs to show evidence that it is using the reclaimed features and infrastructure for maintaining maritime safety and security, offering support for search and rescue operations, scientific research, and other civilian uses.

Apart from the legal implications arising from the merits aspect of the Award, other further implications should not be overlooked. Article 298 allows states to opt out of the compulsory settlement mechanism in disputes related to sovereignty, maritime delimitation, military activities, and other issues. This article was achieved through lengthy

---

22 Besides UNCLOS, international treaty obligations might include, among others, the Convention on International Trade in Endangered Species of Wild Fauna and Flora (CITES) and Convention on Biological Diversity (CBD).

23 "The Tribunal Renders Its Award," Press Release, Permanent Court of Arbitration, July 12, 2016, <http://www.pcacases.com/web/sendAttach/1801>.

24 Hua Chunying, "Foreign Ministry Spokesperson Hua Chunying's Regular Press Conference of April 9, 2015," Embassy of the People's Republic of China in Malaysia, April 9, 2015, <http://www.mfa.gov.cn/ce/cemy/chn/fyrth/t1253375.htm>. [Chinese]

negotiations as a compromise to meet the demands of some states that did not wish to address certain disputes through a third party. The utilization of Article 287 in the South China Sea arbitration case, which obviously involves sovereignty and maritime delimitation, could set an example undermining the true spirit of the dispute settlement mechanism of UNCLOS. Given the predictable result that any award provided by the Arbitral Tribunal will not be able to solve the real dispute between China and the Philippines, the arbitration case is an example of a political game using international law.

China's failure to appear in court demonstrates its continued position of "non-acceptance and non-participation" in the arbitration unilaterally initiated by the Philippines. It does not mean disrespect for the Arbitral Tribunal, the Permanent Court of Arbitration, or international law, nor does it reflect China's inability to fulfill its obligations related to the peaceful settlement of international disputes. China was one of the first countries to participate in international dispute settlement mechanisms, including the Permanent Court of Arbitration. Since the 1980s, the United Nations and other international organizations have called on the international community to set up mechanisms like the Permanent Court of Arbitration to resolve international disputes. To give full play to their functional roles, many international conventions, including UNCLOS, have introduced litigation and arbitral procedures in their dispute settlement mechanisms. This was a good experiment and good starting point, but the result was opposite to what one would want. Since its entry into force in 1994, about twenty cases on maritime disputes have been sitting in the ICJ, while only ten cases were forwarded to arbitral procedures, mainly because the dispute settlement provisions from UNCLOS are very complicated and contain disputes and loopholes. As the Philippines v. China arbitration case has shown, a country that does not accept the arbitral procedures can be portrayed as "not endorsing international law" by an arbitration initiated unilaterally by one party to the dispute.

Beijing maintains that arbitral tribunals should limit their jurisdiction to the scope of a dispute rather than expanding their jurisdiction. The provisional nature of arbitration determines that that purpose of arbitration is to solve the relevant dispute, not to address broader issues. In the case of the South China Sea arbitration, the Tribunal granted itself jurisdiction even though it was aware of China's consistent position on resolving the territorial sovereignty and maritime disputes through bilateral negotiations. It also granted itself jurisdiction know-

> The provisional nature of arbitration determines that that purpose of arbitration is to solve the relevant dispute, not to address broader issues.

ing that China did not wish to participate in the arbitral proceedings and would not accept the awards, and it was aware that rulings responding to the Philippines' appeals would not resolve the disputes. China's will to resort to negotiation in solving the dispute was unfairly neglected.

As far as the South China Sea dispute is concerned, the involvement of the international arbitration has weakened a country's rights in establishing a regional maritime order. The power of arbitration mechanisms has gradually strengthened and continues to expand. China and other countries understand that, as arbitral tribunals expand their jurisdiction and ignore the

na will need to consider its policy options, which relate to how best to engage in negotiations on agreements with other claimants, including the type, pace, scope, and content of these negotiations, and how to engage with extra-regional actors attempting to interfere in the disputes.

While China and ASEAN are working hard to find their way to solve the differences in the South China Sea, other stakeholders' roles should be not ignored either. The South China Sea disputes have evolved from territorial and maritime disputes among the claimant states to a competition between China as a claimant state and the United States as a user state. In order to resolve

> Discussions on exploring other regional and bilateral remedies have emerged among China, other claimant states, and ASEAN, and fostering regional functional cooperation based on the principle of Article 123 of UNCLOS has again come into focus.

legitimate and reasonable claims of the coastal states, tensions between the contracting states of UNCLOS will increase, and it is unlikely that the contents of the Award will be prudently implemented.

Policy Options

Though the arbitration case does not lead to the settlement of the maritime disputes in the South China Sea, it does motivate China and ASE-AN to speed up negotiations on the finalization of a Code of Conduct (COC). Both China and the Philippines have voiced their willingness to open the door for bilateral negotiation. Discussions on exploring other regional and bilateral remedies have emerged among China, other claimant states, and ASEAN, and fostering regional functional cooperation based on the principle of Article 123 of UNCLOS has again become a focus of these discussions. In the wake of the Award, Chi-

this paradox, China and the United States have no choice but to engage each other and maintain regular communications on how they can coexist while ensuring that both can safeguard their respective core interests. After all, the Asia-Pacific region is big enough for both countries to share and exert their respective influence without pointing fingers at each other. As China's rise stands a good chance of triggering a regional power shift, the United States needs to acknowledge China's core interest in ensuring its sovereignty and maritime claims in the South China Sea. Similarly, China must respect the legitimate interests of the United States in the South China Sea, especially freedom of navigation in line with UNCLOS, which is also in China's interest. What would work to serve in both countries' best interest is to explore the fields of developing maritime cooperation (e.g., on issues of search and rescue and humanitarian aid) between China and the United States. Joint efforts in anti-piracy in the

Gulf of Aden have provided one successful example. Providing search and rescue at sea and humanitarian assistance would be areas for these countries to use their naval capabilities to jointly take a lead in the region.

Conclusion

In general, China's legal policy approach to territorial disputes is based on its preference for negotiation and/or consultation directly with the other party. This orientation mostly originates from Chinese culture and history. China's perception of the role

The United States needs to acknowledge China's core interest in ensuring its sovereignty and maritime claims in the South China Sea. Similarly, China must respect the legitimate interests of the US in the South China Sea, especially freedom of navigation in line with UNCLOS, which is also in China's interest.

of international courts in dispute settlement is also passive, and it has opted out of compulsory arbitration for addressing sovereignty issues. Hence, China's position of non-participation in and non-acceptance of the South China Sea arbitration case and its awards has been coherent. China considers the act of initiating arbitration proceedings unfriendly and damaging to Sino-Philippine relations. In addition, China also questioned whether the Arbitral Tribunal had jurisdiction over this case.

The Award has had profound legal implications. First of all, it has had detrimental impacts on China's sovereignty claims and related entitlements. Second, the Arbitral Tribunal expanded its jurisdiction and ignored the legitimate and reasonable claims of the coastal states. Third, this unpleasant result helped the Chinese government justify its position of non-participation and non-acceptance as this ruling has severely harmed China's national interests. Fourth, it raises doubts about the role of UNCLOS in maritime dispute settlement. This has legal implications not just for China but for international law more broadly. Finally, the Award does not lead to the settlement of the maritime disputes between the contracting states of UNCLOS in the South China Sea.

Despite its questionable role in addressing the maritime

disputes in the South China Sea, the arbitration case has motivated China and ASEAN to speed up negotiations on a Code of Conduct. It has also created an opportunity for both China and the Philippines, which have openly expressed their willingness to engage in bilateral negotiations. Discussions on exploring other regional and local remedies have emerged among China, other claimant states, and ASEAN.

Despite its questionable role in addressing the maritime disputes in the South China Sea, the arbitration case has motivated China and ASEAN to speed up negotiations on a Code of Conduct.

These developments also raise important questions about the role that extra-regional actors should play in the disputes. The South China Sea has a complicated past and an uncertain future, but cooperation among nations could stabilize the region and bring tranquility to this important sea.

Nong Hong heads the Institute for China-America Studies (ICAS), an independent, non-profit academic institution based in Washington D.C. She also holds a joint position of research fellow with China Institute, University of Alberta (CIUA), National Institute for South China Sea Studies (NISCSS), and the China Center for Collaborated Studies on the South China Sea, Nanjing University. She received her PhD of interdisciplinary study of international law and international relations from the University of Alberta, Canada and held a Postdoctoral Fellowship in the University's China Institute. She was ITLOS-Nippon Fellow for International Dispute Settlement (2008-2009), and Visiting Fellow at the Center of Oceans Law and Policy, University of Virginia (2009) and at the Max Planck Institute for Comparative Public Law and International Law (2007).

Post-Arbitration South China Sea:

China's Diplomatic Policy Options and Future Prospects

Yan Yan

Abstract

This chapter reviews China's diplomatic policy approach to the South China Sea, the Philippines' arbitration case, and the Award of July 12, 2016. It then discusses the diplomatic implications for China, as the Award has damaged China–Philippines bilateral relations, had reputational costs, increased diplomatic pressure in multilateral fora, strengthened China's distrust of third-party dispute settlement mechanisms, offered justification for its non-participation and non-acceptance policy approach, and complicated future negotiations with rival claimants by challenging China's sovereignty and historical claims in the South China Sea. The chapter then discusses China's diplomatic policy options, which relate to the continuation of its policy of non-participation and non-acceptance, its bilateral relations with the Philippines, clarity about its maritime territorial claims and historic rights, using its occupied features for regional maritime cooperation and confidence-building to reduce diplomatic tensions, managing its diplomatic relations with extra-regional actors, and preparing for a future legal resolution to the disputes.

Introduction

The Philippines issued a Notification and Statement of Claim in January 2013 invoking under Article 287 and Annex VII of UNCLOS a compulsory dispute settlement mechanism to deal with its long-standing disagreements with China over the South China Sea.[1] The following month, China responded with a note verbale and formally rejected the claim with an argument that the Philippines not only violated the previous commitments to settle the dispute through bilateral negotiations but also illegally occupied features over which China had

---

1 "Notification of Statement and Claim," Notification, No. 13-0211, Department of Foreign Affairs, Republic of the Philippines, January 22, 2013, <http://www.philippineembassy-usa.org/uploads/pdfs/embassy/2013/2013-0122-Notification%20and%20Statement%20of%20Claim%20on%20West%20Philippine%20Sea.pdf>.

sovereignty in the South China Sea.[2] China also insisted on solving the disputes through bilateral negotiations by "sovereign States directly concerned", citing the 2002 Declaration on the Conduct of Parties in the South China Sea (DOC). Without China's participation, the arbitral proceedings continued for the following three years and concluded with the Award issued on July 12, 2016.

Without China's participation, aspects of the Award, which overwhelmingly favored the Philippines' legal arguments, were predicted by many legal scholars before it was issued. The Award has implications not only for the South China Sea but also for maritime disputes elsewhere in the world as the arbitrators interpreted many important international legal issues, such as the legal status of maritime features and historic claims. From a diplomatic perspective, the Award serves as an obstacle to the relationship between China and the Philippines and will not be easily overlooked. It also provides a reason for States both in the South China Sea region and beyond to criticize China for non-compliance with international law. On the other hand, it also provides a chance for China to clarify its claims, rethink its policy, and even fight back as some of the Tribunal's conclusions outlined in the Award do not seem to have a well-grounded legal basis.

> The Award has implications not only for the South China Sea but also for maritime disputes elsewhere in the world as the arbitrators interpreted many important international legal issues, such as the legal status of maritime features and historic claims.

The Award will continue to have an impact on China and the Philippines. Moreover, its effects will reverberate throughout the region and into other maritime spaces around the world. Many analysts have speculated about China's reactions to the Award, but many of these have focused on the legal and security aspects of its ongoing and future responses. This chapter evaluates the diplomatic implications of the Award and looks ahead at China's diplomatic policy options with the aim of shedding light on its future prospects in the South China Sea now that the arbitration has ended and a new chapter has begun.

---

2 "Note Verbale No. (13) PG-039 from the Embassy of the People's Republic of China in the Republic of the Philippines," Note Verbale, No. (13) PG-039, Embassy of the People's Republic of China in the Republic of the Philippines, February 19, 2013, <https://perma.cc/WMB2-DDPF>.

Diplomatic Policy Approach

With China's reclamation work in the Spratlys, some argue that China's South China Sea policy approach is now a provocative and assertive one, a sharp departure from the "concealing one's strengths and biding one's time" theory from the 1980s. In fact throughout the years, China's diplomatic policy approach to the South China Sea has been consistent and can be summarized as based on four elements. First of all, the South China Sea dispute should be resolved through peaceful means, with bilateral negotiations between the parties directly involved being the best way forward. Second, China has indisputable sovereignty over the features in the South China Sea. Its sovereignty claims are supported by historical evidence and in accordance with international law, including UNCLOS, as are its claims to relevant surrounding waters. Third, pending a resolution to the disputes, claimant countries could follow the principle of "setting aside disputes and pursuing joint development"[3], as initiated by the paramount leader Deng Xiaoping in the 1970s. Fourth, China is committed to preserving freedom of navigation and overflight and has never interfered with such activities.

Unlike its interpretation of the nine-dash line, China's policy regarding the arbitration case has been firm and clear and has been reiterated many times throughout the arbitral proceedings: it will not accept or participate in the arbitration case. On January 22, 2013, when the Philippines initiated the arbitration, China for the first time declared that it would not accept or participate. On December 7, 2014, China's Foreign Ministry released a "Position Paper of the Government of the People's Republic of China on the Matter of Jurisdiction in the South China Sea Arbitration Initiated by the Republic of the Philippines" (hereinafter "Position Paper"). The document was the first authoritative and comprehensive government statement clarifying the legal basis of China's decision to neither accept nor participation in the case. On October 29, 2015, the day the Award on Jurisdiction and Admissibility was issued, the Chinese government reacted to that award, stating that it is "null and void and has

> Unlike its interpretation of the nine-dash line, China's policy regarding the arbitration case has been firm and clear and has been reiterated many times throughout the arbitral proceedings.

---

3   "Set Aside Dispute and Pursue Joint Development," Ministry of Foreign Affairs, People's Republic of China, November 17, 2000, <http://www.fmprc.gov.cn/mfa_eng/ziliao_665539/3602_665543/3604_665547/t18023.shtml>.

no biding force."[4] On June 8, 2016, China released the "Statement of the Ministry of Foreign Affairs of the People's Republic of China on Settling Disputes Between China and the Philippines in the South China Sea Through Bilateral Negotiation,"[5] again reiterating the same position. The day after the Award was issued on July 12, 2016, China's State Council Information Office published

> The outcome may strengthen China's distrust of third party dispute settlement mechanisms and confirm that its non-participation and non-acceptance was the best choice.

the white paper "China Adheres to the Position of Settling Through Negotiation the Relevant Disputes Between China and the Philippines in the South China Sea."[6]

While "non-acceptance" can be seen as a political statement, "non-participation" requires a legal explanation to the international community. Reasons for such a position have been stated again and again by the Chinese government, diplomats, and scholars. They can be briefly summarized into four points: the two States have long agreed to solve the disputes through bilateral negotiations; the essence of the dispute is, in fact, territorial sovereignty instead of the legal status of certain features in the Spratly Islands, as claimed by the Philippines and its legal team; China's 2006 declaration excludes the territorial disputes from compulsory dispute settlement; and the two States have not engaged in negotiations as required by Article 283 of UNCLOS.

However, the Tribunal was not persuaded by Chinese explanations and provided a final award that greatly favors the Philippines. The outcome may strengthen China's distrust of third party dispute settlement mechanisms and confirm that its non-participation and non-acceptance was the best choice. As China's foreign ministry spokesperson Hong Lei said at the routine press briefing on June 29, "with regard to territorial issues and maritime delimitation disputes, China does not accept any means of third party dispute settlement or any solution imposed on China." It seems that this diplomatic policy approach will continue for the foreseeable future.

Diplomatic Implications of the Award

The Award in the Philippines v. China arbitration case has major implications not only for China and the Philippines but also for the regional and global maritime order. For China, there are several diplomatic implications that are of particular significance. First, the Award affects China–Philippines bilateral relations. It is often regarded as a legal victory of the Philippines over China, but it is still early to reach such a conclusion. Second, China faces reputational costs because of its non-acceptance of and non-compliance with the Award. Third, it faces diplomatic pressure in multilateral forums, especially from the United States, Singapore, and Japan. Fourth, the outcome of the arbitration may strengthen China's distrust of third-party dispute settlement mechanisms as well as other legal means of dealing with disputes. This will confirm China's belief

4   "Statement of the Ministry of Foreign Affairs of the People's Republic of China on the Award on Jurisdiction and Admissibility of the South China Sea Arbitration by the Arbitral Tribunal Established at the Request of the Republic of the Philippines," Ministry of Foreign Affairs, People's Republic of China, November 30, 2015, <http://www.fmprc.gov.cn/mfa_eng/zxxx_662805/t1310474.shtml>.

5   "Statement of the Ministry of Foreign Affairs of the People's Republic of China on Settling Disputes Between China and the Philippines in the South China Sea Through Bilateral Negotiation," Ministry of Foreign Affairs, People's Republic of China, July 8, 2016, <http://news.xinhuanet.com/english/china/2016-06/08/c_135421608.htm>.

6   "China Adheres to the Position of Settling Through Negotiation the Relevant Disputes Between China and the Philippines in the South China Sea," Ministry of Foreign Affairs, People's Republic of China, July 13, 2016, <http://www.fmprc.gov.cn/nanhai/eng/snhwtlcwj_1/t1380615.htm>.

that its non-participation and non-acceptance is the best choice. Finally, since the Award weakens China's sovereignty and historical claims in the South China Sea, negotiation with its neighbors may become much more difficult in the future.

Bilateral Relations

The most obvious diplomatic impact of the Award for China is the degradation of its bilateral relationship with the Philippines. The South China Sea is a defining factor in China–Philippines relations. During the Arroyo administration (2001–2010), bilateral relations between the two countries over the South China Sea were at their most cooperative, as highlighted by the Joint Marine

was released and Vietnam published a statement on the same day, saying that it strongly supported peaceful resolution of the South China Sea dispute and the final outcome of the arbitration, while at the same time reasserting its own sovereignty claims. Malaysia, Indonesia and Singapore then issued similar statements. Extra-regional countries and organizations also expressed their concerns via official channels. Australian Foreign Minister Julie Bishop called for China to abide by the Award and asserted that Australia would continue freedom of navigation exercises. On July 15, 2016, the European Union and its member states also issued a statement expressing their joint opinion of no position on sovereignty issues over the features of the South China Sea but suggesting that the disputed parties clarify

> Since the Award weakens China's sovereignty and historical claims in the South China Sea, negotiation with its neighbors may become much more difficult in the future.

Seismic Undertaking (JMSU) agreement from 2005 to 2008. However the Aquino administration reversed the situation, taking it to a historic low. With the Award in hand, the new president, Rodrigo Duterte, who was inaugurated just two weeks before its release on June 30, 2016, is unlikely to give up the increased bargaining power with China that the Award may offer. On the other hand, his call for a reset in China–Philippines relations and his productive visit to Beijing in October 2016 might signify the turning of a new page in the bilateral relationship.

Reputational Costs

Second, China is facing reputational costs due to its non-participation in the arbitration case and non-acceptance of the Award. As a State party to UNCLOS, the strongest criticism China faces relates to "non-compliance" with international law. That criticism reached a peak after the Award

their claims and pursue them in accordance with international law, especially UNCLOS, and resolve the disputes through peaceful means. The EU also supports the early conclusion of an effective Code of Conduct (COC) between ASEAN and China to manage the disputes and implement the 2002 Declaration on the Conduct of Parties in the South China Sea (DOC).

Diplomatic Pressure

Third, China also faces diplomatic pressure in regional and multilateral forums. The biggest diplomatic test for China may have been the 49th ASEAN Foreign Ministers' Meeting (AMM). It seems that Beijing passed the test, since the joint communiqué produced by ASEAN and issued on

July 24, 2016, does not mention the Award.[7] The joint communiqué contains a single section on international and regional issues, including the South China Sea. It expresses support for general principles such as peaceful dispute resolution, preserving freedom of navigation and overflight, non-militarization, and the early adoption of a COC, but there is no explicit mention of the arbitration case, the Award, or Chinese actions specifically. It has been reported that Cambodia, China's closest neighbor within ASEAN, objected to the proposed wording of the draft communiqué,

In future negotiations on maritime boundary delimitation and sovereignty issues in the South China Sea, rival claimants may attempt to use the Award as leverage against China. As a result, China may need to use its own diplomatic and economic weight as leverage to persuade other claimants and protect its interests.

which had a direct reference to the ruling and the need to respect international law and was supported by Vietnam and the Philippines.[8] Some described this as a "diplomatic victory" for China, but China has argued that extra-regional powers have increased tensions and need to steer clear of the disputes.[9]

Role of Third-Party Dispute Settlement

Fourth, the ruling may destroy China's faith in third-party dispute settlement mechanisms and even international law more broadly. The Award covers a wide scope of maritime issues from historic claims to marine environmental protection as well as issues not included in the Philippines' fifteen submissions to the Tribunal. Although the arbitrators had acknowledged that they did not have jurisdiction over sovereignty issues, the conclusions outlined in the Award touched upon the core aspects of China's South China Sea claims and have major implications for its territorial claims.

Diplomatic Negotiations

Finally, since the Award weakens China's sovereignty and historical claims in the South China Sea, future negotiations with neighboring countries will be complicated by the arbitrators' conclusions. The Tribunal determined that China's historic rights claims to the resources in the South China Sea are incompatible with the regime of exclusive economic zones (EEZs) as elaborated in UNCLOS. Furthermore, the Tribunal held that the Spratly island group is not capable of generating maritime zones collectively and none of the features China claims are entitled to an EEZ.[10] These conclusions are directed at the heart of China's claims and decrease their legitimacy. In future negotiations on maritime boundary delimitation and sovereignty issues in the South China Sea, rival claimants may attempt to use the Award as leverage against China. As a result, China may need to use its own diplomatic and economic weight as leverage to persuade other claimants and protect its interests.

---

7   "Joint Communique of the 49th ASEAN Foreign Ministers' Meeting," Foreign Ministers of the Association of Southeast Asian Nations, July 24, 2016, <http://asean.org/storage/2016/07/Joint-Communique-of-the-49th-AMM-ADOPTED.pdf>.

8   Manuel Mogato, Michael Martina and Ben Blanchard, "ASEAN deadlocked on South China Sea, Cambodia blocks statement," Reuters, July 26, 2016, <http://www.reuters.com/article/us-southchinasea-ruling-asean-idUSKCN1050F6>.

9   Michael Martina and Lesley Wroughton, "China scores a surprising diplomatic victory after South China Sea ruling," Business Insider/Reuters, July 25, 2016, <http://www.businessinsider.com/china-scores-a-diplomatic-victory-after-south-china-sea-ruling-2016-7>.

---

10   "The Tribunal Renders Its Award," Press Release, Permanent Court of Arbitration, July 12, 2016, <http://www.pcacases.com/web/sendAttach/1801>.

Diplomatic Policy Options

China's diplomatic policy options relate to the continuation of its policy of non-participation and non-acceptance, its bilateral relations with the Philippines, clarity about its maritime territorial claims and historic rights, using its occupied features for regional maritime cooperation and confidence-building to reduce diplomatic tensions, managing its diplomatic relations with extra-regional actors, and preparing for a future legal resolution to the disputes.

First of all, since the Award so clearly undermined China's maritime claims in the South China Sea, there is little possibility that China will issues such as fisheries cooperation to demonstrate its good intentions. With the Duterte administration replacing the Aquino administration shortly before the Award, China's was presented with a new policy option as the incumbent president has shown interest in rebuilding relations with China – a stark contrast to his predecessor's policies that had thrown China–Philippines relations into turmoil with the arbitration case. This has paved the way for restoring bilateral relations between the two countries, and Beijing has shown its willingness to improve diplomatic ties and promote cooperation since Duterte's inauguration and the Award. Beijing has expressly stated its desire to resume bilateral talks with the

> A reset of bilateral relations will not only stabilize the current South China Sea situation but also gives China diplomatic credit in regional forums and sets an example for other claimant States to know that third party dispute settlement is not the best option for the dispute.

change its position of accepting it in the future. In the white paper released the day after the Award and other official statements, China has reiterated its position that the ruling is null and void and has no legally binding force. Furthermore, it will never be an option for China to abandon its sovereignty claims to features in the South China Sea, regardless of their status as rocks or islands, because sovereignty is considered a core national interest. In response to the Award, the Chinese Foreign Ministry reiterated its position of "non-acceptance and non-participation" in the arbitration because the Tribunal had no jurisdiction over the case and, as a result, the Award lacks legitimacy. Given the current situation, Beijing will maintain this position for the long term, but it will have to demonstrate its diplomatic adeptness and wisdom in order to face the challenges this policy brings.

Second, as the recently elected Philippine President Rodrigo Duterte has expressed his willingness to reset China–Philippines relations, China could compromise on some less-sensitive Philippines, and Manila has already shown that it is interested in bilateral diplomatic negotiations as well.[11] The uncertainty lies in what role the Award will play in future bilateral talks. Beijing has set as a precondition for talks that the Award could not be considered, but Manila may see this as impossible. China could consider making a compromise by inviting Manila for fisheries cooperation in the waters of the Scarborough Shoal. Former President Fidel Ramos, special envoy to China, has expressed a desire for joint fisheries cooperation in his meetings with Chinese officials and scholars.

All other claimant States are keeping an eye on the development of the China–Philippines dispute to gain insight into the potential implications of following the path of third-party dispute settlement. A reset of bilateral relations will not

---

11   Marlon Ramos, "Duterte calls on China to let Pinoys fish in West Philippine Sea," *Philippine Daily Inquirer*, August 24, 2016, <http://globalnation.inquirer.net/143188/duterte-calls-on-china-to-let-pinoys-fish-in-west-philippine-sea>.

only stabilize the current South China Sea situation but also gives China diplomatic credit in regional forums and sets an example for other claimant States to know that third party dispute settlement is not the best option for the dispute. In October 2016, President Duterte visited China, and Beijing and Manila issued a joint statement. He publicly expressed that the two agreed to resolve the dispute through negotiation and enhance economic and political ties, suggesting a further distancing from the United States. The visit opened a new chapter in the bilateral relationship between China and the Philippines and is expected to stabilize diplomatic interactions over the South China Sea.

The third diplomatic policy option for China relates to a potential clarification of its maritime territorial claims. China could provide a more detailed explanation of its South China Sea claims, particularly in regards to what "historic rights" covers. It could also provide a more extensive counterargument to the contents of the Award to further support its interpretations of international maritime law and improve its reputation after having it damaged by the Award. During the past three years, China has made many efforts to clarify its maritime policy and claims through official channels. In its 2014 position paper, China reaffirmed and clarified its South China Sea claims and their legal, historical, and geographical background, including claiming the Spratly Islands as a group instead of certain single features. The 2016 white paper provides greater detail about China's decades of administration over these features and further clarifies its South China Sea claims. It is worth mentioning that it also confirms that Beijing supports freedom of navigation and overflight in the South China Sea, implying that future baselines of the Spratly Islands will not negate such rights accorded to all states.

Fourth, China could use the infrastructural developments on its occupied features as a foundation for promoting maritime cooperation in the area. This would help to restore confidence and trust with its neighbors to mitigate the negative impacts of the Award. One recent commitment China has made is expressed in paragraph 3 of the joint communiqué signed by China and ASEAN nations at the 2016 ASEAN Foreign Ministers' Meeting (AMM), in which China and ASEAN states agreed not to "inhabit the presently uninhabited islands, reefs, shoals, cays, and other features and to handle their differences in a constructive manner."[12] The joint communiqué shows the goodwill of both China and its neighbors. China could consider using infrastructure on some of its reclaimed features, such as the Mischief Reef, to set up a marine protection center or search-and-rescue center for regional cooperation, to restore confidence and trust and strengthen its ties with surrounding countries.

Fifth, China must consider how best to manage its diplomatic relations with extra-regional actors as related to the South China Sea. For China, the arbitration case and Award reflect ongoing competition with the United States, not only its diplomatic relations with the Philippines or other claimants. Of all extra-regional powers that have sought to become involved in the South China Sea issue, the US, Japan, and Australia have been the three most active players, as further evidenced in their responses of the Award. Although the US claims to be neutral in the South China Sea dispute, it has backed the Philippines on many occasions, especially in support of its resort to arbitration. It also perceives the arbitration case and Award as legitimate and a valid approach and, on many diplomatic occasions, has urged China to abide by the Tribunal's interpretations of international law as detailed in its two awards. On July 12, US Department of State Spokesperson John Kirby stated that "the tribunal's decision is final and legally binding on both China and the Philippines. Our expectation is all claimants are going to abide by it."[13] US Secretary of State John Kerry, when meeting with Laotian Foreign Minister Saleumxay Kommasith, urged ASEAN to reach consensus and issue a joint statement on the Award. On July 25, 2016, the United States, Japan, and Australia issued a trilateral statement during the annual ASEAN foreign ministers meeting in Laos, in which they urged China not to continue its land reclamation and military outpost construction and to comply with the Award. Chinese Foreign Minister Wang Yi responded immediately that the three were "fanning the flames" and escalating

> Although the US claims to be neutral in the South China Sea dispute, it has backed the Philippines on many occasions, especially in support of its resort to arbitration.

---

12   "Joint Statement of the Foreign Ministers of ASEAN Member States and China on the Full and Effective Implementation of the Declaration on the Conduct of Parties in the South China Sea," Association of Southeast Asian Nations, July 25, 2016, <http://asean.org/storage/2016/07/Joint-Statement-on-the-full-and-effective-implementation-of-the-DOC-FINAL.pdf>.

13   John Kirby, "Daily Press Briefing," Office of Press Relations, Bureau of Public Affairs, US Department of State, July 12, 2016, <https://www.state.gov/r/pa/prs/dpb/2016/07/259605.htm>.

the already complicated situation.[14]

The United States is certainly an important factor shaping the future situation in the South China Sea, and it remains unclear what actions the new Trump administration will take as US government and military officials have offered contradictory remarks related to the issue. One thing that is clear is that the Philippines, once its key Southeast Asian defense ally, has distanced itself from the US over anti-drug trafficking and human rights issues, and the future of the relationship between Manila and Washington remains uncertain.

Beijing's diplomatic reactions to the Award have not indicated any anxiety; instead, they show that it was well-prepared for the result. Amid the tension and pressure, a number of countries have publicly come out in support of China's stance in the South China Sea. China has faced criticism that it is trying to line up nations on its side to win global public support for its

Maritime Law"[15] from 2016 to 2020 to maintain freedom and safety of navigation, increase the capabilities of maritime law enforcement agencies, strengthen protection of marine resources and environment, and thus safeguard its maritime interests. It is now the right time to speed up the legislation process and be prepared for potential legal dispute settlement mechanisms.

Conclusion and Future Prospects

Although the Award provided legal clarifications on certain issues, these clarifications remain controversial, and the Award did not serve to ease tensions in the South China Sea. Uncertainties and ambiguities remain, and there are still conflicting interpretations of the Award and international maritime law in general. For China, the diplomatic implications of the arbitral proceedings and Award have been mostly negative. They

> Beijing's diplomatic reactions to the Award have not indicated any anxiety; instead, they show that it was well-prepared for the result.

positions, but most of the countries offering vocal support matter little to the South China Sea dispute. Nevertheless, it is still a wise move for Beijing to find supporters for its positions as it may ease diplomatic tensions and decrease other countries' willingness to pressure Beijing in regional and international multilateral fora.

Finally, China should be prepared for a future legal resolution of the South China Sea dispute, since the Award may encourage other claimants to pursue such an eventual outcome. In March 2016, China announced in its 13th Five-Year Plan that it would introduce a comprehensive "Basic

brought the China–Philippines relationship to a historic low, challenged China's maritime claims in the South China Sea, and unfairly forced upon China a reputation for not respecting international law. China has faced a great deal of criticism and pressure on many diplomatic occasions but has also gained the support of and improved its relations with many nations in and outside of the region. China continues to face diplomatic pressure in multilateral fora, especially from the United States, Singapore, and Japan. Due to the Award's overwhelmingly negative impact on China, it may also give rival claimants more leverage in future negotiations and reinforce China's distrust of third-party dispute settlement mecha-

---

14 "Wang Yi Refuting the Joint Statement by US, Japan and Australia: Peacekeeper or Troublemaker," Ministry of Foreign Affairs, People's Republic of China, July 27, 2016, <http://www.fmprc.gov.cn/mfa_eng/zxxx_662805/t1384823.shtml>.

15 "China to make maritime law in five years," Xinhua, March 5, 2016, <http://news.xinhuanet.com/english/2016-03/05/c_135157406.htm>.

nisms and other legal means of dispute settlement.

China has several diplomatic policy options in responding to the current situation, including restoring bilateral relations with the Philippines, clarifying its maritime claims and their legal bases, provide counter-arguments to the Award, and encourage maritime cooper-

Without backing down on its sovereignty claims, China could pursue a softer policy of economic cooperation in order to gain more diplomatic support from rival claimants and other major stakeholders in the South China Sea.

ation that takes advantage of the infrastructure on its occupied features. China must continue its non-participation and non-acceptance policy approach, but it is time to start preparing for the possibility of third-party dispute settlement mechanisms that it may have to face in the future. Without backing down on its sovereignty claims, China could pursue a softer policy of economic cooperation in order to gain more diplomatic support from rival claimants and other major stakeholders in the South China Sea.

Yan Yan is a deputy director of the Research Center of Oceans Law and Policy in the National Institute for the South China Sea Studies (NISCSS) and currently a PhD candidate in the University of Hong Kong Faculty of Law. She graduated from London School of Economic and Political Studies (LSE) in 2005. Her research focuses on China's maritime policy and strategy, maritime security issues in the South China Sea, the legal regime of peacetime military activities at sea. She speaks in many regional track 1.5 and 2 conferences and seminars on China's maritime policy and regional maritime security issues, such as the 8th Asian Regional Forum (ARF) Inter-sessional Meeting on Maritime Security, and the 10th CSCAP General Conference, and has given lectures in research institutions such as the European Institute for Asian Studies (EIAS). She received the HKU Postgraduate Scholarship in 2013 and Rhodes Academy scholarship for Law of the Sea studies in 2012.

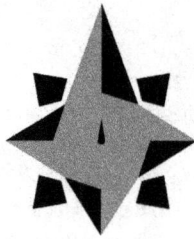

Post-Arbitration South China Sea:

China's Security Policy Options and Future Prospects

Renping Zhang and Duo Zhang

Abstract

Since the Philippines' unilateral initiation of its arbitration case in January 2013, tensions have increased in the South China Sea. Chinese policymakers view the Award issued by the Tribunal on July 12, 2016, as having intensified the disputes in the South China Sea and that the Philippines has spared little effort in disrupting the peace and stability of the region. This chapter first discusses China's security policy approach, which includes setting aside differences and pursuing joint development, exercising restraint, negotiation and coopera- tion with ASEAN, opposition to foreign interference, land reclamation, infrastructure devel- opment, and naval modernization and security cooperation. It then assesses the security implications of the Award for China, which involve law enforcement activities, differing in- terpretations of innocent passage, the frequency of military operations by both claimants and non-claimants, and the intensified monitoring of infrastructure. Following this, it offers an analysis of China's South China Sea security policy options in the post-arbitration context, which relate to naval patrols and maritime law enforcement activities, regional relations and confidence-building measures, infrastructural development of maritime features, and military modernization.

Introduction

On July 12, 2016, an arbitral tribunal rendered its Award in the South China Sea arbitration case between the Republic of the Philippines and the People's Republic of China (PRC). In the Award, the Tribunal concluded that "China has in the course of these proceedings aggravated and extended the disputes be- tween the Parties through its dredging, artificial island-building, and construc- tion activities."[1] The arbitrators concluded that China's "nine-dash line" claims were contrary to UNCLOS where "they exceed the geographic and substantive limits of China's maritime entitlements under UNCLOS". The Philippines also

---

1   Award, PCA Case No. 2013-19, Permanent Court of Arbitration, July 12, 2016, p. 452, <http://www.pcacases.com/web/sendAttach/2086>.

claimed that China's claims to historical rights in the South China Sea were not in accordance with international law, to which the arbitrators agreed. The South China Sea arbitration case has attracted widespread attention in mainstream media and among the general public. China prefers negotiation through dual-track initiatives to find solutions to South China Sea issues. China seeks to resolve the disputes through direct negotiation and dialogue with the parties concerned and, at the same time, China uses all means available to jointly safeguard peace and stability in the region. China holds that it is determined to protect its maritime interests and security in a peaceful manner.

The simple philosophy indicates that everything has its advantages and disadvantages, and the South China Sea arbitration case has in some ways been an enlightening experience for China. First, the Award did not achieve its expected result because it did not resolve the disputes and the parties concerned will still have to negotiate in order to do so. Second, it reinforced China's view that the South China Sea disputes can only be resolved by the parties concerned through bilateral negotiation and relevant efforts. Finally, it helped China to progress towards the rational use of international law in safeguarding its own maritime rights and interests and maintaining regional peace and security.

In the 1970s, former Chinese leader Deng Xiaoping pointed out that "sovereignty belongs to China, disputes can be shelved, and we can pursue joint development," and this is still considered the best way for China to resolve the South China Sea disputes with the parties concerned.[2] The Chinese government aims to demonstrate its sincerity and goodwill without compromising in ways that would be detrimental to its own interests, so it must proceed with its naval modernization, including the deployment of aircraft carriers and large-scale warships in the region, to maintain peace and stability. China makes every effort to work together with all other countries in the region, as well as ASEAN, in a strategic way to promote innovation, interconnectivity, and inclusiveness to make a safer and more

> In the 1970s, former Chinese leader Deng Xiaoping pointed out that "sovereignty belongs to China, disputes can be shelved, and we can pursue joint development," and this is still considered the best way for China to resolve the South China Sea disputes with the parties concerned.

---

2   "China Adheres to the Position of Settling Through Negotiation the Relevant Disputes Between China and the Philippines in the South China Sea," Ministry of Foreign Affairs, People's Republic of China, July 13, 2016, <http://www.fmprc.gov.cn/nanhai/eng/snhwtlcwj_1/t1380615.htm>.

secure South China Sea.

China's Security Policy Approach

In recent years, the international security environment has changed drastically and increased in complexity. All countries face security challenges, and China is no exception. China faces many international and regional security challenges, and maritime security in particular has become a top priority in its national security strategy. China is determined to ensure national maritime security, respond to new types of security issues, and be involved in international and regional security matters for its sustainable development as a maritime nation. China aims to solve maritime disputes with bordering states of the South China Sea in a cautious manner to promote peace and stability in the South China Sea.[3] China's multifaceted security policy approach to South China Sea issues includes setting aside differences and pursuing joint development, exercising restraint, negotiation and cooperation with ASEAN, opposition to foreign interference, land reclamation, infrastructure development, and naval modernization and security cooperation.

> China faces many international and regional security challenges, and maritime security in particular has become a top priority in its national security strategy.

Setting Aside Differences and Pursuing Joint Development

With the precondition that "territorial sovereignty belongs to China", China has long advocated a "set aside differences and pursue joint development" policy approach as proposed by Deng Xiaoping in the 1970s. Now, this policy approach continues to apply in the context of the South China Sea disputes. For China, shelving the dispute can be accomplished without abandoning its territorial sovereignty. China seeks joint development in order to promote mutual understanding through cooperation and create the conditions for resolution of the sovereignty disputes.

Exercising Restraint

China maintains that it has exercised the utmost patience and restraint in the South China Sea to prevent further escalation of the disputes. Even in the face of increasing regional security threats from within and

---

3   *China's Ocean Development Report (2015)*, State Oceanic Administration, People's Republic of China, Beijing: China Ocean Press, May 2015, p. 303.

outside of the region, China has maintained its peaceful policy approach that emphasizes dispute resolution through negotiation, rules-based management and control of the disputes through cooperative mechanisms, mutually beneficial development and cooperation to achieve a win-win

> Chinese Premier Li Keqiang expressed at the East Asia Summit that China was in favor of and advocated a "dual-track" approach to addressing South China Sea issues.

situation, maintaining freedom of navigation, enhancing security, and safeguarding peace and stability in the South China Sea.

Negotiation and Cooperation with ASEAN

In 2002, ASEAN and China agreed to the Declaration on the Conduct of Parties in the South China Sea (DOC).[4] On September 7, 2016, the 19th China-ASEAN Leader's Summit adopted the Guidelines for Hotline Communications among Senior Officials of the MFA of China and ASEAN Member States in Response to Maritime Emergencies and issued the Joint Statement on the Application of the Code of Unplanned Encounters at Sea in the South China Sea.[5] These are important achievements within the framework of implementing the DOC, and fully reflect the determination and confidence of all parties to manage and control disputes within a regional rules-based framework, deepen practical maritime cooperation, and ease

tensions in the South China Sea.

Opposition to Foreign Interference

In November 2014, the Chinese Premier Li Keqiang expressed at the East Asia Summit that China was in favor of and advocated a "dual-track" approach to addressing South China Sea issues.[6] One track is that the relevant dispute should be solved peacefully through friendly consultations and negotiations directly between the states concerned. The other track is that peace and stability of the South China Sea is maintained by China and ASEAN countries. The policy has four implicit meanings:

1. China's stance on the resolution of the relevant disputes through bilateral negotiations will not change.

2. China's position is clear on opposition to foreign countries intervening in the South China Sea.

3. China will never give up resolving the dispute peacefully.

4. China intends to serve as the keeper of peace and stability in the South China Sea.

This statement and others make it clear that Chinese government continues to be consistent in its opposition to foreign intervention in the South China Sea disputes.

Land Reclamation

China holds that its land reclamation in the South China Sea is necessary and purely related to its domestic policy and development. The Chinese government has stated that the work is intended to provide both essential civilian services and military defense, but it is primarily intended to serve non-military purposes. China's plans are to use the artificial islands for civilian services and pro-

---

4   "Declaration on the Conduct of Parties in the South China Sea," Foreign Ministers of ASEAN and People's Republic of China, November 4, 2002, <http://cil.nus.edu.sg/rp/pdf/2002%20Declaration%20on%20the%20Conduct%20of%20Parties%20in%20the%20South%20China%20Sea-pdf.pdf>.

5   Li Keqiang, "Remarks at the 19th China-ASEAN Summit to Commemorate the 25th Anniversary of China-ASEAN Dialogue Relations," State Council, People's Republic of China, September 7, 2016, <http://www.gov.cn/premier/2016-09/08/content_5106318.htm>.

6   "Li Keqiang: 'Dual Track' thinking for Dealing with South China Sea Issues", Xinhua News, November 15, 2014, <http://news.xinhuanet.com/world/2014-11/15/c_1113262929.htm>. [Chinese]

mote maritime safety in the region.[7]

The reclamation and construction has military, operational, and legal implications. As China upholds the principles of international law and freedom of navigation, China's land reclamation efforts in the South China Sea could improve its ability to support civilian ship and aircraft operations in the region on a day-to-day basis and also conduct combat operations in the region.[8]

Infrastructure Development

China's position on infrastructure development is that all of its construction and development on the islands are legal, rational, and reasonable.

search and rescue, meteorological observations, environmental protection, navigational safety, and fisheries protection. China aims to provide better services to all merchant ships, regardless of whether they are Chinese ships or from other countries, operating within or transiting through the region.[9]

Naval Modernization and Security Cooperation

The People's Liberation Army Navy (PLAN) has made great progress in strengthening its capabilities through its naval modernization program. PLAN's vision for modernization ranges from near seas to deep seas defense, and naval mod-

> China, as a major maritime country, must assume more international
> responsibilities than other countries. The scope of its infrastructure
> development is a result of this as it must cope with its international
> responsibilities in the South China Sea, particularly in terms of maritime
> search and rescue, meteorological observations, environmental protection,
> navigational safety, and fisheries protection.

None of them could affect or are directed against any other parties. The infrastructure development is comprehensive and multi-functional, being primarily for civilian purposes and only for basic defense needs if need be. China holds that it is a key player in maintaining regional peace and stability.

China, as a major maritime country, must assume more international responsibilities than other countries. The scope of its infrastructure development is a result of this as it must cope with its international responsibilities in the South China Sea, particularly in terms of maritime

ernization will be required to operate its fleet at longer ranges in order to be capable of protecting its maritime sovereignty. To this end, China has built more modern vessels to operate in its waters.

In terms of security cooperation, China and Russia successfully conducted joint military exercises in September 2016, marking the sixth consecutive joint exercise between the two countries since 2012. The joint exercise aimed to reflect real operations and focused on information technology and standardization, specifically in joint search and rescue, joint onboard inspection, joint anti-air and anti-submarine operations, and

7   "China Adheres to the Position of Settling Through Negotiation the Relevant Disputes Between China and the Philippines in the South China Sea", China Ministry of Foreign Affairs, July 13, 2016, <http://www.fmprc.gov.cn/nanhai/eng/snhwtlcwj_1/t1380615.htm>.

8   Ben Dolven, "Chinese Land Reclamation in the South China Sea: Implications and Policy Options", June 18, 2015, < https://www.fas.org/sgp/crs/row/R44072.pdf>

9   Hua Chunying, "Ministry of Foreign Affairs on US Defense Secretary's Remarks on South China Sea Issues at the Shangri-La Dialogue," Ministry of Foreign Affairs, People's Republic of China, May 30, 2015, <http://www.gov.cn/xinwen/2015-05/30/content_2870863.htm>. [Chinese]

joint seizure and control of islands.[10] Security co-operation between PLAN and the navies of other countries is conducted with the aim of enhancing regional security.

> By definition, Chinese law enforcement activities in its own territorial waters are legitimate and justifiable. Nevertheless, the Award directly targeted the activities of law enforcement agency vessels, fishing boats, and merchant ships operating in these waters.

Security Implications of the Award

The Award of July 12, 2016, has security implications for all of the parties concerned, and impacts claimants as well as non-claimant stakeholders. For China, its security implications relate to law enforcement activities, differing interpretations of innocent passage, the frequency of military operations by both claimants and non-claimants, and the intensified monitoring of infrastructure.

Law Enforcement Activities

For China, the first security implication of the Award is that it affects Chinese law enforcement activities within maritime areas over which it claims sovereignty. By definition, Chinese law enforcement activities in its own territorial waters are legitimate and justifiable. Nevertheless, the Award directly targeted the activities of law enforcement agency vessels, fishing boats, and merchant ships operating in these waters. In Submission 13 of its Memorial submitted to the Tribunal, the Philippines claimed that China had "breached its obligations under the Convention

by operating its law enforcement vessels in a dangerous manner causing serious risk of collision to Philippine vessels navigating in the vicinity of Scarborough Shoal."[11] In its Memorial, it complained of three allegedly dangerous actions conducted by China's law enforcement vessels against Philippine law enforcement vessels on April 10, April 28, and May 26, 2012.[12] The Philippines alleged that China thus violated relevant provisions of the Convention on the International Regulations for Preventing Collisions at Sea (COLREGs) and UNCLOS.[13]

To support its allegations, the Philippines retained Professor Craig H. Allen of the University of Washington, who presented his written opinion to the Arbitration Tribunal on March 19, 2014, and Professor Alan E. Boyle of Essex Court Chambers of the United Kingdom, who gave a statement before the Tribunal on behalf of the Philippines on November 26, 2015. In his opinion, Allen argued:

> PRC vessel FLEC-310 violated the COLREGs on April 28, 2012, when it passed within 200 yards of SARV-002 and 600 yards of SARV-003 at speeds in excess of 20 knots. In addition, PRC public vessels MSV-71, FLEC-303 and FLEC-306 violated the COLREGS on May 26, 2012, when they attempted, on multiple occasions, to cross the bow of RP vessel MSC-3008 at a distance of as little as 100 yards and speeds of up to 20 knots.[14]

It should be noted that the two professors

---

10   Jianing Yao, "China, Russia Conclude Joint Naval Drill," Xinhua, September 19, 2016, <http://eng.mod.gov.cn/DefenseNews/2016-09/19/content_4733271.htm>.

11   Award, PCA Case No. 2013-19, Permanent Court of Arbitration, July 12, 2016, p. 41, <http://www.pcacases.com/web/sendAttach/2086>.

12   Award, PCA Case No. 2013-19, Permanent Court of Arbitration, July 12, 2016, pp. 301–302, <http://www.pcacases.com/web/sendAttach/2086>.

13   Award, PCA Case No. 2013-19, Permanent Court of Arbitration, July 12, 2016, p. 421, <http://www.pcacases.com/web/sendAttach/2086>.

14   Craig H. Allen, "Opinion of Craig H. Allen, Judson Falknor Professor of Law, University of Washington," March 19, 2014, <http://www.pcacases.com/pcadocs/The%20Philippines%27%20Memorial%20-%20Volume%20VII%20%28Annexes%20222-255%29.pdf#page=373>.

retained by the Philippines acknowledged or at least did not deny the basic fact that the alleged incidents took place within the territorial sea of Huangyan Island (Scarborough Shoal), which is claimed by China, and that the Philippine law enforcement vessels allegedly threatened by Chinese law enforcement vessels, in China's view, were not conducting innocent passage through the territorial sea but carrying out illegal activities that were prejudicial to China's territorial sovereignty.[15] Although China maintains that the Award has no legal effect and did not participate in the proceedings, other actors have sought to treat it as legally binding. If used by other coun-

Sea and the Contiguous Zone states, among other things, that "the Government of the People's Republic of China has the right to take all necessary measures to prevent and stop the passage of a ship which is not innocent through its territorial sea."[17] As such, if China exercises sovereignty over Huangyan Island, the only right Philippine vessels have in the relevant territorial sea is innocent passage, and any activities other than innocent passage are prohibited. China, as the coastal State, is entitled to take necessary measures to stop activities of vessels that are prejudicial to Chinese sovereignty, which is common practice worldwide.

When an incompatibility arises between law enforcement activities as authorized by UNCLOS and actions required by the COLREGs, UNCLOS takes precedence over COLREGs.

tries as justification for military action, the security implications for China in regards to law enforcement activities in its claimed waters present a challenge that it may have to face in the future.

Different Interpretations of Innocent Passage

The conclusions set forth in the Award also have security implications for China related to the differing interpretations of innocent passage. The right of foreign vessels to innocent passage is the principal limitation on a country's sovereignty over its territorial seas. UNCLOS defines innocent passage in Article 19(1) as "not prejudicial to the peace, good order or security of the coastal State." Article 25(1) of UNCLOS provides that "the coastal State may take the necessary steps in its territorial sea to prevent passage which is not innocent."[16] Furthermore, Article 8 of the Law of the People's Republic of China on the Territorial

When Chinese law enforcement vessels operate in the vicinity of Huangyan Island, UNCLOS prevails over COLREGs. The different interpretations of innocent passage may have different implication for maritime security. For the purpose of collision avoidance, COLREGs requires ships to keep well clear of each other as a matter of principle, which is contrary to law enforcement practice which often necessitates approaching another vessel. When an incompatibility arises between law enforcement activities as authorized by UNCLOS and actions required by the COLREGs, UNCLOS takes precedence over COLREGs.

UNCLOS, which was adopted by the United Nations at its third Conference on the Law of the Sea, has been widely accepted as the "Constitution for the oceans". From the perspective of jurisprudence, UNCLOS is legally superior to

---

15   Zhang Duo and Zhang Renping, "Chinese law enforcement activities in its own territorial waters legitimate and justifiable," *China Daily*, May 30, 2016, <http://usa.chinadaily.com.cn/epaper/2016-05/30/content_25531538.htm>.

16   United Nations Convention on the Law of the Sea, United Nations, December 10, 1982, <http://www.un.org/Depts/los/convention_agreements/texts/unclos/unclos_e.pdf>.

17   The Law on the Territorial Sea and the Contiguous Zone of the People's Republic of China, Government of the People's Republic of China, February 25, 1992, <http://www.un.org/depts/los/LEGISLATIONANDTREATIES/PDFFILES/CHN_1992_Law.pdf>.

COLREGs.[18] Thus, in the case of incompatibility between the two, the application of Article 25(1) of UNCLOS, which authorizes Chinese law enforcement vessels in Chinese territorial seas to approach its Philippine counterparts as a necessary measure to prevent their prejudicial activities, takes precedence over the application of the COLREGs. Therefore, based on these understandings of innocent passage and sovereignty, in respect to the incidents alleged by the Philippines, the Chinese law enforcement vessels did not violate COLREGs; rather, it was the Philippine vessels that violated UNCLOS by conducting activities other than innocent passage in China's territorial sea.

Boyle and Allen put the horse before the cart by holding that COLREGs prevail over UNCLOS and apply in all circumstances. The absurdity of this logic can be illustrated with the following scenario: when foreign vessels wantonly trample on the sovereignty of a coastal State by entering its territorial sea and conducting activities prejudicial to its sovereignty, the only response the coastal State could make in order not to violate COLREGs would be to order its law enforcement vessels to keep well clear of the intruding foreign vessels and not conduct any preventative activities. Such a situation is entirely not what is intended by the regulations and is out of alignment with the spirit of international law.

> The intention of the Chinese vessels was to drive the intruding Philippine vessels out of the Chinese territorial sea as authorized by Article 25(1) of UNCLOS, without any attempt to threaten the safety of the vessels and personnel on board.

The two professors pointed fingers of blame at Chinese vessels for intentional, deliberate behavior that demonstrated a reckless disregard for the safety of Philippine vessels, but they chose to ignore the fact that the Chinese vessels involved are much faster than their Philippine counterparts, had those Chinese vessels intended to collide with the Philippine vessels, many collisions would have taken place. However, there was no collision. This is because the intention of the Chinese vessels was to drive the intruding Philippine vessels out of the Chinese territorial sea as authorized by Article 25(1) of UNCLOS, without any attempt to threaten the safety of the vessels and personnel on board. The report of the international navigational safety expert appointed by the Tribunal has adverse security implications for China and can be

---

18 Zhang Duo and Zhang Renping, "Chinese law enforcement activities in its own territorial waters legitimate and justifiable," *China Daily*, May 30, 2016, <http://usa.chinadaily.com.cn/epaper/2016-05/30/content_25531538.htm>.

seen as extremely biased.[19]

As described above, Submission 13 by the Philippines was not a professional maritime incident legal evaluation. Given the navigational situation of the law enforcement agency vessels concerned, our analysis of these incidents suggests that China's law enforcement agency vessels were in full compliance with COLREGs. However, it is quite clear to us that expert's view in the report was very much one-sided. Apart from summarizing the situation, the report did not mention the navigation activities, communication, approaches, or signals displayed or given by the vessels in question, including those of the Philippines. The report only spoke of the wrongdoings of Chinese law enforcement agency vessels without examining the behavior of the Philippine side. It is well known that in nearly all cases of collisions at sea, not only one party is solely to blame; in most cases, there is blame to be shared on both sides. Because the expert's report completely disregards relevant details of the law enforcement situation, the Tribunal's conclusions have negative security implications for China by suggesting that its law enforcement activities were in violation of international law.

> Apart from summarizing the situation, the report did not mention the navigation activities, communication, approaches, or signals displayed or given by the vessels in question, including those of the Philippines. The report only spoke of the wrongdoings of Chinese law enforcement agency vessels without examining the behavior of the Philippine side.

Increased Military Operations by Claimants and Non-claimants

Further security implications for China have arisen from the intensification of military operations and activities in the South China Sea following the Award, as regional claimants and non-claimants alike seek to expand their military presence in the maritime area. The Philippines has already coordinated with the US, Vietnam, Malaysia, and Indonesia to organize joint patrols in the South China Sea and to work with countries like India to obtain the naval hardware needed for such patrols. There is no easy solution to regional security in the South China Sea. As combat ships and aircraft in the area increase in number, higher tensions result and impact regional security, increasing the likelihood of maritime incidents. Though unfortunate, this has perhaps been the greatest impact of the Award. Among the many efforts to increase military presence and thus risk armed

---

19   Gurpreet S. Singhota, *Report of the International Navigational Safety*, Hague, Permanent Court of Arbitration, <http://www.pcacases.com/web/sendAttach/1810>.

conflict in the South China Sea, one of the few promising signs was Philippine President Duterte's announcement that the 2016 war games with the US military would be the last.[20]

When the US, Australia, and Japan use freedom of navigation as a justification for their military actions in the South China Sea, regional tensions increase and regional security is threatened due to the heightened risk of maritime incidents. The US has dispatched warships to operate in the South China Sea, assisted several other Southeast Asian claimants in enhancing their naval and air defense capabilities, and sought to pressure its allies into cooperating on joint patrols. With countries emboldened by the Award, some have jumped on board. In September 2016, Japanese Defense Minister Tomomi Inada said that Japan would increase its military involvement in the South China Sea by participating in joint training patrols with the US, conducting bilateral and mul-

amplified by the Award, has significant security implications for China and is detrimental to regional stability and maritime safety.

For China, the worst case scenario would involve increased foreign military operations by multiple countries in its claimed waters because such activities increase the risk of maritime incidents involving two or more countries. With Japan and the US vowing to increase their presence in maritime areas claimed by China, China faces a difficult dilemma about how to confront such challenges that could potentially violate Chinese sovereignty.

Security Policy Options

China holds that peace and stability in the South China Sea should be jointly maintained by China and ASEAN member states. It pursues peaceful

When the US, Australia, and Japan use freedom of navigation as a justification for their military actions in the South China Sea, regional tensions increase and regional security is threatened due to the heightened risk of maritime incidents.

tilateral exercises with other countries in the region, and equipping claimants with military hardware.[21] The increased military presence of the US in the region and its Asia-Pacific rebalancing strategy have posed unprecedented challenges to traditional security in the South China Sea, and the proliferation of maritime securitization efforts by its allies has come to threaten regional stability. Continued US intervention in the region,

development and adheres to security policies that aim to promote stability in the area. China's new security vision emphasizes mutual trust, mutual benefits, equality, and cooperation. China is committed to fostering friendly relations with its neighbors and advancing practical cooperation with ASEAN that is mutually beneficial and encourages sustainable regional development.[22] In line with its goal of promoting peace and stability in the South China Sea, China's major security policy options in the post-arbitration context relate to routine naval patrols and maritime law en-

---

20 Julie M. Aurelio, "2016 PH-US war games will be the last – Duterte," *Philippine Daily Inquirer*, September 28, 2016, <http://globalnation.inquirer.net/145669/2016-ph-us-war-games-will-be-the-last-duterte>.

21 David Brunnstrom, "Japan to conduct training patrols with U.S. in South China Sea," Reuters, September 16, 2016, <http://www.reuters.com/article/us-southchinasea-japan-patrols-idUSKCN11L2FE>.

22 "China Adheres to the Position of Settling Through Negotiation the Relevant Disputes Between China and the Philippines in the South China Sea," China Ministry of Foreign Affairs, July 13, 2016, <http://www.fmprc.gov.cn/nanhai/eng/snhwtlcwj_1/t1380615.htm>.

forcement activities, regional relations and confidence-building measures, infrastructural development of maritime features, and military modernization.

Naval Patrols and Maritime Law Enforcement

China's first security policy option in the post-arbitration environment relates to the frequency and extent of its naval patrols and maritime law enforcement activities. PLAN plays an important role in safeguarding China's maritime sovereignty and security. In recent years, it has increased its capabilities in order to conduct routine naval patrols that contribute to the security and stability of the South China Sea, but it still requires further improvements to its naval capabilities for operating at greater distances. Maritime law enforcement activities are within the mandate of the Chinese Coast Guard and its vessels operate in South China Sea for the purpose of law enforcement. Given the challenges created by the increasing military and civilian activities within maritime areas claimed by China, it has little choice but to increase its naval patrol and maritime law enforcement capabilities if the relevant agencies are to safeguard China's sovereignty claims and protect its own citizens in their use of the South China Sea.

> Given the challenges created by the increasing military and civilian activities within maritime areas claimed by China, it has little choice but to increase its naval patrol and maritime law enforcement capabilities if the relevant agencies are to safeguard China's sovereignty claims and protect its own citizens in their use of the South China Sea.

Regional Relations and Confidence-Building Measures

China's relations with other countries in the region are also an important aspect of its post-arbitration security policy options. Maintaining friendly relations based on mutual trust with its neighbors benefits Chinese security, and confidence-building measures (CBMs) play an important role in this process. China has been a proponent of bilateral and multilateral CBMs. In line with the implementation of the DOC in 2002, which exhorts countries to exercise self-restraint, not take actions that would further complicate the disputes, and undertake cooperation especially on non-traditional security issues, Chinese Premier Li Keqiang announced in September 2016 that the COC should be finalized in mid-2017 and China had also reached an agreement with ASEAN on the implementation of CUES.[23]

Maritime security should be maintained through cooperation between or among littoral states in the South China Sea. Maritime accidents may involve warships, law enforcement agency vessels, merchant fleets, fishing boats, or other vessels. Security risks increase when more naval and civilian vessels operate in the maritime area. Because of the inherent risks of increased maritime activity, effective measures are required in order for all claimants concerned to build confidence and mutual trust. China has been a major advocate of CBMs among relevant parties and is also of the view that foreign involvement jeopardizes these efforts. Because its policy approach of promoting CBMs simultaneously contributes to its national security interests and regional stability, it will continue to move forward with existing approaches and also promote new approaches to preventing and managing maritime incidents and fostering stable regional relations. For regional security, innovative thinking, or the formation of new ideas or methods through incremental change, is of the essence. Interim measures need to be developed new forums designed, and new procedures established in order to create a new approach for building trust and confidence among countries in the region and promoting regional security.

> China has been a major advocate of CBMs among relevant parties and is also of the view that foreign involvement jeopardizes these efforts.

Infrastructural Development of Maritime Features

The third security policy option for China following the arbitral proceedings relates to the development of infrastructure on maritime features. The Chinese government has invested heavily in infrastructural development of its occupied features in the South China Sea, one of the most important sea lines of communications (SLOCs) for global shipping and trade. It has established lighthouses and other facilities on some of the islands to contribute to the safety of vessels navigating through the region, and it has also built facilities necessary for maritime search and rescue and humanitarian aid.

Relative to other South China Sea claimants, China is in a unique position because of its extensive experience in and advanced capabilities for developing infrastructure on maritime

---

23   Li Keqiang, "Speech by Li Keqiang at 19th China-ASEAN Leader's Summit," Government of the People's Republic of China, September 8, 2016, <http://www.gov.cn/premier/2016-09/08/content_5106318.htm>.

features. Rival claimants are limited by logistical, technological, economic, and political factors in their capacity to develop such infrastructure that contributes to the greater good. It is thus China's unique responsibility to do so, and it must continue to improve its facilities and strengthen its capabilities for providing maritime search and rescue services and humanitarian aid. Infrastructure of this nature promotes maritime safety for people from China and other countries and contributes to regional security.

ping lanes has increased in importance. In light of these factors, the Chinese military, particularly PLAN, must continue its process of modernization in order to safeguard China's security interests and promote regional stability.

Conclusion and Future Prospects

China maintains that the Award was a document issued by an ad hoc arbitral tribunal that showed

In the past, China's maritime security policy options were limited to focusing on near-seas defense, but its recent advances increase its options and enable it to shift its security policy approach from solely near-seas defense to a combination of near-seas and far-seas defense.

Military Modernization

China's final security policy option in the post-arbitration context relates to military modernization. China's military has achieved great progress over past couple of years, especially in terms of its naval capabilities. PLAN now has its first aircraft carrier in operation, and a second carrier is under construction. In the past, China's maritime security policy options were limited to focusing on near-seas defense, but its recent advances increase its options and enable it to shift its security policy approach from solely near-seas defense to a combination of near-seas and far-seas defense.[24]

PLAN is expanding its capabilities and operations in order to reduce vulnerabilities in China's near seas and to support its security in deep seas and the South China Sea. China's seaborne trade relies on the security of key SLOCs, including the South China Sea and Strait of Malacca, and as China's economy has become the second largest in the world, the security of maritime ship-

obvious bias against China and that it has no legal effect. In the Award, the Tribunal violated the principle of prudence in interpreting international law and demonstrated a tendency towards legal expansionism and legal radicalism.[25] China neither accepts nor recognizes the Award. Nevertheless, the arbitral proceedings and resulting Award have major security implications for China, particularly as relate to law enforcement activities, differing interpretations of innocent passage, the frequency of military operations by both claimants and non-claimants, and the intensified monitoring of infrastructure. China's security policy options for addressing the disputes and other issues in the South China Sea relate to naval patrols and maritime law enforcement activities, regional relations and confidence-building measures, infrastructural development of maritime features, and military modernization. Increasing foreign involvement, especially by the US and Japan, has had a tremendously adverse impact on the security of China and other South China Sea claimants and is detrimental to region-

---

24 "China's Military Strategy," White Paper, Ministry of National Defense, People's Republic of China, May 25, 2015, <http://www.mod.gov.cn/regulatory/2015-05/26/content_4617812.htm>.

25 Li Xue and Zheng Yuwen, "Legal Defects of the South China Sea Ruling," IPP Review, September 16, 2016, <http://www.ippreview.com/index.php/Home/Blog/single/id/239.html>.

al peace and stability.

All littoral states in the South China Sea have the obligation to promote security and maritime safety in the region. Several factors that should be taken into consideration include maritime incident response, resource management, and confidence building among relevant par-

> The arbitral proceedings and resulting Award have major security implications for China, particularly as relate to law enforcement activities, differing interpretations of innocent passage, the frequency of military operations by both claimants and non-claimants, and the intensified monitoring of infrastructure.

ties. CUES, the COC, and other efforts negotiated among countries concerned are important to safeguarding China's national security interests as well as promoting regional peace and stability, and China – in cooperation with individual countries and ASEAN, one of the most important mechanisms for regional peace and security – will continue to play a major role in the development of such mechanisms.

Renping Zhang is the Director of the Centre for International Maritime Convention Studies at Dalian Maritime University of China. He has been engaged in maritime education and study of maritime conventions over 30 years. His main research and study areas include maritime communication, maritime safety, maritime security, and marine environmental protection.

Duo Zhang is a professor in nautical science at the Training Centre of China COSCO Shipping Corporation Limited at Qingdao Ocean Shipping Mariners College of China. He is a tutor for graduates at Chongqing Jiaotong University of China. He serves as a Secretary of the Seafarers Committee of Asian Shipowners' Association. His other titles include lawyer, arbitrator, and nautical assessor.

Post-Arbitration South China Sea:

Malaysia's Policy Options and Future Prospects

Chow Bing Ngeow

Abstract

Malaysia's policy towards the South China Sea dispute has been different from Vietnam and the Philippines in the sense that Malaysia has opted for a policy approach that is less confrontational with China. There are geographical, historical, and economic explanations for Malaysia's policy approach, but this chapter also argues that Malaysia's view of the importance of ASEAN also shapes the way it looks at China, the South China Sea, and the Philippines vs. China arbitration case. The arbitration award has benefited Malaysia legally, but has not fundamentally changed its major policy stance towards China and the South China Sea disputes. Given its policy stance, Malaysia is unlikely to follow the Philippines in challenging China in an international tribunal or court of arbitration. In the security policy domain, Malaysia has pursued several policies, including strengthening security partnerships with the West, increasing its security presence in Sabah and Sarawak, and maintaining military diplomacy channels with China. It is suggested in this chapter that Malaysia perhaps can also play a bolder role in initiating diplomatic initiatives that could contribute to the stability and peace of the region, such as a Sino-Malaysian fishing agreement and bilateral negotiations over the overlapping claims between Malaysia and China.

Introduction

Amidst rising tensions in the South China Sea since the late 2000s, China–Malaysia ties have also reached new milestones. In 2013, President Xi Jinping visited Malaysia and proposed to elevate the bilateral relationship to a "comprehensive strategic partnership," which Malaysia accepted.[1] In 2014, Xi's visit was reciprocated by Prime Minister Najib Abdul Razak's visit to China, which resulted in the signing of the fourth joint communique in the history of China–Malaysia relations, which affirmed the Sino–Malaysian "comprehensive

---

1   "China, Malaysia agree to lift ties to comprehensive strategic partnership," *Xinhua*, October 4, 2013, <http://news.xinhuanet.com/english/china/2013-10/04/c_132772213.htm>.

strategic partnership."[2] Since the 1990s, top leaders in Malaysia have decided that it is better to capitalize on China's rise and an improving bilateral relationship to derive economic benefits. Today, Malaysia enjoys a large volume of bilateral trade with China, its largest trade partner, and also receives huge investments from China. All these developments stand in contrast to the deterioration of relations between China and the other two major ASEAN claimant states in the South China Sea dispute, Vietnam and the Philippines.

However, Malaysia has also increasingly become very much concerned with China's actions and behaviors in the South China Sea. Malaysian policymakers have long expected that its low-profile approach towards the South China Sea dispute and the history of Sino–Malaysian friendship would make Malaysia less likely to be targeted by China's assertive actions. Such expectations were greatly diminished by several incidents: (1) the oath-taking ceremonies undertaken by PLA Navy officers in waters around James Shoal 2013 and 2014;[3] (2) the incident of the China Coast Guard stopping Malaysian fishermen from fishing in areas around Luconia Shoals in 2015;[4] (3) the continuous presence of a China Coast Guard ship in Luconia Shoals since then; and (4) the sudden appearance of a large number of Chinese fishing vessels near Luconia Shoals in March 2016.[5] Both James Shoal and Luconia Shoals are located off the coast of the state of Sarawak. James Shoal is about 50 nautical miles off the coast of the city of Bintulu, whereas Luconia Shoals is about 80 nautical miles off the coast of the city of Miri. Malaysia patrols around the waters of these two features but does not maintain a naval presence. In more recent

> Malaysian policymakers have long expected that its low-profile approach towards the South China Sea dispute and the history of Sino–Malaysian friendship would make Malaysia less likely to be targeted by China's assertive actions. Such expectations were greatly diminished by several incidents.

2   "Malaysia, China agree to enhance cooperation in various fields," *The Sun Daily*, May 31, 2014, <http://www.thesundaily.my/news/1064241>.

3   Jeremy Page, "Chinese Ships Approach Malaysia," *The Wall Street Journal*, March 27, 2013, <http://www.wsj.com/articles/SB10001424127887324 685104578386052690151508≥; Sui-Lee Wee "Chinese ships patrol area contested by Malaysia," *Reuters*, January 26, 2014, <http://uk.reuters.com/article/uk-china-malaysia-idUKBREA0P06X20140126>.

4   "Presence of China Coast Guard ship at Luconia Shoals spooks local fishermen," *Borneo Post Online*, September 27, 2015, <http://www.theborneopost.com/2015/09/27/presence-of-china-coast-guard-ship-at-luconia-shoals-spooks-local-fishermen/>; "Malaysia to protest over China Coast Guard 'intrusion': Navy chief," *Channel News Asia*, June 9, 2015, <http://www.channelnewsasia.com/news/asiapacific/malaysia-to-protest-over/1903142.html>.

5   Joseph Sipalan, "As Beijing flexes muscles in South China Sea, Malaysia eyes harder response," *Reuters*, June 1, 2016, <http://www.reuters.com/article/us-southchinasea-malaysia-idUSKCN0YM2SV>.

years, Chinese vessels have been less intrusive in the waters surrounding the features where Malaysia claims, occupies, and maintains a naval presence. These features include Swallow Reef, Mariveles Reef, Investigator Shoal, Erica Reef, and Ardasier Reef, all of which are located about 160–180 nautical miles off the coast of Kota Kinabalu, the capital city of the state of Sabah and also where the Malaysian Naval Command Region 2 (the Malaysian navy base covering both Sabah and Sarawak) is located. There were reports that ships from China's maritime enforcement department and fisheries department intruded into waters close to Swallow Reef twice in April 2010, and there may have been more unreported incidents,[6] but the recent pattern generally seems to suggest that Chinese naval activities are more widespread in waters around James Shoal and Luconia Shoals than waters around the five features that the Malaysian Navy maintains a presence.

The recent "island-building" activities undertaken by China, although not directly related to Malaysia's claims, greatly reduce the distance between the active Chinese naval presence and Malaysian naval presence, thereby creating a higher level of risk of incidents occurring between the two. These activities are causing anxiety among Malaysian defense planners, think tankers, and policymakers. Chinese vessels' presence around Luconia Shoals has also been greatly unsettling for Malaysian leaders.

> Chinese vessels' presence around Luconia Shoals has been greatly unsettling for Malaysian leaders.

Many of them, such as Deputy Prime Minister Ahmad Zahid, Minister of the Prime Minister's Department Shahidan Kassim, and Defense Minister Hishammuddin Hussein, have all been notably more vocal in recent years concerning China's actions and behavior in the South China Sea.[7] It should be noted that leaders such as Ahmad Zahid and Hishammuddin Hussein are traditionally China-friendly ministers who have refrained from criticizing China in the past. It should also be noted, however, that vocal dissatisfaction from these Ministers can be read as a sign of Malaysia's growing unhappiness about the situation but not as a sign that Malaysia is undertaking a fundamental change in its South China Sea policy. Malaysia's foreign policy remains very much driven by the Prime Minister. So far, Prime Minister Najib has still been very careful in his statements on the South China Sea and has not publicly uttered anything that could be read as serious criticism of China's actions in the South China Sea. Although plenty of officials in both the

---

6   Dzirhan Mahadzir, "Malaysia's Maritime Claims in the South China Sea: Security and Military Dimension," in Pavin Chachavalpongpun (ed.), *Entering Uncharted Waters? ASEAN and the South China Sea*, Singapore: ISEAS, 2014, pp. 220–221.

7   See Tang Siew Mun, "Why Malaysia is adopting a tougher South China Sea stance," *The Malay Mail*, March 21, 2016, <http://www.themalaymailonline.com/what-you-think/article/why-malaysia-is-adopting-a-tougher-south-china-sea-stance-tang-siew-mun>.

defense and diplomatic sectors as well as analysts in the think tank and strategic studies circles wish that Malaysia could and should undertake a more forceful policy approach,[8] the government has so far still adhered to a China-friendly policy posture.

It is against this backdrop that Malaysia has closely watched developments relating to the arbitration case involving the Philippines and China. Malaysia was not part of the arbitral proceedings and thus feels that it is not bound by the Award. On June 23, 2016, the Embassy of Malaysia in the Netherlands sent a Communication to the Arbitral Tribunal, stating that "Malaysia is not bound by the outcome of the arbitral proceedings or any pronouncement on fact or law to be rendered by the Arbitral Tribunal." The Tribunal agreed, stating that "the legal effect of a judicial or arbitral decision is limited to the Parties and from Article 296(2) of the Convention, which expressly provides that '[a]ny such decision shall

> Malaysia's considerations for upholding ASEAN unity as well as the centrality of ASEAN in the management of regional affairs is, perhaps counterintuitively, also the source of its more restrained policy approach towards China in the South China Sea disputes.

have no binding force except between the parties and in respect of that particular dispute.'"[9] Nonetheless, the Award is likely to have ramifications for the legality of Malaysia's claims in the South China Sea. Malaysia is also trying to derive what lessons can be drawn from this episode in terms of dealing with China over such a complex and contentious issue.

Policy Approach

There have been various explanations, including those related to history, geography and economics, as to why Malaysia has undertaken a China-friendly policy approach despite the two countries' conflicting interests in the South China Sea disputes. This article will attempt to advance an explanation that has received insufficient attention, arguing that Malaysia's considerations for upholding ASEAN unity as well as the centrality of ASEAN in the management of regional affairs is, perhaps counterintuitively, also the source of its more restrained policy approach towards China in the South China Sea disputes.

Geography, History, Economics

In the South China Sea, Malaysia claims eleven features and occupies five of them.[10] All of them are off the coasts of Sarawak and Sabah, the two Eastern Malaysian states. While all these Malaysia-claimed and -occupied features are disputed by China (as well as partly by Brunei, Vietnam, and the Philippines), Malaysia has no claims to the features that are currently occupied and developed by China. Malaysia's claimed features are also located much further from mainland China than the features claimed by Vietnam and the Philippines and therefore considerably safer from the power projection capabilities of the Chinese armed forces. This geographical fact could partially explain why Malaysia has felt that it could afford to have a more stable and positive relationship with China.[11]

Historically, Malaysia was the first country among the original ASEAN Five to recognize China diplomatically, which it did in 1974. The Malay-

---

8   Based on author's interactions and conversations with these people in the past two years.

9   Award, PCA Case No. 2013-19, Permanent Court of Arbitration, July 12, 2016, p. 257, para. 637, <http://www.pcacases.com/web/sendAttach/2086>.

10   Estimates vary based on differing definitions of "occupation".

11   That said, China's building up of its controlled features such as Johnson South Reef and Fiery Cross Reef have considerably diminished this geographical comfort for Malaysia.

sian political elite have believed that since then there has been a "special relationship" between China and Malaysia.[12] This historical relationship may also serve as a partial explanation for Malaysia's less confrontational policy approach regarding China and the South China Sea.

In terms of economics, China is Malaysia's largest trade partner and an increasingly major destination for investment as well. Malaysia has derived so many economic benefits from its positive relations with China that it has decided not to "rock the boat" in its bilateral relationship with the country. A similar economic explanation relates to the Malaysian elite. China's economic activities in Malaysia have greatly benefited the elite, including the top political leadership, and they are thus more likely to support China-friend-

agement of regional affairs may have also contributed to the way Malaysia deals with the South China Sea dispute.

ASEAN's Unity and Centrality

The Malaysian Ministry of Foreign Affairs has stated that "ASEAN is the cornerstone of Malaysia's foreign policy. It is both of geo-political significance and economic relevance to Malaysia and also to the nations within the region. Its renunciation of the use of force and promotion of peaceful settlement of disputes has been the foundation to its peace, stability, and prosperity in the region."[14] Malaysia therefore treasures ASEAN unity and sees ASEAN as the key institu-

> China's economic activities in Malaysia have greatly benefited the elite, including the top political leadership, and they are thus more likely to support China-friendly policies.

ly policies. A case in point is the purchase by a Chinese state-owned enterprise of the assets of the troubled Prime Minister-linked firm One Malaysia Development Berhad (1MDB), which help the firm dodge a looming insolvency crisis.[13] Geographical distance, historical legacy and economic pragmatism all account partly for why Malaysia has taken a different approach to the dispute than Vietnam and the Philippines.

While all these factors play an important role in shaping Malaysia's policy approach in the South China Sea, this chapter attempts to advance here the argument in which the Malaysian declared foreign policy principle of upholding ASEAN unity and ASEAN centrality in the man-

tion for managing regional issues such as the South China Sea. The Ministry's declaration also implies that ASEAN is a central consideration in the process of Malaysian foreign policy. There are, of course, doubts as to whether Malaysia's real foreign policy actions match its rhetoric. However, in the case of the South China Sea dispute, a case can be made that Malaysia means what it says when it declares ASEAN as the cornerstone of its foreign policy.

Indeed, it is this ASEAN-centric South China Sea policy that distinguishes Malaysia from other claimant states in ASEAN. First, the belief in ASEAN unity and its centrality in the management of regional affairs as of critical importance to the maintenance of regional peace and stability has implications in terms of Malaysian attitudes towards the Philippines' decision to bring the South China Sea dispute to the Permanent Court

---

12   Stuart Grudging, "China's assertiveness hardens Malaysian stance in sea dispute," *Reuters*, February 26, 2014, <http://uk.reuters.com/article/uk-malaysia-china-maritime-insight-idUKBREA1P1Z020140226>.

13   "Malaysia's 1MDB sells power assets to China firm for $2.3 billion," *Reuters*, November 23, 2015, <http://www.reuters.com/article/us-malaysia-1mdb-idUSKBN0TC0PT20151123>.

14   "Malaysia's Foreign Policy," Ministry of Foreign Affairs, Malaysia, <http://www.kln.gov.my/web/guest/foreign_policy>.

of Arbitration. Second, Malaysia has believed, and continues to believe, that the best way to engage China on this contentious issue is through ASEAN-based mechanisms, including the Declaration on the Conduct of Parties in the South China Sea (DOC) and the still-being-negotiated Code of Conduct in the South China Sea (COC). Third, conscious of ASEAN centrality, until lately Malaysia has also been more careful than others in engaging extra-regional powers in the dispute.

Preserving ASEAN unity and centrality have become increasingly challenging with the escalation of the South China Sea dispute. Within ASEAN, it is widely believed that two blocs have formed, one with interests more aligned with China (Cambodia and Laos) and one more sus-

An ASEAN-based South China Sea policy also means that Malaysia is not comfortable engaging extra-regional powers into the dispute.

picious and critical of China (Vietnam and the Philippines). Maintaining ASEAN unity means balancing the two blocs, so Malaysia is uncomfortable with actions that are either too aligned with China or too antagonistic towards China, as both kinds of actions are detrimental to the cause of ASEAN unity.

China has so far refused to let ASEAN play a role in the resolution of the dispute and insisted that the South China Sea dispute is between China and certain claimant states who happen to be members of ASEAN, not a dispute between China and ASEAN. However, in practice China has already accepted that ASEAN must play a role, at least in the management of the dispute, and this is manifested in the DOC and the (future) COC. Malaysia's official statements on the South China Sea dispute have always emphasized the importance of the DOC and COC, and in this sense there is a consistent belief that they remain the best mechanisms to achieve several goals: ensur-

ing stability in the region, preserving ASEAN unity and centrality, and engaging China. Malaysia's confidence in and preference for the DOC (and COC) have been quite consistent over the years. This can be seen in the handling of the most recent contentious issue between China and Malaysia over the South China Sea dispute – the incident in March 2016 in which a large number of Chinese vessels appeared in waters close to Sarawak. Malaysia did summon the Chinese ambassador to explain the incident.[15] Two months later in May, Chinese State Councilor Yang Jiechi, the senior government official in charge of foreign policy visited Malaysia and held talks with Malaysian officials concerning the issue. Reportedly, after the meeting, Malaysian Foreign Minister Anifah Aman said that Malaysia and China reached an agreement that both countries would "settle all issues through the DOC and speed up the completion of the COC."[16]

Finally, an ASEAN-based South China Sea policy also means that Malaysia is not comfortable engaging extra-regional powers into the dispute. In this sense, there has been agreement between Malaysia and China over the issue of not involving "outsiders" in the South China Sea disputes. Malaysia appeared to share with China the concern that "internationalizing" South China Sea issues would further complicate the situation. This position against "outsiders' interference" was reinforced with the 2014 joint communique, in which Malaysia and China affirmed that "both sides underscored the importance of maintaining peace, security and stability as well as upholding freedom and safety of navigation in the South China Sea" and further emphasized that all directly concerned

---

15   "Malaysia summons Chinese envoy over South China Sea intrusion," *South China Morning Post*, March 31, 2016, <http://www.scmp.com/news/asia/southeast-asia/article/1932726/malaysia-summons-chinese-envoy-over-south-china-sea>.

16   "Malaysia, China agree to settle South China Sea dispute via conduct declaration," *The Malay Mail*, May 10, 2016, <http://www.themalaymailonline.com/malaysia/article/malaysia-china-agree-to-settle-south-china-sea-dispute-via-conduct-declarat>.

states should "settle their differences by peaceful means, through friendly consultations and negotiations, and in accordance with universally recognized principles of international law" while recognizing that the "intervention or involvement of parties not directly concerned could be counterproductive and further complicate the aforementioned differences."[17] This agreement over not welcoming outside interference appeared to be a strong foundation for China and Malaysia to maintain positive ties despite overlapping claims in the South China Sea. This agreement, nevertheless, has become increasingly untenable with several of China's actions in Luconia Shoals that can be seen as deliberate challenges to Malaysia's claims.

Implications of the Award

The Award was a sweeping legal victory for the Philippines against China. Malaysia was not part of the arbitral proceedings and is not legally bound by the Award. Even so, theoretically, there is much that could be gained from supporting the Philippines in this arbitration case, as the legal implications of the Award seem to strengthen and consolidate Malaysia's claims. Nevertheless, Malaysia's official responses have so far not deviated from its existing South China Sea policy, which emphasizes cautiousness, restraint, and avoidance of actions that can be seen as provocative to China. For the moment, the security implications of the Award are likely to be minimal.

Legal Implications

If the Award can be upheld as a legal precedent, then there are mostly positive implications for Malaysia's claims. The positive implications stem from China's claims to "historical rights to resources within the sea areas falling within the 'Nine-dash line'" having been rendered invalid. Hence, the China Coast Guard's actions in 2015 against Malaysian fishermen and the maritime enforcement agency in waters surrounding Luconia Shoals, which lie within Malaysia's EEZ, would be deemed unlawful. Similarly, James Shoal,

Malaysia's official responses have so far not deviated from its existing South China Sea policy, which emphasizes cautiousness, restraint, and avoidance of actions that can be seen as provocative to China.

which is also well within Malaysia's continental shelf and EEZ, cannot be the "southernmost frontier" of Chinese territory, since it is a permanently submerged feature. The legal benefit to Malaysia extends beyond Malaysia–China dispute. Potentially, other Malaysian-claimed features, such as Amboyna Cay (currently occupied by Vietnam), can also be deemed outside of other countries' EEZs and within that of Malaysia.

On the negative side, the Award also sets a high bar in determining the status of a "habitable island." Since the Tribunal decided that Itu Aba (Taiping) Island, which is currently occupied by the Republic of China (Taiwan) and the largest feature in the South China Sea, is legally a "rock" and not an island under UNCLOS, it could be inferred that the largest and the most well-developed feature occupied by Malaysia, Swallow Reef, can also only generate 12-nautical-mile territorial waters, not a 200-nautical-mile EEZ. This would considerably shrink the size of the potential fishing areas exclusive to Malaysian fishermen.[18] However, Malaysia has in the past refrained from claiming an EEZ from Swallow Reef, so the

17 "Joint Communiqué between the People's Republic of China and Malaysia, in Conjunction with the 40th Anniversary of the Establishment of Diplomatic Relations, Beijing, 31 May 2014," Ministry of Foreign Affairs, Malaysia, May 30, 2014, art. 30, <https://www.kln.gov.my/archive/content.php?t=8&articleId=4184783>.

18 Lam Choong Fah, "Malaysia Should Support the South China Sea Arbitration," [Chinese], Malaysiakini, July 11, 2016, <http://www.malaysiakini.com/columns/348173>.

real negative implications are quite limited. Therefore, if the Award is deemed a valid legal precedent, Malaysia will have gained more than it has lost. For these reasons, there are calls for Malaysia's government to cautiously welcome the Award.[19] However, the Malaysian government's official response has anything but offered overt support to the Philippines.

Diplomatic Implications

Malaysia must carefully calibrate its diplomatic relations with China, ASEAN countries, and non-claimant stakeholders in the aftermath of the Award. The Foreign Ministry's statement on July 12, 2016, is so far the only official document stating the Malaysian government's position on the arbitration case.[20] It mentions that Malaysia takes note of the Award issued by the Tribunal and reiterates the long-standing position held by Malaysia, which includes its commitment to the "full and effective implementation" of the DOC, a call for an early conclusion of the COC, and an urging of all parties to commit themselves to the DOC. The statement notes that Malaysia believes that the disputes can be peacefully resolved with full respect for the "diplomatic and legal process" and relevant international law, including UNCLOS, and urges all parties to exercise self-restraint to avoid complication of disputes, escalation of tensions, and threatening the use of force. This can be read as implicitly criticizing China for its assertive and tension-generating activities, including island building and militarization. The final paragraph of the statement notes that Malaysia "believes China and all relevant parties can find constructive ways to develop healthy dialogues, negotiations and consultations while upholding supremacy of the rule of law for the peace, safety and security for the region."[21]

During 2016 ASEAN Summit in Vientiane, Prime Minister Najib also broke his silence regarding the Award. Queried by a newspaper as to why ASEAN did not raise the issue of the Award in its discussions or statement, Najib opined that the arbitration was essentially unenforce-

> If the Award is deemed a valid legal precedent, Malaysia will have gained more than it has lost.

---

19   Ong Kian Ming, "What the decision on South China Sea means to Malaysia," *Malaysiakini*, July 14, 2016, <https://www.malaysiakini.com/news/348469>.

20   "Press Release: Statement by Malaysia on SCS Arbitration Tribunal," Ministry of Foreign Affairs, Malaysia, July 12, 2016, <http://www.kln.gov.my/web/are_dubai/n2016/-/asset_publisher/ME2g/blog/press-release-:-statement-by-malaysia-on-scs-arbitration-tribunal?redirect=%2Fweb%2Fare_dubai%2Fn2016>.

21   "Press Release: Statement by Malaysia on SCS Arbitration Tribunal," Ministry of Foreign Affairs, Malaysia, July 12, 2016, <http://www.kln.gov.my/web/are_dubai/n2016/-/asset_publisher/ME2g/blog/press-release-:-statement-by-malaysia-on-scs-arbitration-tribunal?redirect=%2Fweb%2Fare_dubai%2Fn2016>.

able because, in arbitration, it would require both parties to agree to the terms. The Philippines' action was essentially "unilateral," so "there is no mechanism for enforcement." Further, Najib also said that China agreed to the COC because China valued "good relations with ASEAN" and expressed "cautious optimism" that the COC would be completed on or before the set mid-2017 deadline. Finally, Najib reiterated the need for ASEAN to uphold solidarity and act as One ASEAN, saying that "[w]hen we have different views, we must be able to harmonize them. We must display the unity of ASEAN."[22] Put into context, this statement displayed a sense that Najib felt the Philippines was not doing enough to have its view "harmonized" with other views in ASEAN and the decision to refer the issue to international arbitration was therefore a "unilateral" action.

> The statement displayed a sense that Najib felt the Philippines was not doing enough to have its view "harmonized" with other views in ASEAN and the decision to refer the issue to international arbitration was therefore a "unilateral" action.

In late October and early November, following Philippine President Duterte's visit to China, Najib also embarked on a visit to China. The visit resulted in both countries reaching economic agreements that amounted to about USD 34 billion and plans for Malaysia to purchase military vessels from China. The visit was also symbolically important, signifying Malaysia's continued willingness to maintain friendly ties with China in spite of the Award and actions in the South China Sea. On the issue, Najib reportedly said that they "agreed that these claims are between two friendly countries, with a high level of trust. There is no reason why it can't be resolved... Of course, it might take some time. A nation's sovereignty is not an easy problem, but it should not jeopardise the peace and stability in the South China Sea and the region."[23]

Security Implications

Whether the Award could lead to a deterioration of Malaysia's security environment in the South China Sea depends on whether or not Chinese naval activities in areas claimed by Malaysia increase as a result of the Award. During the Xiangshan Forum in Beijing in October 2016, the Malaysia Armed Forces chief, General Zulkefli Mohd Zin, told a Reuters

---

22   Azuba Abas, "Handle dispute with care," *New Straits Times*, September 8 2016, p. 3.

23   Lokman Mansor, "Malaysia optimistic South China Sea issue can be resolved," *New Straits Times*, November 3, 2016, <http://www.nst.com.my/news/2016/11/185758/malaysia-optimistic-south-china-sea-issue-can-be-resolved>.

reporter on the sidelines of the forum "that China has exercised restraint over the dispute, and there has been no increase in Chinese military activity in the parts of the South China Sea which Malaysia claims."[24] Thus, for the time being, the security implications are relatively minimal.

Policy Options

Although Malaysia stands to gain from the legal implications of the Award, Malaysia's actions and statements, as illustrated in the previous sections, so far do not indicate that there will be a change to the existing policy approach. In fact, the continuation of this policy approach also im-

Malaysia, covering both land and sea territories, including Malaysia's claims in the South China Sea. The Award does not potentially add anything more to what Malaysia can claim, so there is no imperative for additional domestic legislature at the moment. Given that the Award strengthens rather than weakens the legality of Malaysia's claims in the South China Sea, there might be a temptation to suggest that Malaysia should follow the Philippines' footsteps in bringing its dispute with China to an international body. However, this remains very much a marginal idea, and Malaysia has very little appetite for undertaking such a course of action that would be seen as unnecessarily provocative to China, especially

> Although Malaysia could theoretically attempt to use the international arbitration procedures offered by UNCLOS to its advantage, it is unlikely to do so as continuing to maintain the status quo is in its best interest.

plies that there are only limited policy options in the legal and security domains. However, Malaysia can play a greater role in diplomatic initiatives.

Legal Policy Options

In terms of domestic legislation, Malaysia has completed the basic legislation that established Malaysia's claims over the disputed area. It adopted the Continental Shelf Act in 1966, declared its 12-nautical-mile territorial waters in 1969, declared its 200-nautical mile EEZ in 1980, and enacted an EEZ act in 1984.[25] In 1979, it published *Peta Baru*, the most authoritative official map of

given the fact that the new Philippine president has already seemingly taken a radically different approach to dealing with China on South China Sea issues. Therefore, although Malaysia could theoretically attempt to use the international arbitration procedures offered by UNCLOS to its advantage, it is unlikely to do so as continuing to maintain the status quo is in its best interest.

Diplomatic Policy Options

Malaysia is likely to continue its present policy stance, including emphasizing constructive diplomatic and economic relations with China and pushing for ASEAN to play a central role in regional relations, especially in the process of implementing DOC and negotiating COC. Concomitant with the DOC and COC processes, Malaysia perhaps can also consider some bolder diplomatic initiatives. One of them could be a Sino-Malaysian bilateral fishing agreement. Conflicts over

24   Ben Blanchard, "China berates visiting New Zealand defence minister over South China Sea stance," *Reuters,* October 11, 2016, <http://uk.reuters.com/article/uk-china-security-idUKKCN12B0CC?il=0>.

25   Asri Salleh, *Malaysia's Territorial Disputes, 1963-2008*, Shah Alam: UiTM Press, 2012, p. 2.

fisheries resources in the South China Sea have been the main factor that stoked tensions between ASEAN countries and China and among ASEAN countries as well.[26] For instance, the immediate cause of the recent deterioration of China–Philippines relations involved disputes over fishing rights. Similarly, recent incidents over the South China Sea between Malaysia and China were also related to Chinese fishing vessels. If disputes over fisheries resources could be well managed, chances of the South China Sea dispute flaring up would be significantly diminished.

There has been a history of cooperation between Malaysia and China over fisheries. In 1998, the Sabah state government and the fisheries department of the Guangdong provincial government singed a fisheries cooperation agreement. Several rounds of the "China-Malaysia Forum on Fisheries Cooperation" were also organized in the early 2000s. In 2008, in a visit to China, Malaysia's agricultural minister stated that China could invest in joint ventures with Malaysian companies to fish in Malaysian waters. However, so far there has not been further progress in formulating a bilateral fisheries agreement. On the other hand, China also has signed several similar agreements over fisheries with several countries in the past, including Indonesia, South Korea, Vietnam, and the Philippines. Not all of these fisheries agreements resulted in a reduction of disputes over fisheries resources, but some of them, such as the fisheries agreement with Vietnam over the Beibu Gulf/Gulf of Tonkin, did have an effect. Malaysia and China could begin a joint technical study of the feasibility of a bilateral fishing agreement in the contested South China Sea area. It is true that the Award has denied China's traditional rights, including rights to fisheries resources, within its so-called "nine-dash-line," including those waters within Malaysian EEZ. However, this does not mean that Malaysia must deny China in regards to any cooperative fishing agreement. This could be done based on mutual goodwill without explicit legal implications for the countries' respective claims.

An even bolder initiative would be for Malaysia to consider starting bilateral negotiations with China over the disputed area. Whether Malaysia should negotiate bilaterally with China or multilaterally with other ASEAN claimant states remains a subject of considerable disagree-

> Whether Malaysia should negotiate bilaterally with China or multilaterally with other ASEAN claimant states remains a subject of considerable disagreement.

---

26   Leslie Lopez, "South China Sea - Part One: Fish Wars," *The Straits Times*, April 3, 2016, <http://www.straitstimes.com/asia/south-china-sea-fish-wars>.

ment.[27] Proponents of multilateral negotiation point out that the overlapping claims from multiple claimants in the South China Sea essentially mean that a multilateral negotiation is the only sensible way. However, the total disputed area in the South China Sea is very large, and some sections concern only two parties. Malaysia and China can consider negotiation on sections that only concern them and avoid affecting those of other countries.

A main concern regarding bilateral negotiations is that they would be on an unequal basis given the large disparity in power between China and any of the claimant states. However, in the history of China's boundary negotiations, China has negotiated with neighbors large and small alike, and there is no historical evidence that China has exploited a smaller neighbor in its border negotiations. Another objection to bilateral negotiations concerns the attitudes of fellow ASEAN countries. An ASEAN claimant state going on its own in negotiating with China bilaterally may raise suspicion among fellow ASEAN countries, especially those that are South China Sea claimant states. The other claimant states might argue that any bilateral boundary agreement achieved would need to be harmonized with their respective claims, or there would be a risk of compromising the particular interests of other claimant states and the collective interests of ASEAN as a whole. Again, a counter-argument would be that there are geographical sections of the dispute that would not in any way compromise the claims of others and this should be the starting point for the bilateral negotiations. A successful outcome on limited sections could generate enough goodwill to begin more difficult multilateral negotiations. In this sense, bilateral and multilateral negotiations should not be seen as mutually exclusive.

Security Policy Options

Finally, in the security domain, Malaysia's policy options remain rather limited. Even before the Award, Malaysia has long had several security-related policy plans to "hedge" against a possible future South China Sea conflict scenario. These include increased security cooperation with the US and Japan, the beefing up of its security presence and capabilities in Sabah and Sarawak, and the increase of military diplomacy with China to reduce strategic mistrust.

As have Vietnam and the Philippines, Malaysia has increased security cooperation with the US.

An ASEAN claimant state going on its own in negotiating with China bilaterally may raise suspicion among fellow ASEAN countries, especially those that are South China Sea claimant states.

Combined exercises with the US military involving all service branches of the Malaysian Armed Forces have been undertaken on a regular basis. The most regular exercises involve the Malaysian and US navies under the Cooperation Afloat Readiness and Training (CARAT) program, which were undertaken in recent years off Sabah's east coast.[28] In June 2014, the US Air Force held a combined exercise with its Malaysian counterpart that involved more than a thousand personnel, together with the participation of most advanced US fighter jet, the F-22 Raptor. In September 2014, it was also reported that Malaysia would offer to

---

27   For an overview of the pros and cons of bilateral and multilateral negotiations, see Elina Noor, "The South China Sea Dispute: Options for Malaysia," in Ian Storey and Lin Cheng-yi (eds.), *The South China Sea: Navigating Diplomatic and Strategic Tensions*, Singapore: ISEAS, 2016, pp. 219–221.

28   "Maritime Security Training in Sabah," *The Star*, August 20, 2015, <http://www.thestar.com.my/metro/community/2015/08/20/maritime-security-training-in-sabah-us-navy-and-malaysian-armed-forces-undergo-military-exercise/>.

host the US Navy's spy plane P-8 Poseidon in Sabah, but the Malaysian government subsequently denied such an offer had taken place.[29] Similar reports again resurfaced in late 2015, suggesting that both countries were still in talks about plans to allow the P-8 to operate from Malaysian airstrips over parts of the South China Sea,[30] but there was no subsequent confirmation that the plan was concluded. Instead, in December 2015, it was confirmed that Singapore would host the P-8 plane, but Malaysia would have access to the gathered intelligence.[31]

In addition, Malaysia–Japan security ties have also strengthened. During Japanese Prime Minister Shinzo Abe's visit to Malaysia in 2013, Najib thanked "Japan for helping build the capacity of Malaysia's coast guard in patrolling vast areas and curbing piracy in the Strait of Malacca."[32] In 2015, during the return visit by Najib to Japan, Abe also said that Japan had agreed to cooperate on defense equipment and reinforcing support for Malaysia's maritime law and enforcement body.[33] Japanese security support for Malaysia deepened when, in September 2016, news reports emerged that Japan would provide military vessels previously operated by the Japan Coast Guard to Malaysia during the first half of 2017, free of charge. In addition, "Japan would also provide backing for coast guard training, as well as boat repairs and support for necessary communications equipment."[34]

The increased security cooperation with the US and Japan came in tandem with Malaysia's plans to increase its security presence in Sabah and Sarawak. In 2013, it was reported that Malaysia planned to set up a Marine Corps to be based in Sabah and perhaps modelled after the US Marine Corps.[35] However, perhaps due to budgetary reasons, the plan never materialized. A more recent plan, announced in early 2016, was for a new naval base to be located in Bintulu (overseeing James Shoals). A second naval base in Sarawak is perhaps long overdue given that the naval base in Kota Kinabalu, Sabah (Naval Command Region 2), is overstretched with its mission to protect Malaysian waters in the South China Sea, Sulu Sea, and Celebes Sea. Announcement of the establishment of this new base came after the incident of the appearance of a large number of Chinese fishing vessels around Luconia Shoals, but it is likely that planning of the base came much earlier and was not directly triggered by this inci-

> A second naval base in Sarawak is perhaps long overdue given that the naval base in Kota Kinabalu, Sabah, is overstretched with its mission to protect Malaysian waters in the South China Sea, Sulu Sea, and Celebes Sea.

29   Melissa Chi, "Putrajaya denies letting US use Sabah for spy plane missions," *The Malay Mail*, October 9, 2014, <http://www.themalaymailonline.com/malaysia/article/putrajaya-denies-letting-us-use-sabah-for-spy-plane-missions>.

30   Josh Rogin, "Malaysia and U.S. in Talks to Ramp Up China Spying," *Bloomberg*, September 3, 2015, <https://www.bloomberg.com/view/articles/2015-09-03/malaysia-and-u-s-in-talks-to-ramp-up-china-spying>.

31   "Msia not concerned over P-8 Poseidon spy plane in Singapore," *New Straits Times*, December 9, 2015, <http://www.nst.com.my/news/2015/12/116380/msia-not-concerned-over-p-8-poseidon-spy-plane-singapore>.

32   Abhrajit Gangopadhyay, "Japan and Malaysia Tighten Commercial and Security Links," *Wall Street Journal*, July 25, 2013, <http://www.wsj.com/articles/SB10001424127887323971204578627790278996264>.

33   "Japan and Malaysia bolster defense ties, with eyes on China," *Reuters*, May 25, 2015, <http://www.reuters.com/article/us-japan-malaysia-defence-idUSKBN0OA11720150525>.

34   "Japan to offer Patrol Boats to Malaysia," *Free Malaysia Today*, September 7, 2016, <http://www.freemalaysiatoday.com/category/nation/2016/09/07/japan-to-offer-patrol-boats-to-malaysia/>.

35   Zachery Keck, "Malaysia to Establish Marine Corps and South China Naval Base," *The Diplomat*, October 19, 2013, <http://thediplomat.com/2013/10/malaysia-to-establish-marine-corps-and-south-china-sea-naval-base/>.

dent. Initially, the new naval base was announced under the pretext of protecting Malaysia's oil and gas assets from the Islamic militants in the southern Philippines.[36] However, these militants never really ventured that far to Sarawak; most of their criminal and terrorist activities were confined to areas close to eastern Sabah. Hence, the South China Sea disputes are more likely the reason for creating this new base. This was confirmed in a later report in which the Defense Minister, Hishammuddin Hussien, said that the setting up of a new naval base in Bintulu is necessary because of the "need to monitor asset movements within the Sarawak and South China Sea waters."[37]

In addition to this new naval base, Malaysia has also been strengthening its naval capabilities, most notably with its acquisition of two Scorpène-class submarines. Although acquisitions of these two submarines were made before the recent tensions in the South China Sea, these assets were mainly based in Naval Command Region 2 and mostly likely would be used for strengthening Malaysia's capabilities in the South China Sea. However, it is telling that, in a news conference, when asked about Malaysian maritime capabilities in light of the Chinese ships' intrusions into Malaysian waters, Malaysian Defense Minister Hishammuddin reportedly said, "We will increase our maritime capability anyway... But we have to be realistic. No matter how big we boost our capacity - the navy - will it ever be as big as China's or the US's? No."[38]

Finally, Malaysia has also improved and increased its defense relations with China and the PLA. In 2005, Malaysia signed an MOU on Defense Cooperation with China. Since then, mutual visits of top military and defense officials have

Following the first combined table-top exercise held in 2014, Malaysia and China held their first-ever combined military exercise off the Strait of Malacca in September 2015.

---

36 Joseph Sipalan, "As Beijing flexes muscles in South China Sea, Malaysia eyes harder response," *Reuters*, May 5, 2016, <http://www.reuters.com/article/us-southchinasea-malaysia-idUSKCN0YM2SV>.

37 Esther Landau, "Four initiatives to boost security," *New Straits Times*, September 24, 2016, p. 10.

38 "Asean should get its house in order first: Malaysia's Defence Minister Hishammuddin," The Straits Times, June 4, 2016, <http://www.straitstimes.com/asia/se-asia/asean-should-resolve-their-conflict-over-south-china-sea-instead-of-blaming-china>.

been frequent. Following the first combined table-top exercise held in 2014, Malaysia and China held their first-ever combined military exercise off the Strait of Malacca in September 2015. In a visit to China by Defense Minister Hishammuddin in 2013, he invited Chinese Defense Minister Chang Wanquan to visit Naval Command Region 2 in Kota Kinabalu and also launched a direct communication line between Naval Command Region 2 and the South Sea Fleet of the Chinese Navy. Chang's planned visit never materialized, though. In late 2015, during the visit by the Chinese naval chief, Admiral Wu Shengli, it was announced that Malaysia would allow the Chinese navy to use its port facilities at Naval Command Region 2, fulfilling part of the long-term plan for the Chinese navy to secure "stopover locations"

reflect a Malaysian preference for engagement and dialogue to reduce strategic mistrust and miscalculation. The Malaysia Armed Forces chief, General Zulkefli Mohd Zin, during the aforementioned Xiangshan Forum in Beijing, also reportedly said that "In fact we are establishing military cooperation with China to build up confidence so that we understand one another better."[41]

As mentioned before, all these security policy measures were undertaken before the Award was issued on July 12, 2016. The Award does not change these policies other than perhaps providing an impetus to accelerate some processes. For instance, Japan's announcement that it would freely provide ships to Malaysia occurred after the Award.

Malaysia's policy stance on the South China Sea disputes is influenced by its emphasis on ASEAN unity and centrality.

and supplies along its significant routes. It is also notable that the same naval port is also open to the visits of the military ships of other navies, including the US guided-missile destroyer *Lassen*, which "stopped over at Kota Kinabalu after conducting a patrol less than twelve nautical miles from China's man-made facilities on the [Chinese-occupied] Subi Reef."[39] Another interesting related development is the agreement for Malaysia to purchase four littoral mission ships from China during Najib's visit to China in October–November 2016, the first significant weapon procurement Malaysia has made from China.[40] The increased military ties between Malaysia and China amidst the South China Sea tensions

Conclusion and Future Prospects

In the South China Sea dispute, Malaysia is concerned about China's actions and behaviors, just like Vietnam and the Philippines, but Malaysia has not adopted a confrontational policy. While geography, history, and China's economic influence are all contributing factors, it is suggested here that Malaysia's policy stance on the South China Sea disputes is influenced by its emphasis on ASEAN unity and centrality. A confrontational policy could further jeopardize ASEAN unity and perhaps would open the door for China to interfere in ASEAN issues. Malaysia also continues to have faith in ASEAN-related mechanisms such as the DOC and COC in engaging China and has doubts about the involvement of extra-regional

39 "PLA Navy gains use of port in Malaysia close to Spratly islands," *South China Morning Post*, November 21, 2015, <http://www.scmp.com/news/china/diplomacy-defence/article/1881300/pla-navy-gains-use-port-malaysia>.

40 Sue-Lin Wong, "China and Malaysia sign deals on navy vessels," *Reuters*, November 1, 2016, <http://www.reuters.com/article/us-china-malaysia-idUSKBN12W3WF>.

41 Ben Blanchard, "China berates visiting New Zealand defence minister over South China Sea stance," *Reuters*, October 11, 2016, <http://uk.reuters.com/article/uk-china-security-idUKKCN12B0CC?il=0>.

powers.

While Malaysia stands to gain legally from the Award, the official response so far has been limited to the continuation of its current policy stance, and there is very little indication that Malaysia is interested in pursuing a legal course of action on its own in the South China Sea dispute. At the moment, China's reactions to the Award have not resulted in an increase of naval activities in areas that Malaysia claims, so the security implication of the Award remain minimal.

Malaysia has been pursuing several security-related policy measures, including strengthening its security partnership with the Unit-

> While Malaysia stands to gain legally from the Award, the official response so far has been limited to the continuation of its current policy stance, and there is very little indication that Malaysia is interested in pursuing a legal course of action on its own in the South China Sea dispute.

ed States, beefing up its security presence in Sabah and Sarawak, and maintaining military-to-military ties with China to reduce strategic distrust. However, the efficacy of these policies may still be limited. It is suggested here that Malaysia can perhaps utilize its good relationship with China and other ASEAN countries to launch diplomatic initiatives that can help ease tensions, including a bilateral fishing agreement and bilateral claims negotiations that concern only Malaysia and China.

Chow Bing Ngeow is a Senior Lecturer at the Institute of China Studies, University of Malaya. He has published several articles in academic journals such as *Journal of Contemporary China*, *Contemporary Southeast Asia*, *Issues and Studies*, and others.

Post-Arbitration South China Sea:

Philippines' Legal Policy Options and Future Prospects

Jay L. Batongbacal

Abstract

The Philippines' arbitration case against China demonstrates its reliance upon a stable, clear, and rules-based allocation of maritime rights and resources under the United Nations Convention on the Law of the Sea (UNCLOS) in order to pursue and protect its interests in the South China Sea. This approach of using "right v. might" has paid off handsomely as seen in its nearly complete success in persuading the Arbitral Tribunal to rule in its favor, resulting in an authoritative interpretation and application of UNCLOS to its maritime disputes with China over rights, resources, and jurisdiction in the South China Sea. This legal victory will form the basis of its future policies and positions in the South China Sea disputes, and will likely influence the policies and positions of other Southeast Asian claimants against China's expansive claims.

Introduction

In the Award of July 12, 2016, the Philippines achieved a stunning legal victory against China when it won almost all of the principal submissions it made before the Arbitral Tribunal constituted under Annex VII of the United Nations Convention on the Law of the Sea (UNCLOS).[1] Only a part of its penultimate submission which involved military activities in or around Second Thomas Shoal,[2] and the final submission found to not raise an actual dispute between the parties,[3] were not considered by the Tribunal in the Philippines' favor. In all other respects, the Tribunal found that China was in breach of multiple

---

1   Award, PCA Case No. 2013-19, Permanent Court of Arbitration, July 12, 2016, <http://www.pcacases.com/web/sendAttach/2086>.

2   Award, paras. 1153–1162.

3   Award, paras. 1191–1201.

provisions of international law.[4] In doing so, the Tribunal also established guidance for the interpretation and application of UNCLOS, particularly the proper determination of maritime zones around contested features in the Spratly Islands group and Scarborough Shoal, which enables the Philippines to take a firm and legally-supported position in all future diplomatic and legal exchanges against China's expansive claims to rights, jurisdictions, and resources within the area encompassed by its nine-dash line illustrated in the map it submitted to the United Nations in 2009.[5]

Policy Approach

As a smaller country with very little hard power at its disposal and limited means with which to address the great power imbalance among the claimants in the South China Sea disputes, the Philippines places great emphasis on the system of stable, clear, and rules-based allocation of maritime rights and resources under UNCLOS in order to protect and pursue its maritime economic and security interests in the sea areas adjacent to its western coast and within the South China Sea.

The policy imperatives for securing its fishing and petroleum interests in its EEZ and continental shelf along its western seaboard, referred to domestically as the "West Philippine Sea",[6] are particularly strong. Up to 17% of the total annual national fisheries production have

> As a smaller country with very little hard power at its disposal and limited means with which to address the great power imbalance among the claimants in the South China Sea disputes, the Philippines places great emphasis on the system of stable, clear, and rules-based allocation of maritime rights and resources under UNCLOS

---

4   Specifically, the Tribunal found China had breached Articles 56, 58(3), 60, 77, 80, 94, 123, 192, 194(1), 194(5), 197, 206, 279, 296, and 300 of UNCLOS and Rules 2, 6, 7, 8, 15, and 16 of the Convention on the International Regulations for Preventing Collisions at Sea.

5   "Note Verbale CML/17/2009," Permanent Mission of the People's Republic of China to the United Nations, May 7, 2009, <http://www.un.org/depts/los/clcs_new/submissions_files/mysvnm33_09/chn_2009re_mys_vnm_e.pdf>; "Note Verbale CML/18/2009," Permanent Mission of the People's Republic of China to the United Nations, May 7, 2009, <http://www.un.org/depts/los/clcs_new/submissions_files/vnm37_09/chn_2009re_vnm.pdf>.

6   Contrary to popular understanding and mass media usage, the term "West Philippine Sea" is not meant to be synonymous with the "South China Sea" but rather intended to distinguish and separate the sea area under Philippine jurisdiction from the rest of the area of the South China Sea. See "Administrative Order No. 29: Naming the West Philippine Sea of the Republic of the Philippines, and for other purposes," Office of the President of the Philippines, September 5, 2012, <http://faolex.fao.org/docs/pdf/phi152482.pdf>.

historically been derived from fishing activities within this area,[7] and it also happens to encompass its most promising offshore petroleum province currently producing a strategically significant proportion of the country's indigenous energy.[8] From the Philippine perspective, the increasing maritime assertiveness of China in recent years culminated with unilateral actions within the Philippine-claimed EEZ and continental shelf, in some cases as close as only 50–60 nautical miles off the Philippine mainland. This left the Philippines with no choice but to invoke the compulsory dispute settlement provisions of UNCLOS in order to protect and vindicate its exclusive rights to and jurisdiction over limited, but strategically significant, resources.

Legal clarification of its rights and the nature and status of competing claims in the South China Sea was also essential for it to be able to secure firm support from its security partners like the United States and the international community at large in terms of pursuing its interests in the West Philippine Sea. External powers have historically stayed neutral with respect to the complicated and intractable South China Sea disputes on account of numerous unsettled legal uncertainties. The clarification provided by the arbitration case allows the Philippines to obtain better support and greater leverage vis-à-vis China's expansive claims. This legal policy approach, sometimes called "lawfare" and portrayed as "right vs. might", was a key feature of the foreign policy of President Benigno Aquino III and his administration. This policy approach was sustained up until the actual promulgation of the Award on July 12, 2016.

> The clarification provided by the arbitration case allows the Philippines to obtain better support and greater leverage vis-à-vis China's expansive claims.

In the aftermath of the arbitral proceedings, however, President Rodrigo Duterte, who assumed office only weeks prior to the Award, chose not to follow through with this approach and instead re-engaged China in friendly bilateral negotiations that heavily relied on finding areas of cooperation and developing economic linkages between the

---

7   Noel Barut, "National Report on the Fish Stocks and Habitats of Regional, Global, and Transboundary Significance in the South China Sea: Philippines," in *National Reports on the Fish Stocks and Habitats of Regional, Global, and Transboundary Significance in the South China Sea*, UNEP/GEF South China Sea Project, 2007, pp. 89–144, <http://www.ais.unwater.org/ais/aiscm/getprojectdoc.php?docid=3514>.

8   The Northwest Palawan Basin hosts the Philippines' only natural gas production platform, the Malampaya Deepwater Gas-to-Power Project that presently supplies nearly 40% of the electrical power of Luzon. See "Malampaya: The Future of Energy Now," Press release, Shell Philippines, June 26, 2015, <http://www.shell.com.ph/aboutshell/media-centre/news-and-media-releases/2015/malampaya-the-future-of-energy-now.html>; "5th Philippine Energy Contracting Round (PERC5): Figures and Maps," Department of Energy, Republic of the Philippines, <https://www.doe.gov.ph/figures-and-maps-petroleum>.

two countries. At least for now, the "lawfare" approach appears to have been temporarily suspended while the two countries seek to renew their bilateral ties in other areas such as trade, development assistance, economic linkages, and infrastructure development.

Legal Implications of the Award

Regardless of improvements in the political and economic relations between the two countries, the Award has made a difference in their legal situation insofar as the South China Sea disputes are concerned. For the Philippines, the legal implications of the Award include: (1) legal clarity about maritime entitlements, (2) delineation of the geographic scope for joint exploration and development, (3) confirmation of the illegality of certain Chinese actions, (4) legal justification for future Philippine maritime law enforcement operations, (5) legal justification for future Philippine maritime resource exploration and exploitation, and (6) limitation of the geographic scope of unresolved sovereignty issues. Even though China refuses to recognize the validity and binding effect of the Award, the reasoning and analysis

general categories of claims submitted for arbitration. These policy areas are:

1. The nature, extent, and legal status of China's entitlements and claims within the South China Sea in general, including those represented by the "nine-dash line" map;

2. The legitimacy of China's historic claims to marine resources encompassed by the nine-dash line but located within the West Philippine Sea;

3. The legitimacy of China's activities, particularly those involving fishing, maritime law enforcement, and artificial island building, within the West Philippine Sea; and

4. The legitimacy of China's island-building activities pending the resolution of its territorial and jurisdictional disputes with the Philippines in the South China Sea.

As far as the Philippines is concerned, the legal nature, extent, and legal status of China's claims in the South China Sea have been evaluated and precisely defined through the arbitra-

Even though China refuses to recognize the validity and binding effect of the Award, the reasoning and analysis of the Tribunal remain a strongly argued disposition of various aspects of the South China Sea disputes that are sure to have their own influence over international legal thinking.

of the Tribunal remain a strongly argued disposition of various aspects of the South China Sea disputes that are sure to have their own influence over international legal thinking.

Legal Clarity about Maritime Entitlements

The arbitration has provided legal clarity and provided legal foundations for the Philippines' political and diplomatic positions with respect to its maritime jurisdictional disputes with China in terms of the key policy areas implicated in the

tion case. The territorial disputes concerning sovereignty over land features such as islands and rocks, including their adjacent 12-nautical-mile territorial seas, remain unresolved and subject to continuing talks and future resolution by the parties. Beyond those sea areas, however, the Philippines considers the jurisdictional disputes to have been resolved to the extent that the arbitration has identified (a) exactly what "historic claims" China has been making, (b) the geographical area where such claims apply, and (c) the legal status or legitimacy of such claims under prevailing international law.

According to the Tribunal, China's entitlements and claims to resources and jurisdiction in the South China Sea are properly determined not by China's nine-dash line map but by the system of maritime zones defined by UNCLOS.[9] China can claim no more than 12-nm territorial seas extending from its mainland coast and Hainan, and around islands and rocks in the South China Sea that it claims. The Philippines does not dispute China's entitlement to 12-nm territorial seas, nor does it dispute the 200-nm EEZ and con-

teria for its application[10] and its eventual finding that none of the major land features in the Spratly Islands are entitled to their own 200-nm EEZ or continental shelf,[11] the Philippines is entitled to exercise exclusive sovereign rights to its EEZ and continental shelf extending up to 200-nm from its archipelagic baselines.[12] This jurisdiction is effective throughout the entire area of the EEZ and continental shelf, unless the sea and seabed areas are included within the 12-nm territorial enclaves around disputed islands and rocks.

The Tribunal further concluded that each

> The Philippines does not dispute China's entitlement to 12-nm territorial seas, nor does it dispute the 200-nm EEZ and continental shelf measured from and adjacent to its southern mainland coast and Hainan.

tinental shelf measured from and adjacent to its southern mainland coast and Hainan. However, the Philippines effectively disputes China's claim to sovereignty over the islands, rocks, and 12-nm territorial seas surrounding them, within the area of the Spratly Islands that is included in the Philippines' Kalayaan Island Group claims. The latter is a necessary outcome of the deliberate exclusion of all sovereignty issues from the arbitration. In so doing, the Tribunal accepted the Philippine approach of legally and geographically separating the territorial disputes and sovereignty issues over the island and rocks (including their territorial seas) from the jurisdictional disputes to sovereign rights over the waters around them.

The Tribunal's perspective is that beyond 12 nm from the shores of China's mainland, Hainan, and the islands and rocks it claims within the Spratly Islands and Scarborough Shoal, jurisdiction over sea areas is allocated in accordance with the EEZ, continental shelf, and high seas regimes under UNCLOS as interpreted by the arbitrators. In light of the Tribunal's interpretation of UNCLOS Article 121(3) resulting in detailed cri-

high-tide elevation in the Spratly Islands, whether occupied by China, the Philippines, or other States, is entitled to at most 12-nm territorial seas (and implicitly 24-nm contiguous zones) under UNCLOS, but sovereignty over these features and their adjacent zones remains disputed and open to future dispute resolution between the parties concerned.

Beyond 200 nm from the Philippines, the area is comprised of either high seas open to all or EEZs and continental shelves measured from the mainland coasts of other countries, but the seabed beneath may be subject to claims to a continental shelf beyond 200 nm in accordance with the provisions of UNCLOS Article 76. It may be noted that, at this point, the Philippines may

---

10   Award, paras. 475–553.

11   Award, paras. 554–626.

12   The archipelagic baselines encompassing the main archipelago of the Philippines are defined in Republic Act No. 9522. See Republic Act No. 9522: An Act to amend certain provisions of Republic Act No. 3046, as amended by Republic Act No. 5446, to define the archipelagic baselines of the Philippines, and for other purposes, Congress of the Philippines, March 10, 2009, <http://www.lawphil.net/statutes/repacts/ra2009/ra_9522_2009.html>.

---

9   Award, paras. 261–262 and 276–278.

make a submission for a continental shelf beyond 200 nm encompassing the seabed area around the Spratly Islands in accordance with the provisions of UNCLOS Article 76 and the standards established by the "Scientific and Technical Guidelines of the Commission on the Limits of the Continental Shelf."[13]

Delineation of the Geographic Scope for Joint Exploration and Development

In light of the Tribunal's affirmation that UNCLOS determines the rights and entitlements of the Philippines and China with respect to the maritime areas of the South China Sea[14] and that UNCLOS does not permit the maintenance of historic

> The Philippines cannot legally consider proposals for joint exploration and exploitation for petroleum resources within its continental shelf on the basis of Chinese historic claims, and any such proposals must be undertaken on the basis of UNCLOS and national legislation.

rights to natural resources in the EEZ, continental shelf, high seas, or international seabed area,[15] the Philippines cannot recognize the legitimacy of Chinese claims to any rights and/or resources within the former's 200-nm EEZ and continental shelf on the basis of historic claims and beyond 12 nm from any of the contested islands or rocks, regardless of whether these are characterized as being based on historic "rights," "waters," "title," or "facts". The Tribunal found that China's claims

to fishery resources in Philippine waters, whether understood to be either historic rights since previous times or as high seas freedoms prior to the extension of coastal state jurisdiction, were relinquished and abandoned in exchange for the establishment of the EEZ regime under UNCLOS.[16] In any case, China could not validly establish and maintain historic claims to fishery or any other resources or jurisdictions since there is no evidence that (1) such claims were ever specifically expressed previously despite ample opportunity in various diplomatic fora to do so (most notably, during the UNCLOS negotiations),[17] (2) exclusive usage and/or control over them had ever been exercised,[18] or (3) any such claims been accepted by any other State.[19] The Philippines cannot legally consider proposals for joint exploration and exploitation for petroleum resources within its continental shelf on the basis of Chinese historic claims, and any such proposals must be undertaken on the basis of UNCLOS and national legislation.

China's construction of large, massive artificial islands on seven of the features it currently occupies and controls while the arbitration case was still ongoing particularly drew the Tribunal's censure. In no uncertain terms, the Award determined that such actions were clearly contrary to international law because they aggravated and extended the dispute,[20] caused permanent and irreparable harm to the marine environment,[21] and directly prejudiced the rights of the Philippines by permanently destroying ev-

---

13 "Scientific and Technical Guidelines of the Commission on the Limits of the Continental Shelf," Commission on the Limits of the Continental Shelf, May 13, 1999, <http://www.un.org/depts/los/clcs_new/commission_guidelines.htm>.

14 Award, para. 277.

15 Award, paras. 239–247.

16 Award, paras. 257, 263, and 271.

17 Award, paras. 251–254.

18 Award, para. 270.

19 China had never explained or clarified the nature and extent of its claims in the South China Sea until 2009 with the submission of its nine-dash line map to the United Nations and subsequent acts and statements; but since that time, States have expressly objected to its claims. See Award, para. 275.

20 Award, para. 1181.

21 Award, para. 1178.

idence of the natural conditions of the features and impeding the fair determination of their maritime entitlements under UNCLOS.[22]

Confirmation of the Illegality of Certain Chinese Actions

The Arbitral Tribunal assessed the legality of some of China's activities in the South China Sea, including interference with Philippine petroleum exploration activities,[23] the use of environmentally-destructive fishing methods such as the harvesting of coral and giant clams,[24] the construc-

with and preventing traditional fishing activities in Scarborough Shoal.[30]

Legal Justification for Future Maritime Law Enforcement Operations

In this light, the Philippines cannot consider the repetition of similar kinds of activities and operations in the future as legal and may consider it entirely justifiable to actively intervene and prevent them from recurring. Since the Award has provided an authoritative determination of the respective rights and jurisdictions of the parties in large

> Within its EEZ, the Philippines may lawfully insist upon and assert exclusive sovereign rights to regulate the exploration and exploitation of natural resources of the water column and the seabed.

tion of artificial islands,[25] and the government's failure to prevent Chinese fishermen from fishing in the Philippine EEZ.[26] It found that China acted in a manner incompatible with its obligations under UNCLOS in these respects since they contravened the Philippines' exclusive sovereign rights within and jurisdiction over its EEZ and continental shelf[27] and also violated China's own obligations to preserve and protect the marine environment.[28] The Tribunal also found that China operated its maritime law enforcement ships in a manner contrary to the provisions of COLREGS and increased the risk of serious collisions with Philippine ships.[29] It also determined that China acted contrary to international law in interfering

areas of the South China Sea, the Philippines would also have the option, in case of recurrence and depending on the precise location of future similar breaches, to seek relief against China on the basis of state responsibility for wrongful acts. Examples of other potential actions include calling for and mobilizing diplomatic pressure, filing complaints with and seeking sanctions by international organizations, or seeking compensation and reparations for damages. Moreover, the Tribunal's de-legitimization of the construction of artificial islands in the South China Sea allows the Philippines to consider any existing and/or new artificial island-building activities to be a continuing violation of international law, which could adequately justify future actions to prevent their recurrence.

Legal Justification for Future Maritime Resource Exploitation

The Award clearly vindicates the Philippines' exclusive sovereign rights to its own EEZ and conti-

---

22   Award, para. 1179.

23   Award, para. 209.

24   Award, para. 826–851.

25   Award, paras. 852–905.

26   Award, paras. 718–728.

27   Award, paras. 716, 757, 1043.

28   Award, paras 992–9923.

29   Award, para. 1109.

---

30   Award, para. 814.

nental shelf, measured from its archipelagic baselines and extending up to 200 nm into the South China Sea. Within this area, the Philippines may lawfully insist upon and assert exclusive sovereign rights to regulate the exploration and exploitation of natural resources of the water column and the seabed in accordance with Parts V and VI of UNCLOS. This includes its primary and exclusive jurisdiction to regulate all fishing and petroleum development activities. Any further attempts by China to seek some form of access to rights and resources within these areas on any basis other than UNCLOS and Philippine national law, particularly on the basis of ambiguous and unsupported historic "rights," "title," "waters," or "facts," may be lawfully rejected by the Philippines.

Limitation of the Geographic Scope of Unresolved Sovereignty Issues

The Award, however, does not resolve the issue of sovereignty over the islands and rocks within the Spratly Islands, including their respective adjacent 12-nm territorial seas. As far as the Philippines is concerned, these resulting enclaves, which still collectively represent a substantial maritime area, are still in dispute between the Philippines and China and an appropriate subject for future dispute resolution through diplomatic negotiations. Only within these enclaves may Chinese historic claims be considered as possible issues for discussion and negotiation, since they would then form part and parcel of the issues included in the sovereignty disputes. Activities within and around these disputed areas are likewise subject to discussions and negotiations for the purpose of ensuring that the disputes are managed and eventually resolved peacefully. It is important to note that on account of the pending sovereignty disputes, the parties are equally bound by international law to not act in a manner that aggravates and extends the disputes, causes serious irreparable damage to the marine environment, prejudices the rights of the other, or contravenes the UN Charter. In the meantime, the parties are also bound to ensure that they do not resort to the use of force or the threat of the use of force in their future interactions over the disputes, and make every effort to mitigate and prevent opportunities for possible escalation into armed conflict.

> The Award does not resolve the issue of sovereignty over the islands and rocks within the Spratly Islands,.

Legal Policy Options

The conclusion of the arbitral proceedings has created several legal policy options for the Philippines, which relate to (1) the entrenchment of legal positions on entitlements, rights, and delimitation; (2) re-engagement with China on the basis of legal positions; and (3) engagement with other rival claimants and ASEAN on the basis of legal positions. The Award has provided the Philippines with an enormous amount of legal, political, and diplomatic leverage that it can employ against China in its bilateral relations or deploy in its multilateral relations with other states and international organizations with direct or indirect interests in the South China Sea. However, its legal options remain limited on account of immutable geographical and geopolitical realities. The use of armed force to resolve the disputes in its favor is completely out of the question. Not only does the Philippines eschew the use of force as a means of pursuing interests with the international community, it also must acknowledge that with respect to its basic sovereignty claims to the Kalayaan Island Group within the Spratly Islands, all non-claimant countries, including its allies, and organizations remain neutral and will not support such use of force. Therefore, its only policy framework for addressing and eventually resolving the South China Sea disputes must be based on the peaceful modes of dispute settlement enumerated in the Charter of the United Nations and Part XV of UNCLOS.

> The Award has provided the Philippines with an enormous amount of legal, political, and diplomatic leverage that it can employ against China in its bilateral relations or deploy in its multilateral relations with other states and international organizations with direct or indirect interests in the South China Sea.

Entrenchment of Legal Positions on Entitlements, Rights, and Delimitation

The scope of the arbitration case initiated by the Philippines comprehensively settles and entrenches its legal positions with respect to its 200-nm EEZ and continental shelf. It would be unreasonable to expect the Philippines to easily and arbitrarily give up any aspect of its hard-won legal victory, especially in light of the fact that the Award has so clearly adjudged that it is China that has been in engaged in multiple breaches of international law.

Although China insists that it does not, and will never, recognize the Award, any changes in the legal situation between the two parties inconsistent with the terms of the Award, particularly resulting in an accommodation of China's legally-unfounded claims and a denigration of the Philippines' rights and jurisdictions under UNCLOS, would probably only be possible under one of two conditions: a transactional exchange of legal rights for economic benefits or an accommodation coerced through unilateral actions. In either case, even if the Philippines might be criticized for caving in to Chinese demands, China will still bear the long-term reputational costs of having imposed illegitimate claims upon a smaller, weaker neighbor. No national leader in the Philippines, no matter how friendly to China, can be expected to politically survive the repercussions of either situation. For this reason, it cannot be reasonable to expect the Philippines to change its position regarding the Award, particularly its binding force and determination of the parties' maritime rights and jurisdiction.

In legal terms, these two tracks will manifest through continued efforts to create legally-sound and possibly binding bilateral arrangements, such as bilateral agreements concerning fishing and petroleum development activities, economic and security cooperation arrangements, or trade, as well as multilateral arrangements such as a code of conduct, provisional and non-prejudicial agreements, or other formal and informal regional arrangements with regional or extra-regional states. These do not preclude the Philippines from possibly seeking recognition, implementation, and compliance with the Award at the appropriate time and place, despite China's refusal to accept it.

The clarification of the maritime entitlements, limitation of the scope of the disputes, and identification of legally unacceptable actions also pro-

The clarification of the maritime entitlements, limitation of the scope of the disputes, and identification of legally unacceptable actions also provide the Philippines with a good basis for seeking security partnerships and alliances with other countries with which it shares common interests.

Re-engagement with China on the Basis of Legal Positions

This leaves the Philippines with limited options that are fundamentally based on two tracks. It must work diplomatically toward re-engaging and improving Philippines-China relations in order to reduce tensions and the possibility of reigniting another round of unilateral actions and escalating the South China Sea disputes. At the same time, it must increase its resilience against the possible deployment by China of hard power approaches intended to coerce or force a settlement of the South China Sea disputes in its favor by strengthening, building, and diversifying its security alliances and partnerships. The extent to which these two tracks can be pursued will be defined and confined by the legal positions established in the Award.

vide the Philippines with a good basis for seeking security partnerships and alliances with other countries with which it shares common interests, particularly in navigation, overflight, and access to resources in the South China Sea. The Award's effect of declaring what parts of the South China Sea can be considered as legally appurtenant to the Philippines and limiting the geographic scope of legitimate disputes between claimants, can serve as the basis for establishing common interests to be protected and pursued. This is an important first step considering the diversity of resources available and territorial and jurisdictional claims in the South China Sea.

These options present the best suitable means for the Philippines to protect and preserve its exclusive rights and interests in its EEZ and continental shelf, while at the same time, leaving the doors open to possible joint cooperation related to shared interests in the remaining disputed areas comprised of 12-nm territorial sea enclaves around all the high-tide elevations in the Spratly Islands area.

Engagement with Other Rival Claimants and ASEAN on the Basis of Legal Positions

The fundamental jurisdictional allocations and framework that underlies the approach to these areas need not be limited to its dealings with China, but most likely can also be the basis for its dealings with other regional claimants such as Vietnam, Malaysia, and Brunei, with whom the Philippines is more likely to find common ground and interests on the basis of the Award even though they are technically not bound by it. The Award can therefore provide the basis for the development of a consistent and unified regional position on maritime rights and jurisdiction in the South China Sea among Southeast Asian countries in the immediate term, despite China's non-acceptance of the Award.

> The Award can therefore provide the basis for the development of a consistent and unified regional position on maritime rights and jurisdiction in the South China Sea among Southeast Asian countries in the immediate term, despite China's non-acceptance of the Award.

A clear and common position derived from the adoption of the Award's interpretation and application of UNCLOS to the South China Sea mutually supports and reinforces the legal and diplomatic positions of all the smaller Southeast Asian nations, not only the Philippines, in their attempts to bilaterally and unilaterally negotiate with China for the management and future settlement of the disputes. These would therefore be the best means of pursuing and protecting Philippine interests in the West Philippine Sea and the South China Sea.

Conclusion and Future Prospects

In summary, the Award has provided the Philippines with very strong legal leverage that can be used in its bilateral relations and discussions with China and in multilateral relations with other parties both within and beyond the region. It has provided legal clarity about maritime entitlements, delineated the geographic scope of joint exploration and development, confirmed the illegality of certain Chinese actions, provided legal justification for future Philippine maritime law enforcement operations, provided legal justification for future Philippine maritime resource exploration and exploitation, and limited the geographic scope of unresolved sovereignty issues. These create some policy options that may be pursued in future dealings with the South China Sea disputes, such as the entrenchment of legal positions on entitlements, rights, and delimitation; re-engagement with China on the basis of its legal positions; and engagement with other rival claimants and ASEAN on the basis of its legal positions.

While the arbitration has settled a significant proportion of the competing claims to maritime rights, resources, and jurisdiction between the Philippines and China, especially those concerning activities and incidents that occurred beyond 12-nm from any island or rock in the Spratly Islands and within the Philippines' 200-nm EEZ and continental shelf measured from its archipelagic baselines, the territorial and sovereignty disputes remain untouched and unresolved and are an appropriate subject for further dispute settlement negotiations. The conclusion of the arbitration case provides the Philippines with a clear legal basis and framework for decision- and policy-making on the regulation and proper management, including through international cooperation, of the marine resources in both the West Philippine Sea and South China Sea. This framework will also determine its long-term approach to the management and eventual resolution of the South China Sea disputes.

> China's continued refusal to accept and recognize the Award poses the principal challenge to the Philippines' policy framework.

Of course, China's continued refusal to accept and recognize the Award poses the principal challenge to the Philippines' policy framework. However, since the Award contains a detailed and comprehensive disposition of all of China's jurisdictional and substantive objections to the proceedings and the submissions of the Philippines and is considered under UNCLOS to be legally binding on both parties, there can be little doubt on the part of non-parties to the arbitration as to the value of the case, which has served to bring greater legal clarity to prevailing international law.

With the legal situation in the South China Sea having been largely clarified by the Award, the Philippines is open to engaging in legitimate and legal means for management and resolution of the South China Sea disputes in accordance with international law. As it must consider itself firmly bound by the conclusions of the Award in all its future actions and interactions in the South China Sea, its legal policy options and approach have become simpler and more predictable as long it stays consistent with UNCLOS. This can increase its bargaining power as it can be confident about its legal rights and entitlements. The Philippines may incur some risks, such as if it feels legally obligated to respond militarily to foreign incursions and violations of its rights and entitlements, but it may also consider more opportunities to instead explore maritime cooperation and seek greater reliance on peaceful modes of dispute settlement under UNCLOS. Any deadlock that ensues in its relations may be attributed to insistence on an illegitimate and extra-legal approach that would undermine the progressive development of international law necessary for the continuing evolution of a global community. Idealistic as it may seem, the Philippines' "right v. might" legal approach to the maritime disputes firmly sets abstract legal rights and maritime entitlements on the basis of international law agreed upon by all states

> This is likely to be a watershed moment and game-changer in the future evolution of the South China Sea disputes.

against China's application of tangible political, military, and economic power to unilaterally reshape the South China Sea situation and incorporate the maritime area into its national territorial boundaries. This is likely to be a watershed moment and game-changer in the future evolution of the South China Sea disputes, not only between China and the Philippines, but between China and other rival claimants and major non-claimant stakeholders as well.

Jay L. Batongbacal is a lawyer and Associate Professor at the University of the Philippines College of Law and Director of the UP Institute for Maritime Affairs & Law of the Sea. He holds the advanced degrees of Master of Marine Management and Doctorate in the Science of Law, both from Dalhousie University in Canada.

Post-Arbitration South China Sea:

Philippines' Diplomatic Policy Options and Future Prospects

Richard Javad Heydarian

Abstract

This chapter provides an overview of the diplomatic implications of the Republic of the Philippines' (RP) landmark legal victory against the People's Republic of China (PRC) at The Hague, where an arbitration body, constituted under the aegis of the United Nations Convention on the Law of the Sea (UNCLOS) exercised jurisdiction on and granted a favorable award on the bulk of the Southeast Asian country's key legal arguments. The chapter looks at the specific diplomatic implications of the legal verdict, not only for the RP and PRC but also for the broader region and beyond. It also evaluates the Philippines' foreign policy under the newly-elected administration of Rodrigo Duterte, who has signaled a significantly divergent position on the maritime disputes, extended an olive branch to Beijing, and has refused to flaunt the legal conclusions of the arbitration case to taunt China. For the new Philippine government, the priority is to revive long-frozen diplomatic ties with China, hence its reticence to openly call for compliance with the Award, while shifting to direct engagement rather than diplomatic confrontation. Finally, the chapter argues that the conclusion of the arbitral proceedings has served as a springboard to revive diplomatic relations between the RP and PRC. In fact, the Duterte administration has opted for a pragmatic and conciliatory approach to the South China Sea dispute, raising hopes for peaceful management of the disputes.

Introduction

While the South China Sea disputes are by no means novel, given the ancient claims of empires, kingdoms, and colonies across the resource-rich strategic waterway,[1] recent years have witnessed a dangerous uptick in regional maritime tensions. While no claimant state can credibly profess strategic innocence – several Southeast Asian claimant states, including Vietnam, the Philippines and Malaysia, have built military and civilian structures on disputed land fea-

---

1   Bill Hayton, *South China Sea: The Struggle for Power in Asia*, Yale University Press: London, 2014.

tures over the past decades – analysts from the Philippines and other countries have determined that the PRC in particular has made a disproportionate contribution to the uptick in the age-old spats. In the past two years alone, China has engaged in massive island-building efforts, particularly in the Spratly Islands. While the PRC is certainly not the first country to have built advanced military facilities in the area, the sheer scale, speed and sophistication of its construction and reclamation activities in the area dwarf that of all other claimant states' combined. According to one estimate, China reclaimed more than 2,900 acres (1,170 hectares) of land between December 2013 and June 2015. To put that into perspective, in less than two years, the PRC reclaimed seventeen times more land than all other claimants combined over the past four decades.[2]

> The militarization of the disputes erodes regional and international trust and confidence in the PRC's intentions and rhetoric about its 'peaceful rise'.

Of great concern to the Philippines and other Southeast Asian countries like Vietnam is China's decision, prospective and verified, to deploy advanced military assets to the area, including high-frequency radars, fighter jets, mobile artillery platforms, and potentially, as in the Paracel Islands, surface-to-air missile systems.[3] There is genuine concern that China will soon establish an exclusion zone in the Spratlys, declaring an Air Defense Identification Zone (ADIZ), which may render reconnaissance and re-supply activities by other claimant states in the area almost impossible or too risky to try. Adding to regional concerns are the PRC's deployment of ever-larger flotilla of fishermen-cum-militia forces, well-equipped law enforcement vessels, and, more recently, advanced naval vessels, which collectively contribute to the increasingly securitized atmosphere in the area.[4] The militarization of the disputes erodes regional and international trust and confidence in the PRC's intentions and rhetoric about its 'peaceful rise'. It also encourages other claimant states to increase their military presence in the disputed areas, raise their defense

---

2   Dean Yates, "China's land reclamation in South China Sea grows: Pentagon report," Reuters, August 21, 2016, <http://www.reuters.com/article/us-southchinasea-china-pentagon-idUSKCN0QQ0S920150821>.

3   "Another Piece of the Puzzle," Asia Maritime Transparency Initiative, Center for Strategic and International Studies, n.d., <https://amti.csis.org/another-piece-of-the-puzzle/>.

4   Minnie Chan, "Beijing ready to impose air defence identification zone in South China Sea pending US moves," *South China Morning Post*, June 1, 2016, <http://www.scmp.com/news/china/article/1960954/beijing-ready-impose-air-defence-identification-zone-south-china-sea>.

spending, and even welcome, particularly in the case of the Philippines and Vietnam, deeper military cooperation with external powers such as the US and Japan. A combination of growing mistrust, particularly between China and its neighbors, and military buildup, both by claimant states and external powers, makes any diplomatic resolution of the dispute more difficult if not impossible.

China has sought to justify its maritime assertiveness by invoking the doctrine of "historic rights", laying claim to much of the South China Sea, which cuts well into the 200-nautical-mile exclusive economic zone (EEZ) of archipelagic Southeast Asian states like the Philippines and Malaysia. In 2012, China provoked uproar in Manila, when it began a *de facto* occupation of the disputed Scarborough Shoal after a dangerous standoff between Chinese coast guard forces and a Filipino naval frigate. Perturbed by China's perceived encroachment into what it considers its national waters, bereft of sufficient military capability to protect its interests, and failing to achieve any satisfactory outcome through bilateral negotiations, the Philippines employed legal warfare (lawfare), which culminated in what many experts consider as a landmark victory under the aegis of the United Nations Convention on the Law of the Sea (UNCLOS). Yet, after the Permanent Court of Arbitration announced the much-anticipated Award of an arbitral tribunal constituted under Article 287 and Annex VII of UNCLOS, the regional strategic landscape took a surprising turn, largely thanks to the election of a new leader in the Philippines.

> After the Permanent Court of Arbitration announced the much-anticipated Award of an arbitral tribunal constituted under Article 287 and Annex VII of UNCLOS, the regional strategic landscape took a surprising turn, largely thanks to the election of a new leader in the Philippines.

Diplomatic Policy Approach

To the surprise of many Filipinos and international observers, the newly-elected Philippine government under President Rodrigo Duterte has shown little interest in adopting a confrontational post-arbitration strategy against China. Instead, Duterte has called for direct bilateral engagement and peaceful, non-adversarial management, if not resolution, of the disputes. With Duterte in office, the Philippines has not mobilized significant international support in the post-arbitration phase, and Duterte has even pushed back against perceived meddling by external powers in the South China Sea disputes. Unsure about the strategic utility of the Award, the administration has instead opted for direct engagement with China – a remarkable departure from the Philippines' confrontational strategy under the Benigno Aquino administration.

In a matter of months, the RP has transformed itself from being one of PRC's most strident critics into a potential partner for peace. For the Duterte administration, the first priority is to prevent

> To the surprise of many Filipinos and international observers, the newly-elected Philippine government under President Rodrigo Duterte has shown little interest in adopting a confrontational post-arbitration strategy against China.[5]

outright conflict in the area, especially in light of Beijing's decision to up the ante in contested waters. There is a basis for its concern. Shortly after the Award was issued, the China's People's Liberation Army Air Force (PLAAF) deployed fighter jets and a nuclear-capable long-range bomber to the Scarborough Shoal. This was in addition to reports that China is also deploying a growing number of vessels and fishermen to the contested areas, not to mention potential plans for establishing military facilities on the Scarborough Shoal.[5]

Reports also show that the PRC has warned Japan against intervention in the South China Sea disputes, with Premiere Li Keqiang remarking, "We cannot accept the ruling. If it is implemented [by Japan and America], there will be conflict." Against the backdrop of rising post-arbitration tensions, the Association of Southeast Asian Nations (ASEAN) did not manage to even mention the Award, much less call for compliance by concerned parties. Statements from other major Western powers, from the United States to the European Union, were also relatively anodyne. Instead of pressuring the PRC into compliance, the common refrain among regional actors was the necessity for calm and patient diplomacy.[6]

The Republic of China (Taiwan), also a claimant, expressed outright opposition to the Award and threatened to deploy an additional naval vessel to the Spratlys, lamenting its exclusion from the process and the unfavorable conclusion on the status of ROC-occupied Itu Aba (Taiping) Island, which was determined to be a "rock" and not an "island" under UNCLOS. By most indicators, the PRC has prevented a post-arbitration diplomatic backlash, at least for the time being, and Duterte has played an important role in facilitating this process. Recognizing the clear and present danger of full-scale military escalation, the Duterte administration has constantly reiterated his preference for peaceful settlement of the disputes based on dialogue.

Diplomatic Implications of the Award

For the Philippines, which skillfully limited its case to questions of "sovereign rights" and maritime entitlement claims, the Award was better than expected. Not only did it convince the court to exercise jurisdiction on almost all key items of its Memorial, but it also secured favorable conclusions on almost all of them. The Award, in accordance with Article 296 as well as Article 11 of Annex VII of UNCLOS, is final and binding. Even the most optimistic Filipino experts did not expect such a sweepingly favorable denouement, though it must be said that, in October 2015, the Tribunal raised hopes in Manila when it rejected China's invocation of exemption clauses (Art. 298, Section 2, Part XV) under UNCLOS to dismiss the case. It

---

5   Franz-Stefan Gady, "China Flies Nuclear-Capable Bomber Over Disputed Feature in South China Sea," *The Diplomat*, July 19, <http://thediplomat.com/2016/07/china-flies-nuclear-capable-bomber-over-disputed-feature-in-south-china-sea/>.

6   Hiroyuki Akita, "Two contrasting theories about China's provocative actions," *Nikkei Asian Review*, August 29, 2016, <http://asia.nikkei.com/Politics-Economy/Policy-Politics/Two-contrasting-theories-about-China-s-provocative-actions>.

is unsurprising that the Award was not well-received in China, which dismissed it as 'null and void' and launched a concerted Public Relations blitzkrieg to question the credibility of the arbitration body. In terms of its potential diplomatic implications for the Philippines, the Award was momentous for several reasons.

Increased Bargaining Power

First of all, the Award, which was beneficial for the Philippines and detrimental to China's interests from a legal standpoint, may have the effect of increasing the Philippines' bargaining power in future diplomatic negotiations with China or other rival claimants. The Award questioned the

that China's island-building activities have no legal bearing because they were mostly superimposed over low-tide-elevations, which can neither generate sovereignty claims nor any maritime entitlements of their own. However, Hughes Reef, Johnson South Reef, and Scarborough Shoal were determined to be "rocks," which can at most generate 12 nautical miles of territorial sea. The Tribunal also censured China for "violat[ing] the Philippines sovereign rights" to explore and exploit natural resources within its EEZ, while declaring that Beijing's massive reclamation activities are "incompatible with the obligations" of UNCLOS signatories, since they "inflict irreparable harm to the maritime environment" and destroy "evidence of the natural condition of" features in the Spratlys. Therefore, the Tribu-

> The Award, which was beneficial for the Philippines and detrimental to China's interests from a legal standpoint, may have the effect of increasing the Philippines' bargaining power in future diplomatic negotiations with China or other rival claimants.

basis of the PRC's doctrine of "historic rights" by juxtaposing it with prevailing international law. Although it did not fully nullify China's expansive claims in adjacent waters because the Tribunal had no justification over the competing sovereignty claims to high-tide land features in the South China Sea, it nevertheless significantly compressed the extent to which the PRC can, per modern international law, make legitimate claims in the area. More specifically, the Tribunal ruled that the PRC's "nine-dashed-line" was "incompatible" with prevailing international law because "there was no evidence that the PRC had historically exercised exclusive control over the waters or their resources."[7]

Moreover, the Tribunal also concluded that there are no naturally-formed islands in the Spratlys and therefore no overlapping EEZs between the RP and PRC. Moreover, it determined

nal reinforced the legal basis for the RP's claims that it is entitled to explore and exploit natural resources within its EEZ.[8]

The Award carries significant implications for the PRC. First and foremost, non-compliance with the Award of an international arbitral tribunal constituted under the aegis of UNCLOS, puts into question the country's commitment to its obligations under the existing global order. It would be hard for China to continuously profess 'peaceful' intentions and portray itself as a responsible great power if it refuses to comply with prevailing international legal principles and the decisions made by arbitral tribunals formed under UNCLOS. As a global maritime power, the PRC has a long-term interest in preserving the sanctity of UNCLOS in particular and international law more broadly. A predictable, rule-based international order is indispensable to the long-term devel-

---

7   Award, PCA Case No. 2013-19, Permanent Court of Arbitration, July 12, 2016, <http://www.pcacases.com/web/sendAttach/2086>.

8   Award, PCA Case No. 2013-19, Permanent Court of Arbitration, July 12, 2016, <http://www.pcacases.com/web/sendAttach/2086>

opment of any major commercial power like the PRC.

The Award has also strengthened the Philippines' diplomatic bargaining power because it can now call upon external powers to effectively 'enforce' the Award by pushing back against China's 'excessive' claims (i.e., claims not in accordance with UNCLOS) in the disputed areas. The Philippine government can, for instance, call upon concerned naval powers such as the US, Japan, Australia, India and France to invoke Award as a basis for conducting expanded, sustained and multilateral Freedom of Navigation Operations (FONOPs) close to low-tide elevations currently controlled by PRC, even if they have been artificially augmented into island-like features.

> Unless Beijing recalibrates its behavior in adjacent waters, it could potentially face multiple arbitration cases initiated by estranged neighbors. Even if other claimant states fall short of actually filing arbitration cases, they can now credibly threaten to do so.

For the past year, the US Navy has been conducting FONOPs unilaterally and without a clear legal basis. However, the Award, which declared the bulk of Chinese-occupied land features in the Spratlys to be low-tide elevations, provides a clear legal pretext not only for the expansion of those operations but also for turning them into expanded, multilateral operations along with other naval allies. The Philippine government, however, seems to have opted for a non-confrontational post-arbitration approach.

Effectiveness of Lawfare

Second, the Philippines proved that UNCLOS could serve as the basis for launching a successful lawfare offensive against China. With the RP overcoming jurisdiction hurdles and leveraging

UNCLOS to conclude an auspicious arbitration case against the PRC, fellow Southeast Asian nations such as Vietnam are also in a position to credibly threaten, if not actually adopt, a similar lawfare strategy to protect their interests in the South China Sea. Aside from Vietnam, Indonesia, which is concerned about its interests in the Natuna islands, and Japan, which is worried about the escalating disputes in the Senkaku/Diaoyu Islands, have also expressed their interest in exploring a lawfare approach against China. Thus, the PRC faces the prospects of a post-arbitration 'legal multiplier'. That is to say, unless Beijing recalibrates its behavior in adjacent waters, it could potentially face multiple arbitration cases initiated by estranged neighbors. Even if other claimant states fall short of actually filing arbitration cases, they can now credibly threaten to do so. Thus, the arbitration case has strengthened their diplomatic leverage in any prospective negotiation with China.

Defense of Entitlement Claims

Third, the Award could serve as a roadmap for management, if not resolution, of the disputes between the PRC and RP as well as among other claimant states. It could serve as a basis for the clarification of actual claims in accordance to prevailing international law and their harmonization based on cooperative schemes such as joint development agreements. The Philippines and other Southeast Asian claimant states could also invoke the verdict as a basis to explore and exploit natural resources within their EEZs, specifically areas where the PRC, per the Award, has no overlapping claims with other claimant states. In an event that the PRC decides to unilaterally exploit natural resources in areas where it has no legitimate sovereign rights, per the Award, the aggrieved coastal state could initiate another arbitration case. For instance, if a Chinese energy company (e.g., CNOOC, CNPC, SINOPEC) unilaterally exploited hydrocarbon resources in the RP's EEZ, the latter would have the option of filing a suit against the involved Chinese company for violating its sovereign rights.[9]

Diplomatic Policy Options

While the RP can claim that it has achieved a legal victory against the PRC, the reality on the ground suggests otherwise. Beijing continues to exert control over Philippines-claimed land features such as Scarborough Shoal and Mischief Reef, both of which fall within the RP's EEZ, and has refused to even acknowledge the Award as

cial envoy to the PRC. After a five-day 'ice-breaker' trip to Hong Kong, where Ramos met senior Chinese officials and scholars, Beijing extended an invitation for more substantive negotiations in China, with Duterte making a high-profile state visit to Beijing aimed at restoring frayed bilateral relations in late-October 2016.[10]

This policy shift, however, has created some tensions in its relations with traditional partners such as the US and Japan, which would prefer that Manila use the Award as a basis to rally international support against China in the South Chi-

> The Duterte administration's policy shift has created some tensions in its relations with traditional partners such as the US and Japan, which would prefer that Manila use the Award as a basis to rally international support against China in the South China Sea.

a legally binding document. The Philippines has also struggled to garner the support of ASEAN countries on the issue, with ASEAN failing to even mention the Award in any of its subsequent joint statements. Thus, the primary diplomatic option ahead for the Philippines seem to be engagement rather than confrontation with China.

For the new Filipino president, a single issue, particularly the ongoing maritime spats, should not define overall bilateral relations with Beijing. Instead, Duterte is interested in reviving investment ties with the PRC, particularly in the realm of public infrastructure development, which have suffered in recent years. Duterte has made it clear that he will not flaunt the Award to taunt the PRC. This means the RP, as a form of confidence-building measure, will approach bilateral negotiations with the PRC with minimal emphasis on Award, at least in formal diplomatic statements. To kick start negotiations, Duterte appointed a trusted friend, former president Fidel Ramos, as a spe-

na Sea. However, it seems that the priority of the Duterte administration has been to avoid conflict and re-open communication channels with China, even if this may lead to some temporary setbacks in diplomatic relations with Washington. If anything, Duterte has signaled his preference for partial decoupling from existing security agreements with the US in favor of more cordial ties, if not an outright alliance, with China.[11]

Conclusion and Future Prospects

Instead of leading to further confrontation between the RP and the PRC, the conclusion of the arbitral proceedings has actually enhanced their resolve to bridge their differences through diplomacy, leading to a decline in tensions in the South

9   Antonio T. Carpio. "How the Philippines Can Enforce the South China Sea Verdict," *Wall Street Journal*, July 17, 2016, <https://www.wsj.com/articles/how-the-philippines-can-enforce-the-south-china-sea-verdict-1468774415>.

10   Richard Javad Heydarian, "Can Ramos Break the Ice in Philippines-China Relations," Asia Maritime Transparency Initative. Center for Strategic and International Studies, August 16, 2016, <https://amti.csis.org/can-ramos-break-ice-philippines-china-relations/>.

11   Richard, Javad Heydarian, "Duterte Shakes Up Philippine Foreign Policy," *Asia Unbound*, Council on Foreign Relations, October 3, 2016, <http://blogs.cfr.org/asia/2016/10/03/duterte-shakes-up-philippine-foreign-policy/>.

China Sea. Duterte is expected to hold informal talks with high-level Chinese officials to facilitate a speedy resolution of the maritime disputes, re-normalizing frayed ties with Beijing. Establishing a joint-fisheries agreement in the Scarborough Shoal, which the two sides are looking at, would be a potentially game-changing compromise.[12] The neighbors will most likely also explore confidence-building measures such as the establishment of military-to-military hotlines, institutional-

> While the successful completion of a mutually satisfactory agreement is far from certain, the RP and PRC are moving closer to re-normalization of bilateral ties after years of acrimony and diplomatic confrontation.

ized communication between their marine law enforcement agencies, as well as marine scientific and environmental cooperation schemes in contested waters.

While the successful completion of a mutually satisfactory agreement is far from certain, the RP and PRC are moving closer to re-normalization of bilateral ties after years of acrimony and diplomatic confrontation. Much of this has to do with the Duterte administration's pragmatic foreign policy outlook and the realization that translating *de jure* victory into *de facto* gains requires careful and deliberate diplomacy.

Richard Javad Heydarian is an Assistant Professor in political science at De La Salle University, and, most recently, the author of *Asia's New Battlefield: US, China, and the Struggle for Western Pacific* (Zed, London). He is an Opinion Writer for Al Jazeera English, and a regular contributor to the Asia Maritime Transparency Initiative of the Center for Strategic & International Studies (CSIS). *The Manila Bulletin*, a leading national daily, has described him as one of the Philippines' "foremost foreign affairs and economic analysts". He has contributed to global think tanks such as Brookings Institution and Council on Foreign Relations (CFR), and has written for and/or been interviewed by ABC, BBC, *Bloomberg*, CNN, CNBC, *Christian Science Monitor, Foreign Affairs, The Guardian, The Economist, The Financial Times, The New York Times, The Washington Post, The Wall Street Journal, Spiegel, Straits Times,* and *The Nation,* among other major publications. He is currently working on a book on "Obama's Asia policy" (Palgrave, Macmillan).

---

12   Richard, Javad Heydarian, "Duterte Shakes Up Philippine Foreign Policy," *Asia Unbound*, Council on Foreign Relations, October 3, 2016, <http://blogs.cfr.org/asia/2016/10/03/duterte-shakes-up-philippine-foreign-policy/>.

Post-Arbitration South China Sea:

Philippines' Security Policy Options and Future Prospects

Rommel C. Banlaoi

Abstract

Despite its legal victory, the Philippine government continues to face a lingering security dilemma in the South China Sea. This is attributable to the fact that the problems in the South China Sea are not only legal. The Tribunal's decisions have tremendous security implications not only for the Philippines and China but also for other claimants and even non-claimants as well. This chapter examines security issues facing the Philippines in the post-arbitration environment in the South China Sea. It describes the current security policy approach of the new administration under President Rodrigo Duterte, which has been cautious, pragmatic, and reconciliatory towards China. The chapter also explores the security implications of the Award for the Philippines, particularly the safety of Filipino fishermen in the Scarborough Shoal, the protection of the Philippine government's natural gas and oil exploration projects in the Reed Bank, and the security of Philippine troops pursuing resupply and rotation missions in the nine Philippines-occupied features in the Kalayaan Island Group (KIG). Finally, it describes the security policy options available to the Duterte administration for easing the Philippines' security dilemma in the post-arbitration environment in the South China Sea, including rethinking security alliance with the United States; strengthening its strategic partnerships with Japan and Australia; promoting strategic cooperation with members of the Association of Southeast Asian Nations (ASEAN), particularly with Vietnam, Indonesia and Malaysia; and engaging China constructively in functional areas and on non-traditional security issues.

Introduction

On July 12, 2016, after several months of intense deliberations, the Arbitral Tribunal rendered its Award in the high-profile international arbitration case filed by the Philippines against China regarding ongoing maritime disputes in the South China Sea. The Philippine government regards the Award as a grand legal victory by a small nation against a big nation's excessive maritime claims.

Though the Chinese government has maintained its position of vehemently rejecting the result of the international arbitration after not participating in the arbitral proceedings, close friends of the Philippine government have nevertheless celebrated this triumphant moment. Former Philippine President Benigno Aquino III, who initiated the filing of the case, even described this legal victory as a "victory for all" nations.[1]

However, the complex maritime disputes in the South China Sea are not only a legal problem that requires a legal solution. The South China Sea disputes are largely a security issue that warrants appropriate security responses not only by claimants but non-claimants as well, particularly major powers that have strongly expressed their interests in the security of the South China Sea.

Close friends of the Philippine government have celebrated this triumphant moment. Former Philippine President Benigno Aquino III, who initiated the filing of the case, even described this legal victory as a "victory for all" nations.

Although the arbitral proceedings were initiated under the Aquino administration, it was not until after the Duterte administration had taken office that the Tribunal released its Award. During his presidential campaign, then Mayor of Davao City Rodrigo Duterte had already begun to articulate his security approach to the South China Sea and relations with China. While committed to advancing Philippine security interests in the South China Sea and steadfast about protecting the Philippines' sovereign rights in the maritime domain referred to locally as the West Philippine Sea (WPS), President Duterte has been mindful of the fact that many ramifications of the dispute cannot be addressed by using a legal approach alone. Thus, in his first Cabinet Meeting on June 30, 2016, President Duterte preemptively warned his officials not to "taunt or flaunt" the conclusions of the Tribunal.[2]

Given the current situation in the South China Sea in the post-arbitration security environment, the Duterte administration is pursuing a new security approach towards China that is cautious, pragmatic, and reconciliatory. Pursuing this new security approach aims to address the main security implications of the Award for the Philippines, which relate to the safety of Filipino fishermen in the Scarborough Shoal, the protection of the Philippine government's natural gas and oil explora-

---

1   Nikko Dizon, "Aquino on arbitral court ruling: 'A victory for all'," *Philippine Daily Inquirer*, July 13, 2016, <http://globalnation.inquirer.net/141043/aquino-on-arbitral-court-ruling-a-victory-for-all>.

2   Kathrina Sharmaine Alvarez, "Duterte warns against using tribunal ruling vs China to 'taunt or flaunt'," *GMA News*, June 30, 2016, <http://www.gmanetwork.com/news/story/571930/news/nation/duterte-warns-against-using-tribunal-ruling-vs-china-to-taunt-or-flaunt>.

tion projects in the Reed Bank, and the security of Philippine troops pursuing resupply and rotation missions in the nine Philippines-occupied features in the KIG. In order to confront the Philippines' continuing security dilemma in the post-arbitration South China Sea security environment, the Duterte administration is pursuing the following policy options: rethinking its security alliance with the United States; strengthening strategic partnerships with Japan and Australia; promoting strategic cooperation with ASEAN members, particularly with Vietnam, Indonesia and Malaysia; and engaging China constructively in functional areas and on non-traditional security issues.

Security Policy Approach

In stark contrast to the policies of its predecessor, the Duterte administration is currently pursuing a security policy approach that is cautious, pragmatic, and reconciliatory towards China. When President Duterte assumed his post on June 30, 2016, the arbitral proceedings and resulting Award were at the top of his security policy agenda. Expecting a favorable Award from the Arbitral Tribunal, he strictly instructed his cabinet officials to be more circumspect in their reactions to the Award in order not to "put the country in an awkward position" vis-à-vis China, which he recognized as an influential neighbor.[3] While President Duterte has strongly expressed his commitment

> In stark contrast to the policies of its predecessor, the Duterte administration is currently pursuing a security policy approach that is cautious, pragmatic, and reconciliatory towards China.

to abide by the decisions of the Tribunal, he has also articulated his keen interest in repairing the Philippines' damaged political ties with China. In his speech during his first cabinet meeting, he reiterated his desire to pursue bilateral talks with China to address their maritime disputes as his government did not want "to declare any fighting with anybody."[4] He stressed, "If we can have peace [with China], I'll be very happy."[5] Even his Foreign Affairs Secretary Perfecto Yasay, Jr., declared during the same cabinet meeting that he was averse to the idea of is-

---

3   Kathrina Sharmaine Alvarez, "Duterte warns against using tribunal ruling vs China to 'taunt or flaunt'," *GMA News*, June 30, 2016, <http://www.gmanetwork.com/news/story/571930/news/nation/duterte-warns-against-using-tribunal-ruling-vs-china-to-taunt-or-flaunt>.

4   "Full Speech of President Rodrigo Roa Duterte during his First Cabinet Meeting," June 30, 2016, <https://www.youtube.com/watch?v=ATqYDmOZd4k>.

5   "Full Speech of President Rodrigo Roa Duterte during his First Cabinet Meeting," June 30, 2016, <https://www.youtube.com/watch?v=ATqYDmOZd4k>.

suing a strong statement on the Award arguing that "The first thing that we will do is to study its implications and ramifications. What does it mean when we win? There are lots of nuances that we do not know as yet."[6] Then, when the Award was issued on July 12, 2016, Secretary Yasay only declared:

> Our experts are studying the award with the care and thoroughness that this significant arbitral outcome deserves.
>
> In the meantime, we call on those concerned to exercise restraint and sobriety.
>
> The Philippines strongly affirms its respect for this milestone decision as an important contribution to ongoing efforts in addressing disputes in the South China Sea.
>
> The decision upholds international law, particularly the 1982 UNCLOS.
>
> The Philippines reiterates its abiding commitment to efforts of pursuing the peaceful resolution and management of disputes with the view of promoting and enhancing peace and stability in the region.[7]

Though the Philippine public criticized Secretary Yasay for issuing a cold and pro forma statement on the Award,[8] it indicated that the Duterte administration was taking a very cautious approach to the South China Sea disputes. As a lawyer himself and a former local chief executive of Davao City in Mindanao for more than twenty years, President Duterte has formed the habit of

taking a pragmatic approach to many pressing policy problems under his leadership. The principle of pragmatism, therefore, informs President Duterte's current security policy approach to the South China Sea disputes. President Duterte is also pursuing a more reconciliatory approach towards China to peacefully manage their differences on South China Sea issues. President Duterte's current security policy approach towards the South China Sea disputes is a paradigm shift from the highly legalistic and adversarial approach of the previous Philippine government under President Aquino III.[9]

> As a lawyer himself and a former local chief executive of Davao City in Mindanao for more than twenty years, President Duterte has formed the habit of taking a pragmatic approach to many pressing policy problems under his leadership.

President Duterte has already articulated his cautious, pragmatic, and reconciliatory approach towards the South China Sea dispute in his recent speeches, statements, and actions. Though some of his statements appeared to be indicative of a hardline approach, such as when he warned China not to invade Philippine territory as "it will be bloody and we will not give it to them [China] easily,"[10] his overall approach towards the South China Sea dispute, however, has remained cautious, pragmatic, and reconciliatory. This approach

---

6   For more analysis where this quotation comes from, see Rommel C. Banlaoi, "Arbitration ruling and Philippines-China relations under Duterte administration," *China-US Focus*, July 7, 2016, <http://www.chinausfocus.com/foreign-policy/arbitration-ruling-and-philippines-china-relations-under-the-duterte-administration/>.

7   Perfecto Yasay, Jr., "PH foreign affairs chief's statement on arbitration ruling," ABS-CBN News, July 12, 2016, <http://news.abs-cbn.com/news/07/12/16/read-ph-foreign-affairs-chiefs-statement-on-arbitration-ruling>.

8   Janvic Mateo, "Netizens asks: Why so sad Yasay?" *Philippine Star*, July 14, 2016, <http://www.philstar.com/headlines/2016/07/14/1602694/netizens-ask-why-so-sad-yasay>.

9   Rommel C. Banlaoi, "Duterte Presidency: Shift in Philippine-China Relations," *RSIS Commentaries*, May 20, 2016, <https://www.rsis.edu.sg/rsis-publication/rsis/co16121-duterte-presidency-shift-in-philippine-china-relations/>.

10 "'It will be bloody': Duterte's warning to China if it attacks the Philippines in festering sea dispute'," *South China Morning Post* / Agence France-Presse, August 24, 2016, <http://www.scmp.com/news/asia/southeast-asia/article/2008509/it-will-be-bloody-dutertes-warning-china-if-it-attacks>.

sometimes conveys a message of strategic ambiguity and lack of policy clarity prompting foreign observers to declare that the Duterte government is unpredictable.[11] However, during his election campaign, President Duterte has already articulated his crystal clear agenda in mind: advancing Philippine national security interests.[12]

President Duterte's cautious approach was the advice of four former Philippine presidents who attended his first meeting of the National Security Council (NSC) on July 28, 2016. During the meeting, former presidents Fidel V. Ramos, Joseph E. Estrada, Gloria Macapagal Arroyo, and Benigno Simeon Aquino III urged President Duterte to handle the South China Sea dispute with caution and restraint. The NSC meeting was a major milestone for the country because, for

nila's stance on the Award.

Security Implications of the Award

The Philippines' legal victory in the arbitration case has concomitant security concerns that cannot be addressed by a legal approach alone. The Award has tremendous security implications for the Philippines that relate to the safety of Filipino fishermen in the Scarborough Shoal, the protection of the Philippine government's natural gas and oil exploration projects in the Reed Bank, and the security of Philippine troops pursuing resupply and rotation missions in the nine Philippines-occupied features in the KIG.[13]

It was during this meeting that President Duterte also laid out his pragmatic approach when he announced his decision to simultaneously maintain the Philippines' security alliance with the United States and improve bilateral ties with China amidst turbulence caused by the maritime dispute.

the first time in its history, all living past presidents attended it. It was also the first time that the meeting was convened by a newly elected Philippine president during their first month in office. It was during this meeting that President Duterte also laid out his pragmatic approach when he announced his decision to simultaneously maintain the Philippines' security alliance with the United States and improve bilateral ties with China amidst turbulence caused by the maritime dispute. President Duterte also reiterated his reconciliatory approach towards China when he stressed the need to promote conversation with Beijing while at the same time asserting Ma-

Safety of Filipino Fishermen in Scarborough Shoal

One security implication of the Award relates to the safety of Filipino fishermen relying on the maritime resources of the South China Sea, particularly in the Scarborough Shoal. In the Award, the Tribunal declared that, under the United Nations Convention on the Law of the Sea (UNCLOS), the Scarborough Shoal was a rock entitled to only a 12-nautical-mile territorial sea, contrary to China's claim that it is an island that can generate a 200-nautical-mile exclusive economic zone (EEZ). The Tribunal also concluded that China had violated the Philippines' sovereign rights when the China Coast Guard denied Filipino fishermen full access to the shoal and declared China's maritime law enforcement activities at Scarborough

11 Sampa Kundu, "Understanding Duterte: The unpredictable President of the Philippines," IDSA Comment, July 14, 2016, <http://www.idsa.in/idsacomments/understanding-duterte-president-of-the-philippines_skundu_140716>.

12 Nestor Corrales, "Country's interest is top priority: Duterte," *Philippine Daily Inquirer*, April 24, 2016, <http://newsinfo.inquirer.net/781420/countrys-interest-is-top-priority-duterte>.

13 For more insights prior to the release of arbitral award, see Aileen S.P. Baviera, "The Philippines and the South China Sea Dispute: Security Interests and Perspectives" in Ian Storey and Lin Cheng-yi (eds.), *The South China Sea Dispute: Navigating Diplomatic and Strategic Tensions*, Singapore: Yusok Ishak Institute, 2016, pp. 161–185.

Shoal as unlawful.[14]

Though the Philippine Bureau of Fisheries and Aquatic Resources (BFAR) reported in May 2016 that Filipino fishermen could already fish in the waters of the Scarborough Shoal as a sign of goodwill by China to improve relations with the Duterte government,[15] there were reports that the China Coast Guard continued to bar Filipino fishermen from fishing in the area, particularly after the announcement of the Award in July 2016.[16] With the Award, the Duterte government

> The Award reaffirms the sovereign right of the Philippine government to develop the resources of the Reed Bank, but there are still security anxieties about whether or not to pursue the project, particularly in the context of China's continuing maritime patrol operations in the area.

did not discourage Filipinos from fishing in Scarborough Shoal waters but urged them to be careful because of the presence of Chinese maritime security vessels in the area. In a media interview on August 23, 2016, President Duterte said that he had already called on China not to prevent Filipinos from fishing in the Scarborough Shoal in order to help improve the bilateral ties between

the two countries.[17] However, China has continued to intensify its presence in the Scarborough Shoal, and these actions further exacerbate the Philippines' security dilemma in the area.

Protection of Exploration Projects in the Reed Bank

Another security implication relates to the Philippine government's protection of natural gas and oil exploration projects in the Reed Bank. The Tribunal determined that the Reed Bank was a submerged feature that rightfully belonged to the Philippines' continental shelf. Thus, China violated the Philippines' rights when law enforcement vessels hamper its oil and natural gas exploration activities in the Reed Bank. The Philippine government has a Sampaguita oil field project at the Reed Bank called Service Contract (SC) 72, formerly known as Geophysical Survey Exploration Contract (GSEC) 101. The Philippine Department of Energy suspended the implementation of this project when it initiated its arbitral proceedings in January 2013, citing a force majeure.

The Award reaffirms the sovereign right of the Philippine government to develop the resources of the Reed Bank. However, the PXP Energy Corporation (formerly Philex Petroleum Corporation), which holds a substantial stake in the implementation of SC72, has not yet received instructions from the Philippine government on the next step for exploration following the arbitral proceedings. With China's continuing rejection of the Award, there are still security anxieties about whether or not to pursue the project, particularly in the context of China's continuing maritime patrol operations in the area.

14   Award, PCA Case No. 2013-19, Permanent Court of Arbitration, July 12, 2016, <http://www.pcacases.com/web/sendAttach/2086>.

15   Kristine Daguno-Bersamina, "BFAR: Pinoy fishermen can now freely fish in Scarborough Shoal," *Philippine Star*, May 21, 2016, <http://www.philstar.com/headlines/2016/05/21/1585503/bfar-pinoy-fishermen-can-now-freely-fish-scarborough-shoal>.

16   JC Gotinga, "Filipino fishermen still barred from Scarborough Shoal," CNN Philippines, July 15, 2016, <http://cnnphilippines.com/news/2016/07/15/scarborough-shoal-filipino-fishermen-chinese-coast-guard.html1>.

17   Christina Mendez, "Duterte to China: Let Filipinos fish in Scarborough," *Philippine Star*, August 23, 2016, <http://www.philstar.com/headlines/2016/08/23/1616685/duterte-china-let-filipinos-fish-scarborough>.

Security of Philippine Troops in the KIG

Finally, there are still serious issues related the security of Philippine troops pursuing resupply and rotation missions to the nine Philippines-occupied features in the KIG. Of particular concern to the Philippine government is the safety of Philippine troops at Second Thomas Shoal, where a rusty Philippine naval ship has been grounded and is maintained as an active mission to safeguard its claims to the feature. China Coast Guard vessels continue to patrol around the shoal prompting fears among government and military officials that China could utilize its maritime law enforcement agency to compel the Philippine troops assigned there to leave their post.

(Pag-asa) Island.

There is no doubt that the post-arbitration environment in the South China Sea has unleashed panoply of security challenges for the Philippine government. Surmounting these security challenges requires policy options that are cautious, pragmatic, and reconciliatory.

Security Policy Options

Aware of the aforementioned security implications and the current security situation in the post-arbitration South China Sea, the Philippine government is now pursuing several key policy options, including rethinking its security alliance

> There is no doubt that the post-arbitration environment in the South China Sea has unleashed panoply of security challenges for the Philippine government.

Though the Tribunal affirmed that Second Thomas Shoal was a submerged feature that belongs to the Philippines' continental shelf, the Award failed to clarify whether China's harassment of Filipino troops at Second Thomas Shoal had violated the Philippines' rights. China's construction of an artificial island at Mischief Reef, which is close to Second Thomas Shoal, has led to a strong Chinese presence in the area. The situation, considered a "new normal", has heightened the security apprehensions of Philippine troops assigned to the shoal. Though the Tribunal declared China's construction of facilities on Mischief Reef, which started in 1995, to be illegal under international law, arguing that the Mischief Reef is part of the Philippines' continental shelf, China's construction of an artificial island there indicates that China has no intention to leave. Instead, it has committed itself to fortifying its presence in the area. China's construction of six other artificial islands in the Spratlys has also exacerbated Philippine security anxieties in the maritime domain, particularly with Subi Reef being in close proximity to the Philippine's Thitu

with the US, strengthening its strategic partnerships with Japan and Australia, promoting strategic cooperation with ASEAN members, and engaging China constructively in functional areas and on non-traditional security issues.

Rethinking the Philippines–US Security Alliance

President Duterte has articulated a critical view of the Philippines' security relations with the US. During his visit to China from October 18–21, 2016, he announced his intention to "separate" from the US "militarily" and "economically". Though Duterte clarified that his declaration should not be interpreted as cutting diplomatic ties with its long-time security ally, his many "anti-American" overtures since he assumed office in June 2016 have already made the US uncomfortable with the new Philippine president, especially when he suggested stopping Philippine–US joint patrols in the South China Sea and removing American troops stationed in Mindanao. It is apparent that Duterte is calling for a rethinking of the Philippines' security alliance with the US as an option for easing tensions in the post-arbitration South China Sea security environment.

At present, the Philippine government is implementing a force modernization program to strengthen its autonomous territorial defense, but its existing budgetary capacity is not sufficient to develop the "minimum credible defense force" that it desires. Thus, the Philippine government, particularly the Department of National Defense (DND), continues to seek the assistance of and defense cooperation with the US.

When US Secretary of State John Kerry visited the Philippines in July 2016, Philippine Foreign Affairs Secretary Yasay assured Kerry of the Duterte administration's desire to see the full implementation of the Enhanced Defense Cooperation Agreement (EDCA) signed in 2014 and declared by the Philippine Supreme Court as constitutional on July 26, 2016.[18] Duterte, however, is very critical of the EDCA's implementation and has thus called for a rethinking of the Philippines' security alliance with the US for pragmatic considerations: to get more benefits for the Philippines from the alliance and to make sure that the alliance will not target any country, particularly China.

> The Philippine government is implementing a force modernization program to strengthen its autonomous territorial defense, but its existing budgetary capacity is not sufficient to develop the "minimum credible defense force" that it desires.

Strengthening Strategic Partnerships with Japan and Australia

Aside from the US, the Philippines is also strengthening its strategic partnerships with two other American allies: Japan and Australia. Through its Official Development Assistance (ODA), Japan is donating ten patrol ships to the Philippine Coast Guard. Japan is also involved in maritime capacity building for the Philippines' National Coast Watch Commission. In February 2016, Japan and the Philippines signed a defense agreement for the sharing of defense technologies to upgrade the capacity of the Armed Forces of the Philippines (AFP) in the conduct of intelligence, surveillance, and reconnaissance operations in maritime areas. Japan is also willing to provide the AFP with five second-hand Beechcraft TC-90 King Air reconnaissance planes from the Japan Maritime Self-Defense Force (JMSDF). The AFP, for its part, has

---

18 Rose-An Jessica Dioquino, "Yasay assures Kerry of EDCA implementation under Duterte admin ," *GMA News*, July 27, 2016, <http://www.gmanetwork.com/news/story/575306/news/nation/yasay-assures-kerry-of-edca-implementation-under-duterte-admin>.

expressed its willingness to acquire surplus submarines and P-3C Orion long-range reconnaissance planes from Japan. The Philippines and Japan are currently discussing the prospects of forging a Status of Visiting Forces Agreement (SOVFA), which the Philippines already has with the US and Australia. In fact, the Philippines already acquired three Balikpapan-class landing craft heavy (LCH) vessels from Australia in March 2016.[19] In 2015, the Philippine Navy acquired two naval vessels from Australia: the BRP Ivatan (formerly HMAS Tarakan) and BRP Batak (formerly HMAS Brunei).[20] Increased tensions in the South China Sea have prompted countries outside the region to strengthen their defense cooperation with claimants, including the Philippines. Since the Award provides a legal confirmation of some of the Philippines' maritime claims, it may serve to make potential security partners such as Japan and Australia even more willing to engage in defense cooperation with the Philippines.

> Since the Award provides a legal confirmation of some of the Philippines' maritime claims, it may serve to make potential security partners such as Japan and Australia even more willing to engage in defense cooperation with the Philippines.

Promoting Strategic Cooperation with ASEAN Members

The Philippines is currently promoting strategic cooperation with other ASEAN countries not only for the purpose of concluding a Code of Conduct (COC) in the South China Sea but also in order to strengthen coordinated patrols, information sharing, and the establishment of communication procedures. Among its partners in ASEAN, Philippine strategic relations with Vietnam are the most advanced. In January 2015, the Philippines and Vietnam signed the Agreement for Strategic Partnership, which included provisions for the strengthening of naval cooperation between the two countries. On August 1, 2016, the Philippines also signed the Framework Agreement for Trilateral Cooperation with Indonesia and Malaysia to promote coordinated patrols along their re-

---

19   Ridzwan Rahmat, "Philippines receives three additional ex-RAN landing craft", *IHS Janes 360*, March 29, 2016, <http://www.janes.com/article/59058/philippines-receives-three-additional-ex-ran-landing-craft>.

20   Ridzwan Rahmat, "Philippines receives three additional ex-RAN landing craft", *IHS Janes 360*, March 29, 2016, <http://www.janes.com/article/59058/philippines-receives-three-additional-ex-ran-landing-craft>.

spective maritime borders. President Duterte, in fact, decided to conduct his first foreign visits to ASEAN countries to demonstrate the importance of strengthening ties with neighboring countries. Duterte visited Laos during the ASEAN Summit (September 6–8, 2016), Indonesia (September 8–9, 2016), Vietnam (September 28–29, 2016), and Brunei (October 16–18, 2016). Following his Brunei visit, Duterte proceeded to China for a state visit on October 18–21, 2016.

Engaging China Constructively in Functional Areas and on Non-Traditional Security Issues

Though the South China Sea dispute continues to be a thorny issue in relations between China and the Philippines following the arbitration, Presi-

(40) "… exchange views on issues regarding the South China Sea[, including] handling the disputes … in an appropriate manner[;] … maintaining and promoting peace and stability, freedom of navigation in and over-flight above the South China Sea, addressing their territorial and jurisdictional disputes by peaceful means … through friendly consul-tations and negotiatuns by sovereign states directly concerned".

(41) "… commit to the full and effective im-plementation of DOC in its entirety, and work substantively toward the early conclusion of a Code of Conduct in the South China Sea (COC) based on consensus."

(42) "… continue discussions on confi-

> Duterte has expressed his desire to mend ties with China. He visited China in October 2016 for this purpose and signed thirteen agreements covering many functional areas and non-traditional security issues and issued a 47-point joint statement.

dent Duterte has expressed his desire to mend ties with China. He visited China in October 2016 for this purpose and signed thirteen agreements covering many functional areas and non-tradi-tional security issues and issued a 47-point joint statement. In the statement, South China Sea is-sues were mentioned specifically, with the rele-vant points stating that both sides would:

(18) "… enhance cooperation between their respective Coast Guards, to address maritime emergency incidents, as well as humanitari-an and environmental concerns in the South China Sea … in accordance with universally recognized principles of international law in-cluding the 1982 UNCLOS."

dence-building measures to increase mutual trust and confidence …, [including] a bilateral consultation mechanism … [and] explor[ing] other areas of cooperation.[21]

Prior to visiting China, Duterte sent former President Ramos to meet friends in China to re-kindle their bilateral ties. On August 13, 2016, the former president met Madam Fu Ying, former Chinese ambassador to the Philippines and now Chairman of the Foreign Affairs Committee of the National People's Congress, in Hong Kong. He also met Dr. Wu Shicun, President of China's

21 "Joint Statement of the Republic of the Philippines and the People's Republic of China," Philippine Information Agency, October 21, 2016, <http://pia.gov.ph/news/articles/1141477032859>.

National Institute for South China Sea Studies. After their meeting, they agreed to promote the following areas of cooperation between the Philippines and China in view of the two countries' long history of friendship and the prospect of further cooperation for the sake of future generations:

- Encouraging marine preservation;
- Avoiding tension and promoting fishing cooperation;
- Anti-drug and anti-smuggling cooperation;
- Anti-crime and anti-corruption cooperation;
- Improving tourism opportunities;
- Encouraging trade and investment facilitation; and
- Encouraging track II (think tank) exchanges on relevant issues of mutual concern and interest.[22]

Conclusion and Future Prospects

As the Award demonstrated, the South China Sea disputes between the Philippines and China are not only a legal issue. They are a security issue requiring appropriate security responses. The Philippine government under President Duterte is currently pursuing a cautious, pragmatic, and reconciliatory approach towards China to peacefully manage the South China Sea disputes in the post-arbitration environment.

The Award gave the Philippines a legal victory on the issue, but it has also had security implications for the Philippines, particularly in terms of protecting the interests of Filipino fishermen in the Scarborough Shoal, securing the Philippine government's natural gas and oil exploration projects in the Reed Bank, and ensuring the safety of Philippine troops conducting resupply and rotation missions in the KIG.

To promote its national security interests in the post-arbitration

---

22 "Former President and Special Envoy Fidel V. Ramos meets Chinese diplomats in Hong Kong," Philippine Information Agency, August 13, 2016, <http://news.pia.gov.ph/article/view/1141471014584/former-president-and-special-envoy-fidel-v-ramos-meets-chinese-diplomats-in-hongkong>.

South China Sea, the Philippine government is pursuing various security policy options, which include rethinking its security alliance with the US, strengthening strategic partnerships with Japan and Australia, promoting strategic cooperation with ASEAN members, and constructively engaging China in functional areas and on non-traditional security issues. Though pursuing these policy options is giving the international

Though pursuing these policy options is giving the international community mixed signals because of the inherent strategic ambiguity and lack of policy clarity, President Duterte has a clear policy agenda in mind.

community mixed signals because of the inherent strategic ambiguity and lack of policy clarity, President Duterte has a clear policy agenda in mind: to advance Philippine national security interests in order to overcome the country's security dilemma in the post-arbitration era.

Rommel C. Banlaoi is the Chairman of the Philippine Institute for Peace, Violence and Terrorism Research (PIPVTR), a non-government policy think-tank, and a Director of its Center for Intelligence and National Security Studies (CINSS), which manages its South China Sea Studies Program. He is a Professorial Lecturer at the Department of International Studies of Miriam College, the Philippines and the Vice President of the Philippine Association for Chinese Studies (PACS). He is a member of the board of the China-Southeast Asia Research Center on the South China Sea (CSARC), a member of the International Panel of Experts of the Maritime Awareness Project (MAP) of the National Bureau of Asian Research (NBR) and Sasakawa Peace Foundation, and an Adjunct Research Professor at the National Institute of South China Sea Studies (NISCSS) in Hainan, China. He earned his PhD in International Relations at Jinan University, Guangzhou, China, and finished his BA and MA in Political Science at the University of the Philippines, where he also worked on his PhD in Political Science (ABD status). He is the author of *Philippine Security in the Age of Terror* (CRC Press/Taylor and Francis, 2010).

Post-Arbitration South China Sea:

Taiwan's Legal Policy Options and Future Prospects

Chen-Ju Chen

Abstract

Through an analysis of official statements and government actions, this chapter looks into the Republic of China (ROC) in Taiwan's positions on the South China Sea disputes before and after the change in ruling political party from the Kuomintang (KMT) to the Democratic Progressive Party (DPP) in May 2016. Differences exist between these two parties in terms of their views on the ROC's international legal status, cross-strait relations, the "Taiwan Authority of China" term used in the Award of July 12, 2016, and the historical and inherency concepts used in the ROC's territorial claims in the South China Sea. Nevertheless, the ROC's legal policy approach has been mostly maintained, and includes reiteration of its territorial claims, emphasis on Itu Aba (Taiping) Island's legal status as an island, support for freedom of navigation and overflight, proposals for the peaceful settlement of the disputes, and its position of non-acceptance of the Award, which is determined to have no legally-binding effect on the ROC. The legal implications of the Award for the ROC relate to its U-shaped line claim and the legal status of Itu Aba, both of which were implicitly targeted in the content of the Award. In light of these implications, the ROC's legal policy options relate to potential clarification of its U-shaped line claim and the governance of Itu Aba (Taiping) Island in the post-arbitration context.

Introduction

Since the Republic of the Philippines initiated arbitral proceedings against the People's Republic of China (PRC) on February 19, 2013, in regards to the South China Sea maritime territorial disputes, the Republic of China (ROC) in Taiwan[1] has paid close attention to the procedures and developments in the arbitra-

---

1   In practice, the terms ROC and Taiwan, are often used interchangeably. Given that the government's official statements on South China Sea issues have used "the ROC," this chapter mostly conforms to that usage.

tion case. The Philippines' submissions and the contents of the Award of July 12, 2016, have two major legal implications for the ROC's interests in the South China Sea. These relate to the ROC's eleven-dash (or U-shaped) line claim and its occupied features, particularly Itu Aba (Taiping) Island, which is the largest naturally formed feature in the Spratly Islands and has had a permanent ROC presence since the 1950s. At different stages during and after the arbitral proceedings, the ROC has officially reiterated its positions on the South China Sea disputes and taken actions to support its claims and safeguard its interests. Towards the end of the arbitral proceedings, democratic elections in January 2016 led to a transfer of power between ruling political parties with President Tsai Ing-wen being inaugurated in May 2016. The previous administration led by former President Ma Ying-jeou of the Kuomintang (KMT) and the current administration led by the Democratic Progressive Party (DPP) hold different views on the ROC's international legal status and cross-strait relations. Moreover, the two administrations seem to have different policies for managing the South China Sea disputes, and some doubts have been raised about the ROC's shifting South China Sea policy approach since the DPP took office.

> The two administrations seem to have different policies for managing the South China Sea disputes, and some doubts have been raised about the ROC's shifting South China Sea policy approach since the DPP took office.

On July 12, 2016, the Tribunal in the South China Sea arbitration case issued its Award, making legal conclusions related to the interpretation and application of the United Nations Convention on the Law of the Sea (UNCLOS).[2] In the Award, the arbitrators concluded that the PRC's "claims to historic rights, or other sovereign rights or jurisdiction, with respect to the maritime areas of the South China Sea encompassed by the relevant part of the 'nine-dash line' are contrary to the Convention and without lawful effect...".[3] Therefore, the PRC had no legal basis to claim historic rights to resources within the sea areas falling within the 'nine-dash line.'[4] Although directed at the PRC's claims, the Award also implicitly made legal conclusions affecting the

---

2   United Nations Convention on the Law of the Sea, United Nations, December 10, 1982, <http://www.un.org/Depts/los/convention_agreements/texts/unclos/unclos_e.pdf>.

3   Award, PCA Case No. 2013-19, Permanent Court of Arbitration, July 12, 2016, para. 278, <http://www.pcacases.com/web/sendAttach/2086>.

4   "The Tribunal Renders Its Award," Press Release, Permanent Court of Arbitration, July 12, 2016, <http://www.pcacases.com/web/sendAttach/1801>.

ROC's eleven-dash line claim from which the PRC's nine-dash line is derived. In addition, the arbitrators concluded that none of the Spratly Islands were islands as defined by UNCLOS and were thus not capable of generating exclusive economic zones (EEZs).[5] These conclusions in particular have been detrimental to the ROC's territorial claims and rights in the South China Sea. When the ROC forms policies on and exercises its rights in the South China Sea, it must consider the challenges resulting from the Award and issues of compliance with differing interpretations of international law and the law of the sea.

This chapter analyzes the ROC's official statements and relevant actions from a legal perspective and makes comparisons between the ROC's pre- and post-inauguration positions on the South China Sea. It further investigates the Award's legal implications for the ROC and its legal policy options in the wake of the arbitration case. Based on the ROC's current approach and the major issues faced, it then concludes with a discussion of the future prospects for the ROC's legal position and role in the South China Sea disputes.

Policy Approach

The ROC's policy approach can be analyzed based on observations of the ROC's statements before and after the Award. Under the KMT administration, the arbitration case already garnered global attention. In

> MOFA made clear its position on the South China Seas disputes well before the Tribunal issued its Award on Jurisdiction and Admissibility on October 29, 2015.

that context, the ROC's Ministry of Foreign Affairs (MOFA) made clear its position on the South China Seas disputes in its "Statement on the South China Sea" released on July 7, 2015,[6] well before the Tribunal issued its Award on Jurisdiction and Admissibility on October 29, 2015. Following that first award, the government reiterated its position in another statement released on October 31, 2016.[7] After the DPP took office, even more attention has been paid to the ROC's South China Sea policies, the arbitral proceedings, and the DPP administration's reactions to the Award. Following the Award of July 12, 2016, in which the

---

5 Award, para. 646.

6 "Statement on the South China Sea," Ministry of Foreign Affairs, Republic of China, July 7, 2015, <http://www.mofa.gov.tw/en/News_Content.aspx?n=0E7B91A8FBEC4A94&sms=220E98D761D34A9A&s=EDEBCA08C7F51C98>.

7 "ROC government reiterates its position on South China Sea issues," Ministry of Foreign Affairs, Republic of China, October 31, 2015, <http://www.mofa.gov.tw/en/News_Content.aspx?n=1EADDCFD4C6EC567&s=F5170FE043DADE98>.

arbitrators overwhelmingly concluded in favor of the Philippines' and against the arguments and interests of the PRC and ROC, the ROC's MOFA immediately reiterated its position on the South China Sea disputes with regards to its claims, rights, and the content of the Award.[8] Through these statements, the key aspects of the ROC's legal policy approach can be understood to include reiteration of its territorial claims, emphasis on Itu Aba (Taiping) Island's legal status as an island, support for freedom of navigation and overflight, proposals for the peaceful settlement

any claims to sovereignty over, or occupation of, these areas by other countries, irrespective of the reasons put forward or methods used for such claim or occupation.[9]

This built upon its statement of July 7, 2015, which emphasized the historical basis for its claims, explaining:

the ROC maintains that the South China Sea Islands were recorded long ago in ancient Chinese historical records and local chronicles, even since the Han dynasty. During World War

The ROC's legal policy approach includes reiteration of its territorial claims, emphasis on Itu Aba (Taiping) Island's legal status as an island, support for freedom of navigation and overflight, proposals for the peaceful settlement of the disputes, and its position of non-acceptance of the Award, which is determined to have no legally-binding effect on the ROC.

of the disputes, and its position of non-acceptance of the Award, which is determined to have no legally-binding effect on the ROC.

Reiteration of Territorial Claims

In its statement on October 31, 2015, the ROC reiterated its territorial claims, stating:

[w]hether from the perspective of history, geography, or international law, the Nansha (Spratly) Islands, Shisha (Paracel) Islands, Chungsha Islands (Macclesfield Bank), and Tungsha (Pratas) Islands (together known as the South China Sea Islands), as well as their surrounding waters, are an inherent part of ROC territory and waters. As the ROC enjoys all rights to these islands and their surrounding waters in accordance with international law, the ROC government does not recognize

II, the South China Seas Islands were occupied by Japanese forces. Called "Shinnan Gunto" and placed under the Kaohsiung Prefecture's jurisdiction in 1939, these islands were administered by Taiwan's 'Governor-General' office. By World War II's end, Japan withdrew from the South China Sea Islands. In 1946, the ROC reclaimed these islands and set up outposts on the Tungsha (Pratas Islands), Shisha (Paracel Islands), and Nansha Islands (Spratly Islands). Since then, to support its sovereignty, the ROC has conducted various administrative measures. Such measures include the publication of a cross-reference table for the South China Sea Islands' new and old names and the publication of the Location Map of the South China Sea Islands in 1947 that delineates the scope of ROC territory and waters in the region.[10]

---

8   "ROC position on the South China Sea Arbitration," Ministry of Foreign Affairs, Republic of China, July 12, 2016, <http://www.mofa.gov.tw/en/News_Content.aspx?n=1EADDCFD4C6EC567&s=5B5A9134709EB875>.

9   "ROC government reiterates its position on South China Sea issues," Ministry of Foreign Affairs, Republic of China, October 31, 2015, point 1.

10   "Statement on the South China Sea," Ministry of Foreign Affairs, Republic of China, July 7, 2015, point 2.

As for this claim's legal basis, according to Article 2 of the 1952 Treaty of Peace between the ROC and Japan, which is pursuant to Article 2 of the 1951 San Francisco Peace Treaty, Japan renounced all rights, titles, and claims to the Nansha Islands (Spratly Islands) and Shisha Islands (Paracel Islands). From the ROC's perspective, by then, the ROC had formally restored the territory and waters" concept as it implied ties with Chinese history, geography, and views on international law, the statement of July 12, 2016, merely restated the ROC's "entitlement to the sovereignties over the South China Sea Islands, which form part of its territory"[13] without mentioning the historical and inherency concepts. Thus, these differences suggest that the ROC

> The ROC government's attitude has changed slightly with the DPP taking office, and it has shifted its approach to advocating territorial sovereignty over the islands and waters of the South China Sea.

ritories that Japan had taken from the Chinese during World War II. As the ROC further stressed in its statement of October 31, 2015:

> [t]he South China Sea Islands were first discovered, named, and used, as well as incorporated into national territory, by the Chinese. Furthermore, the San Francisco Peace Treaty, which entered into effect on April 28, 1952, as well as the Treaty of Peace between the ROC and Japan, which was signed that same day, together with other international legal instruments, reconfirmed that the islands and reefs in the South China Sea occupied by Japan should be returned to the ROC.[11]

Over these areas, the ROC does not recognize other States' claims to occupation or sovereignty.[12]

In these official statements, a key issue that should be noted is that, although the 2015 statements elaborated "an inherent part of ROC

government's attitude has changed slightly with the DPP taking office, and it has shifted its approach to advocating territorial sovereignty over the islands and waters of the South China Sea.

Emphasis on Itu Aba (Taiping) Island's Legal Status as an Island

The ROC's statements emphasized not only its effective control (a basis for sovereignty claims under international law) of Itu Aba (Taiping) Island but also the island's legal status. Along with the documents released in 2015[14] that provided evidence of the ROC's control of and sovereignty over Itu Aba (Taiping) Island, the ROC's statements further discussed the island's legal status under international law. In the statement of October 31, 2015, it argued that, from legal, economic, and geographic perspectives, Itu Aba (Taiping) Island indisputably qualified as an island. This argument was supported by the requirements set forth in Article 121 of UNCLOS. Itu Aba (Taiping) Island is an "island" because it can sustain human habitation and economic life of its own,

---

11 "ROC government reiterates its position on South China Sea issues," Ministry of Foreign Affairs, Republic of China, October 31, 2015, point 2.

12 Chen-Ju Chen, "Philippines v. China Arbitration Case: Taiwan's Legal Perspectives on the Arbitral Proceedings," in Fu-Kuo Liu and Jonathan Spangler (eds.), *South China Sea Lawfare: Legal Perspectives and International Responses to the Philippines v. China Arbitration Case*, Taipei: South China Sea Think Tank / Taiwan Center for Security Studies, January 29, 2016, pp. 58-59, <http://scstt.org/reports/2016/525/>.

13 "ROC position on the South China Sea Arbitration," Ministry of Foreign Affairs, Republic of China, July 12, 2016.

14 Dustin K. H. Wang (eds.), *Compilation of Historical Archives on the Southern Territories of the Republic of China*, Taipei: Ministry of the Interior, 2015, pp. 128 and 161.

and under the same article, it is categorically not a "rock". To firmly defend this position, MOFA, along with its statement of July 7, 2015, released a document that detailed the island's environment, natural resources, life, and development.[15] From the ROC's perspective, Itu Aba (Taiping) Island's fresh water supplies and other conditions enable it to meet the criteria required by Article 121(3) of UNCLOS for an island to be entitled to an EEZ. As such, the ROC maintains that Itu Aba (Taiping) Island's legal status cannot be subject to discussion or reinterpretation by other claimants.[16]

To further raise awareness of the evidence demonstrating Itu Aba (Taiping) Island's "island" status, the ROC has sent many high-ranking government officials to visit Itu Aba since late 2015.

> Itu Aba (Taiping) Island's fresh water supplies and other conditions enable it to meet the criteria required by Article 121(3) of UNCLOS for an island to be entitled to an EEZ.

These visits are viewed as actions taken against the Philippines' attempt at "legally downgrading" the island through its arbitration case.[17] In January 2016, then-ROC President Ma Ying-jeou visited Itu Aba to promote his South China Sea Peace Initiative.[18] These visits, combined with the Chinese (Taiwan) Society of International Law's *Amicus Curiae* submission on March 23, 2016,[19] have drawn global attention to the ROC's long-standing occupation and administration of Itu Aba (Taiping) Island as well as its status as a fully entitled island under international maritime law.

With the Award falling in the Philippines' favor, the MOFA's statement of July 12, 2016, reiterated the ROC's territorial claims over and views on the status of Itu Aba (Taiping) Island. The Ministry of the Interior (MOI) further supported the ROC's stance on the issue. In a press conference, Minister of the Interior Yeh Jiunn-rong drew further attention to the "Location Map of the South China Sea Islands" published by the MOI in 1947. This publication specified that the Tungsha (Pratas), Shisha (Paracel), Chungsha (Macclesfield Bank), and Nansha (Spratly) islands and their surrounding waters were part of the ROC territory.[20] These official statements can be considered significant actions taken by the Tsai administration. Such actions contrast the previous "U-Shaped line" term's absence in the ROC's diplomatic responses under the Ma administration due to concerns over diplomatic pressure by other countries, particularly the United States. Such actions also contrast earlier doubts about whether the Tsai administration would abandon or simply not mention the U-shaped line claim.

On August 16, 2016, Yeh went to Itu Aba (Taiping) Island as the DPP's first high-ranking government official to visit since Tsai's inauguration

15 "Our Island: The Atlas of Taiping Island of the Republic of China (Taiwan), Vol. 1," Ministry of Foreign Affairs, Republic of China, July 7, 2015, <http://www.mofa.gov.tw/Upload/RelFile/1125/150640/848fe97d-1e7c-4ad1-95f4-86b922f9fceb.pdf>.

16 Chen-Ju Chen, "Philippines v. China Arbitration Case: Taiwan's Legal Perspectives on the Arbitral Proceedings," pp. 59-60.

17 "Minister leads group at opening rites for Itu Aba facilities," *Taipei Times*, December 13, 2015, <http://www.taipeitimes.com/News/front/archives/2015/12/13/2003634679>.

18 Yuan-Ming Chiao, "Ma visits Taiping, asserts nation's claim," *The China Post*, January 29, 2016, <http://www.chinapost.com.tw/taiwan/national/national-news/2016/01/29/457279/p2/Ma-visits.htm>.

19 "Amicus Curiae Submission by the Chinese (Taiwan) Society of International Law," Chinese (Taiwan) Society of International Law, March 23, 2016, <http://csil.org.tw/home/wp-content/uploads/2016/03/SCSTF-Amicus-Curiae-Brief-final.pdf>.

20 "ROC gives strong response over South China Sea award," *Taiwan Today*, July 13, 2016, <http://taiwantoday.tw/ct.asp?xItem=246203&ctNode=2175>.

in May 2016 and took the opportunity to reaffirm the ROC's territorial sovereignty claims.[21] On his visit, Yeh restated that the ROC maintained all rights over the South China Sea islands and their surrounding waters in accordance with international law and UNCLOS. Yeh further stated that "while we will not assert excessive claims, we will also not give up any rights."[22] He also announced an important policy to transform Itu Aba into a scientific hub for research on climate change and China Sea."[24] With such statements and a history of actions to support them, the international community has been assured by the ROC of its enduring support for freedoms of navigation and overflight in relevant South China Sea areas. These assurances comply with the UN Charter and other relevant international norms. In terms of implementation, by not interfering with other countries' legal activities, the ROC has, in practice, acted to ensure that all countries can exer-

> The international community has been assured by the ROC of its enduring support for freedoms of navigation and overflight in relevant South China Sea areas. These assurances comply with the UN Charter and other relevant international norms.

marine ecology.[23] This suggests that the current government's policy to govern this island has moved from a more traditional military-based approach to a more non-traditional and environmentally friendly one.

Support for Freedom of Navigation and Overflight

The ROC government has also emphasized its commitment to international law by abiding by and advocating the freedoms of navigation and overflight that are guaranteed to countries under international law. It has stressed that it "has consistently adhered to ... freedom of navigation and over-flight as stipulated in the UN Charter and other relevant international law and regulations ... [and has not] interfered with other nations' freedom of navigation or overflight in the South

cise their rights to unimpeded navigation and overflight through ROC-claimed territory where it is guaranteed to them under international law.[25]

Peaceful Settlement of Disputes

As part of its legal policy approach, the ROC has also insisted that the territorial disputes be managed and resolved through peaceful means. The statement of October 31, 2015, stressed that the ROC "has consistently adhered to the principles of peaceful settlement of international disputes ... as stipulated in the UN Charter and other relevant international law and regulations. In fact, the ROC has defended Taiping Island and other islands without ever getting into military conflict with other nations."[26]

As for the means of dispute settlement, the ROC urged in its statement of July 12, 2016, that

21   Stacy Hsu, "Interior Minister pays a visit to Itu Aba," *Taipei Times*, August 17, 2016, <http://www.taipeitimes.com/News/front/archives/2016/08/17/2003653278>.

22   "Interior minister visits Taiping, reasserts ROC sovereignty," *Taiwan Today*, August 17, 2016, <http://taiwantoday.tw/ct.asp?xItem=247058&ctNode=2175>.

23   "Interior minister visits Taiping, reasserts ROC sovereignty," *Taiwan Today*, August 17, 2016, <http://taiwantoday.tw/ct.asp?xItem=247058&ctNode=2175>.

24   "ROC government reiterates its position on South China Sea issues," Ministry of Foreign Affairs, Republic of China, October 31, 2015, point 4.

25   Chen-Ju Chen, "Philippines v. China Arbitration Case: Taiwan's Legal Perspectives on the Arbitral Proceedings," pp. 60-61.

26   "ROC government reiterates its position on South China Sea issues," Ministry of Foreign Affairs, Republic of China, October 31, 2015, point 4.

the South China Sea disputes, in the spirit of setting aside differences and promoting joint development, be settled peacefully through multilateral negotiations. To advance South China Sea peace and stability, the ROC maintains that negotiations must be conducted on the basis of equality and has expressed its willingness to work with all concerned parties.[27]

Aside from these statements, Taiwan has complemented its legal and diplomatic rhetoric with concrete actions, particularly through the development of Itu Aba (Taiping) Island, which has focused on not only on defense but also emergency, humanitarian, scientific, environmental, and other uses that solidify its role as a regional peacemaker. These goals are in contrast to the offensive military power expansion and lawfare approaches of rival claimants, which risk destabilizing the region. To build Itu Aba into a location that contributes to regional peace, is ecologically sustainable, has low carbon emissions, and can support humanitarian aid operations, the ROC has set up solar photovoltaic systems, improved navigation facilities, and developed its regional maritime rescue capabilities. To facilitate normal and emergency communications for global humanitarian rescue operations, a communications network was completed in December 2013. In order to reduce regional tensions and maintain regional peace, the government has "call[ed] on the coastal states of the South China Sea to respect the provisions and spirit of the UN Charter and UNCLOS, and to exercise restraint, safeguard peace and stability in the South China Sea, uphold the freedom of navigation and overflight through the South China Sea, refrain from taking any action that might escalate tensions, and resolve disputes peacefully."[28]

> Taiwan has complemented its legal and diplomatic rhetoric with concrete actions, particularly through the development of Itu Aba (Taiping) Island, which has focused on not only on defense but also emergency, humanitarian, scientific, environmental, and other uses that solidify its role as a regional peacemaker.

Non-Acceptance and Non-Legally-Binding Force of the Award

Immediately following the Award, the ROC's statement of July 12, 2016, stressed that the Award was completely unacceptable and without legally binding force on the ROC because: (1) the arbitrators exceeded

---

27 "ROC position on the South China Sea Arbitration," Ministry of Foreign Affairs, Republic of China, July 12, 2016.

28 "ROC government reiterates its position on South China Sea issues," Ministry of Foreign Affairs, Republic of China, October 31, 2015, point 5.

the scope of their jurisdiction by concluding on issues not directly related to the South China Sea disputes, including Taiwan's international legal status by addressing Taiwan with the inappropriate and demeaning nomenclature "Taiwan Authority of China";[29] (2) the Tribunal severely jeopardized the South China Sea islands' legal statuses by expanding its authority and declaring all Spratly Islands to be rocks that do not generate extended maritime zones including EEZs, even though some of these islands, including Itu Aba, do not fall within the scope of the Philippines' submissions; (3) the ROC's sovereignty and entitlement claims in the South China Sea are based on international law and the law of the sea; and (4) the ROC, from a procedural view, was not invited to participate in the proceedings, nor were its views solicited or taken into consideration by the Tribunal. Thus, the ROC has insisted the Award has no legally binding force on the ROC and expressed its resolute attitude towards safeguarding its national territory and relevant maritime rights.[30]

> The arbitrators exceeded the scope of their jurisdiction by concluding on issues not directly related to the South China Sea disputes, including Taiwan's international legal status by addressing Taiwan with the inappropriate and demeaning nomenclature "Taiwan Authority of China".

Legal Implications of the Award

The Award's legal implications for the ROC relate to two major issues: the U-shaped line claim and Itu Aba's legal status. In terms of the ROC's U-shaped line claim, the arbitrators determined that the PRC's nine-dash line, which was derived from the ROC's earlier claims, was not in accordance with UNCLOS. This has raised doubts about the legality of the ROC's claims that served as the foundation for those of the PRC. In terms of Itu Aba's legal status, the Award interpreted Article 121(3) of UNCLOS in an exceptionally narrow manner, concluding that none of the features in the Spratly Islands, including Itu Aba, were capable of sustaining human habitation or an economic life of their own.

---

29 It should be noted that the term "Taiwan Authority of China" had been previously used by the Philippines in its supplemental written submission submitted on March 16, 2015. However, in all of the ROC's statements responding to the South China Sea arbitration case, the statement of July 12, 2016, was the first time that it had raised the issue. Only under the Tsai administration and following the Award did the government respond officially to highlight the error. See "Supplemental Written Submission of the Philippines," Arbitration under Annex VII of the United Nations Convention on the Law of the Sea, Permanent Court of Arbitration, March 16, 2015, <http://www.pcacases.com/pcadocs/Supplemental%20Written%20Submission%20Volume%20I.pdf>.

30 "ROC position on the South China Sea Arbitration," Ministry of Foreign Affairs, Republic of China, July 12, 2016.

Territorial Claims

On the ROC's U-shaped line and the PRC's nine-dash line, the Tribunal concluded that the PRC had no legal basis to claim historical resource rights within the sea areas falling within the nine-dash line. As the PRC rejected the Tribunal's jurisdiction and did not participate in the proceedings, the Tribunal proceeded on the basis of the PRC's official statements from 2009, 2013, and subsequent statements that suggested that its South China Sea claims were historically based[31] and looked into the nature of the PRC's claimed South China Sea rights.[32] The Tribunal then concluded, without considering that those waters form part of its territorial sea or internal waters, that the PRC's historical rights claim to the living and non-living resources within the nine-dash line were incompatible with UNCLOS.[33]

In the ROC's case, the U-shaped line first appeared in its 1947 "Location Map of the South China Sea Islands". However, the "U-shaped line" term has never been formally used in official documents or laws with the exception of the publication of the baselines plus limits of the territorial sea and contiguous zone of both the Tungsha and Chungsha (Huangyan) Islands promulgated by the ROC's Executive Yuan on February 10, 1999, in which the ROC claimed that "all islands and rocks of Spratly Islands within the traditional U-Shaped line of the ROC all belong to its territory."[34] This was the only instance in which the ROC officially used the "U-shaped line" term. To date, the U-shaped line's contents have not been

clarified.[35] The ROC's 1993 South China Sea Policy Guidelines claimed that "the South China Sea area within the historic water limit is the maritime area under the jurisdiction of the Republic of China, in which the Republic of China possesses all rights and interests,"[36] the aftermath and development of which have been examined by several Taiwanese scholars.[37] In December 2005, these Policy Guidelines were suspended by the DPP administration in office at the time.[38]

Legal Status of Itu Aba (Taiping) Island

As for the legal status of islands and rocks, the Award is the first international adjudication to formally interpret Article 121(3) of UNCLOS. It investigated the text of Article 121(3) in a rig-

> As for the legal status of islands and rocks, the Award is the first international adjudication to formally interpret Article 121(3) of UNCLOS.

orous manner by detailing its six elements: (a) "rocks", (b) "cannot", (c) "sustain", (d) "human habitation", (e) "or", (f) "economic life of their own."[39] Also examined in detail were the objective and purpose of UNCLOS and Article 121(3)'s *travaux préparatoires*.[40] With the Philippines' rele-

---

31   Award, paras. 182, 185, and 817.

32   Award, paras. 207–214.

33   Award, para. 232.

34   Dustin K. H. Wang (eds.), *Compilation of Historical Archives on the Southern Territories of the Republic of China*, pp. 196–197.

35   Chun-I Chen, "Legal Aspects of the ROC's Position on the U-Shaped Line," *Prospect Journal*, April 15, 2016, pp. 20–21, <http://nccur.lib.nccu.edu.tw/bitstream/140.119/97954/1/01__Legal_Aspects.pdf>.

36   South China Sea Policy Guidelines, republished in Kuan-Ming Sun, "Policy of the Republic of China towards the South China Sea: Recent Developments," *Marine Policy*, 19, 1995, p. 408.

37   Kuan-Hsiung Wang, "The ROC's Maritime Claims and Practices with Special Reference to the South China Sea," in Nien-Tsu Alfred Hu and Ted L. McDorman (eds.), *South China Sea: Troubled Waters or a Sea of Opportunity*, Oxon: Routledge, 2013, pp. 62-63.

38   Yann-Huei Song, "Possibility of US Accession to the LOS Convention and its Potential Impact on State Practices and Maritime Claims in the South China Sea," in Yann-Huei Song and Keyuan Zou (eds.), *Major Law and Policy Issues in the South China Sea*, Oxon: Routledge, 2016, p. 116.

39   Award, paras. 478–506.

40   Award, paras. 507–538.

vant submissions requesting that the Tribunal consider whether or not certain features under the PRC's control (Scarborough Shoal, Johnson Reef, Cuarteron Reef, and Fiery Cross Reef) generated extended maritime zone entitlements as well as claiming Mischief Reef and Second Thomas Shoal were part of the Philippines' EEZ and continental shelf,[41] the Tribunal also decided to go beyond what was requested of it and investigated other insular features located within 200 nautical miles of Mischief Reef and Second Thomas Shoal, including Itu Aba. In doing so, it concluded that "none of the high-tide features in the Spratly Islands are capable of sustaining human habitation or an economic life of their own within the meaning of those terms in Article 121(3) of the Convention."[42] Although Itu Aba was only raised during the merits hearings, not in the Philippines' initial submissions, the Tribunal nevertheless made conclusions regarding Itu Aba's legal status in its discussions of the application of Article 121(3) when determining the legal statuses of Mischief Reef and Second Thomas Shoal. The decision, which legal scholars and policy makers have argued was based on incomplete evidence and beyond the scope of the Tribunal's jurisdiction, that Itu Aba is incapable of generating a 200-nm EEZ or continental shelf has been seriously detrimental to the ROC's interests and its capacity to safeguard its territorial claims in the region.

> Although Itu Aba was only raised during the merits hearings, not in the Philippines' initial submissions, the Tribunal nevertheless made conclusions regarding its legal status.

Legal Policy Options

Given the Award's content, there are two broad policy issues related to these two legal implications that merit consideration: the maintenance and ambiguity of the U-shaped line claim and the governance of Itu Aba (Taiping) Island in light of the Award's potential effects on its legal status.

U-Shaped Line Claim

Given the U-shaped line's historical development and the Award's conclusions on the matter, the ROC has been presented with major several options: abandon its U-shaped line claim, clarify its U-shaped line claim to be in accordance with the Tribunal's interpretation of UNCLOS, or maintain its policy of ambiguity over its U-shaped line claim. Furthermore, if it opted to clarify its claims, it would have to consider the var-

---

41   Award, para. 385.

42   Award, para. 646.

ious ways of doing so. These legal policy options for the ROC's U-shaped line have also long been a concern for the United States, which has urged the ROC to clarify the contents of the U-shaped line claim.[43] The ROC's claims about the Spratly Islands in the 1999 publication of the baselines plus limits of the territorial sea and contiguous zone of the Tungsha and Chungsha (Huangyan) Islands, implied that the U-shaped line refers to its island territories. Nonetheless, the ROC has never fully clarified the U-shaped line's contents and continues to maintain a certain level of ambiguity on the issue. Although clarifying its U-shaped line claims could avoid accusations of incompatibility with or breaching of UNCLOS, the Tsai administration's attitude toward these options seem to suggest that it will continue to maintain ambiguity for several reasons. First, the administration has not explicitly abandoned the U-shaped line but just avoided using the term in response to the Award.[44] Second, because clarification would have to be compliant with international law and the law of the sea, it could trigger negative reactions from either the PRC or US depending on the way in which it was clarified and introduce contradictions regarding the ROC's role in US–ROC–PRC triangular relations. Thus, it may be the best choice for the ROC in the near-term to maintain the "status quo" of cautious ambiguity regarding its claims.

Governance of Itu Aba (Taiping) Island

As for Itu Aba's legal status, which, in the view of Taiwanese lawmakers, the arbitrators sought to "legally downgrade" in their Award, the Tsai administration's responses, including its official statements and Yeh's visit, seem to continuously advocate maintaining effective control over the

feature, which mirrors the general public's feelings on the issue. However, questions still remain about whether the ROC should consider Itu Aba a rock or an island, how to govern the feature in light of the arbitrators' conclusions, whether or not – and, if so, how – more evidence about its legal, historical, geographic, and geological nature should be provided and disseminated, and whether other legal procedures to further assess its legal status should be considered.

As for whether the ROC should consider Itu Aba a rock or an island, the ROC has not published the baselines of the Itu Aba or the Spratly Islands, so the claims to Itu Aba's EEZ and continental shelf entitlements have not been completed yet. Although the ROC's official statements insisted on its status as an island, in practice, it is still difficult to deduce the government's real

> The administration has not explicitly abandoned the U-shaped line but just avoided using the term in response to the Award.

intentions because of the lack of official maritime delimitation submissions. This question, in turn, also links to other issues such as whether or to publish the baselines of Itu Aba (Taiping) Island or the Spratly Islands and, if the government were to do so, how to draw these baselines as doing so would involve explicitly recognizing the legal status of other features within 200 nm of the feature.

As for how to govern Itu Aba in light of the arbitrators' conclusions, its governance must comply with international law and the law of the sea. The ROC's current policy plan to turn Itu Aba (Taiping) Island into a hub for scientific research and humanitarian aid operations seems not to go too far in terms of a concrete, long-term plan for administration of the feature.

In terms of whether or not to research and disseminate more evidence about Itu Aba's legal, historical, geographic, and geological nature, the ROC government – through its official statements, visits, and invitations – and the Chinese

---

43   Lynn Kuok, *Tides of Change: Taiwan's evolving position in the South China Sea*, Washington D.C., Brookings Institution, May 2015, pp. 15–16, <https://www.brookings.edu/wp-content/uploads/2016/06/taiwan-south-china-sea-kuok-paper.pdf>

44   Li-hua Chung, "Tsai to avoid 'U-shaped line': source," *Taipei Times*, July 15, 2016, <http://www.taipeitimes.com/News/front/archives/2016/07/15/2003651053>.

(Taiwan) Society of International Law – through its *Amicus Curiae* submission – tried hard before the Award was issued to demonstrate to the Tribunal and the international community that Itu Aba qualified as a fully entitled island under the provisions of UNCLOS. Providing more evidence may or may not change the result or the perspectives of other relevant actors on the matter.

This leads the final important aspect of the ROC's legal policy options regarding Itu Aba's governance: whether or not other legal procedures to further assess its legal status should be

and related entitlements, the arbitrators' conclusions, which overwhelmingly supported the Philippines' arguments, still have important legal implications for the ROC and are, on the whole, detrimental to its interests in the South China Sea. In particular, these legal implications relate to the ROC's U-shaped line claim and the legal status of Itu Aba (Taiping) Island, both of which were targeted in the Award. The ROC's corresponding legal policy options, which relate to the possibility of clarifying its claims and the governance of Itu Aba, are complex, and the government will have

Influential Taiwanese politicians have called publicly for the government to file the case with the International Tribunal for the Law of the Sea.

considered. In answering this question, several challenging legal issues will need to be considered. These relate to whether or not decisions on side issues in the arbitration case are legally binding, whether or not non-parties to the arbitration are legally bound by the Award, how different State practices might impede the force of this arbitral award as it is only "a subsidiary means for the determination of rules of law" according to Article 38(1)(d) of the Statute of the International Court of Justice, and whether or not it would be possible for the ROC to initiate further international arbitral proceedings to determine the legal status of Itu Aba (Taiping) Island. Each of these complex issues deserves further analysis in the coming years, and such analyses must take into account that influential Taiwanese politicians have already called publicly for the government to file the case with the International Tribunal for the Law of the Sea.[45]

Conclusion and Future Prospects

Although the ROC was not a party to the arbitration case and has insisted that the Award has no legally binding effect on its territorial claims

to proceed cautiously while continuing to analyze the potential effects of its actions with regards to these policy options over the coming years.

Chen-Ju Chen is currently an Associate Professor at the Department of Law, National Chengchi University, Taiwan. She obtained her LL.B. at National Taiwan University, LL.M. at National Taiwan Ocean University, LL.M. in International Legal Studies at Georgetown University Law Center, United States, along with Dr. iuris at the Faculty of Law, University of Hamburg, Germany with the Max Planck Society's scholarship. In 2010, her doctoral dissertation *Fisheries Subsidies under International Law* was published by Springer. Upon returning to Taiwan, she has participated in several government-funded research projects regarding the marine environment, underwater cultural heritage protection, the Taiwan-Japan Fisheries Agreement, and South China Sea issues. Following events involving Taiwan's maritime affairs, such as the various cases of marine pollution, bullet trajectory of Guangdaxing in 2013, along with the South China Sea Arbitration, she has focused on researching relevant law of the sea issues and published several papers in both Chinese and English.

---

45   Stacy Hsu, "Lu calls for action on Itu Aba ruling," *Taipei Times*, July 22, 2016, <http://www.taipeitimes.com/News/taiwan/archives/2016/07/22/2003651544>.

Post-Arbitration South China Sea:

Taiwan's Diplomatic Policy Options and Future Prospects

Jonathan Spangler

Abstract

Taiwan has taken a multifaceted approach to the Philippines v. China arbitration case and the South China Sea more broadly that has attempted to highlight its commitment to abiding by international law and promoting regional cooperation by shelving sovereignty disputes. The extent to which the Tribunal's conclusions in its Award were detrimental to Taiwanese interests and addressed issues beyond the Philippines' fifteen submissions took many policymakers, analysts, and legal experts by surprise. For Taiwan, the Award threatens to have profound diplomatic implications for its (1) capacity to participate in dispute management negotiations, (2) leverage in pushing for regional cooperation, (3) relations with mainland China, and (4) relations with countries and other actors that have sided with the Tribunal despite the controversy regarding some of its conclusions. In the post-arbitration context, Taiwan's diplomatic policy options have become more limited, less feasible in terms of near-term implementation, and will require greater domestic and international commitment to accomplish in the long term. Nevertheless, the ROC government still has various policy options available to it. This chapter considers three of its diplomatic policy options for which it must make important choices in the post-arbitration context, including (1) whether it should maintain a hardline or flexible position on issues of territorial sovereignty, entitlements, and the inclusivity of international legal and diplomatic mechanisms; (2) whether or not – and if so, how – it should continue its vociferous advocacy of the "shelve disputes, promote cooperation" framework; and (3) whether or not it should clarify its eleven-dash line territorial claims to be in accordance with the Tribunal's interpretations of international law.

Introduction

Taiwan, which was unable to participate in or present its views in the arbitration case initiated by the Philippines against China, has nevertheless been dealt a major blow as a result of the conclusions outlined in the Award. Having consistently made efforts to clearly and publicly explain the different aspects of its multifaceted policy approach to the South China Sea, its stance, approach, and the evidence presented received scarce consideration by the arbitrators involved in the case in the formulation of their Award. Taipei Economic and Cultural Office in the Philippines Representative Gary Song-huann Lin sums up much of the frustration experienced by Republic of China (ROC) policymakers, legal experts, and scholars, expressing that "a peaceful, law-abiding and non-threatening Taiwan/ROC has turned out to be the biggest innocent victim of the [Award]" and that, for "the government and people of Taiwan/ROC, the tribunal's decision is unacceptable, unfair and double standards."[1] Despite the surprise and resentment that the Award has generated in Taiwan, the ROC government must now move forward, recalibrate its policy approach, and consider its policy options in the post-arbitration context.

Policy Approach

> The ROC government must now move forward, recalibrate its policy approach, and consider its policy options in the post-arbitration context.

Taiwan's policy approach to the Philippines v. China arbitration case and the South China Sea more broadly is influenced by several key factors including its (1) historical presence and role as claimant in the South China Sea, (2) currently occupied features, (3) unique legal status and relations with China, (4) pivotal role in regional relations, and (5) democratic political system. As with all actors involved in the disputes, the context within which the ROC government operates drives its policy approach, presenting it with a discrete but dynamic set of options and limitations that must be continuously assessed in the formulation of its policy. To fully appreciate the ROC's policy approach, these contextual factors first merit attention.

First, the ROC government, after its founding in 1911, has publicly made sovereignty claims to South China Sea features and waters since at least mid-1933 when it established the Water and Land Map Examination Committee tasked with mapping the ROC's territorial claims. It has also maintained a permanent presence on Itu Aba (Taiping) Island in the Spratly Islands since 1956 and the Pratas (Dongsha) Islands since the 1950s. Prior to that, it had also temporarily occupied features, erected stone markers, held flag-raising ceremonies, or otherwise attempted to stake its claims in the South China Sea beginning in the 1940s, including stints on Woody

---

1   "ROC stance on South China Sea award garners headlines in Philippines," Taiwan Today, July 27, 2016, <http://www.taiwantoday.tw/ct.asp?xItem=246546&ctNode=2194&mp=9>.

(Yongxing) Island in the Spratly Islands, Itu Aba (Taiping) Island, and the Pratas (Dongsha) Islands. Regardless of whether or not rival claimants, major stakeholders, and international organizations concur with the historical details or legal relevance of these events, the ROC government's policy is nevertheless influenced by its own understanding of the historical record.

Second, the ROC government currently continues to occupy Itu Aba (Taiping) Island and the Pratas (Dongsha) Islands. These are key features in the South China Sea because of their geographic size and location; the longevity of their occupation; the presence of flora, fauna, and marine life; and several other characteristics such as the availability of freshwater on Itu Aba (Taiping) Island. Taiwan has no choice but to take these into account in formulating its maritime policy and, indeed, can use some of them to its advantage in pursuing its interests.

Third, Taiwan's unique legal status and relations with China are another key contextual factor shaping its policies. The Chinese Civil War was a game-changer for the ROC government that resulted in it abandoning the mainland and retreating to the island of Taiwan in the last three months of 1949 after the establishment of the PRC on October 1, 1949. Its subsequent loss of representation as a United Nations member state on October 25, 1971,[2] has since hindered its capacity to be involved in international organizations and engage in normal state-to-state diplomatic relations with other countries. Its unique legal status of *de facto* but not *de jure* statehood combined

> The ROC government has publicly made sovereignty claims to South China Sea features and waters since at least mid-1933 when it established the Water and Land Map Examination Committee tasked with mapping the ROC's territorial claims.

with the precarious nature of cross-strait relations continue to influence its policy approach to the South China Sea and many other issues.

Fourth, since relocating to Taiwan, the ROC has maintained a pivotal role in regional relations despite the daunting challenges it faces without full recognition by the international community and as a renegade province in the eyes of PRC policymakers. It has been at the center of key agreements such as the Peace Treaty with Japan (i.e., San Francisco Peace Treaty); was involved in the first United Nations Conference on

---

2   "Restoration of the lawful rights of the People's Republic of China in the United Nations," United Nations General Assembly Resolution 2758, October 25, 1971, <https://documents-dds-ny.un.org/doc/RESOLUTION/GEN/NR0/327/74/IMG/NR032774.pdf>.

the Law of the Sea (UNCLOS I) from 1956-1958;[3] has developed an advanced economy; and has created a robust armed forces capable of defending Taiwan proper and its outlying islands. Moreover, it has long been a crucial ally for the US and a partner for Japan and other countries in the region as well as a powerful force in the triangular relations with each of these countries and the PRC. Its pivotal role in China-Taiwan-US and China-Taiwan-Japan relations has an impact on much of its foreign policy, including that related to the South China Sea.

Fifth, following the lifting of martial law in 1987, Taiwan has emerged as a vibrant demo-

> Taiwan has been at the center of key agreements such as the San Francisco Peace Treaty, was involved in the first United Nations Conference on the Law of the Sea from 1956-1958, has developed an advanced economy, and has created a robust armed forces capable of defending Taiwan proper and its outlying islands.

cratic political system with an active civil society and has been widely recognized as a model for other countries in the region. As with all healthy democracies, its domestic politics and vocal citizenry have the potential to shape both its domestic and foreign policies regarding all high-profile issues. Its maritime policies have been no exception as, in the end, Taiwanese political administrations all have the people to answer to and must formulate their policies accordingly. Each of

these five contextual factors has played and will continue to play a significant role in shaping the ROC's policy approach to the South China Sea.

With those contextual factors in mind, the President Ma Ying-jeou administration's multifaceted approach included (1) a reassertion of its claims based on the map issued by the ROC government in 1947; (2) strategic ambiguity in terms of its entitlements within the map's eleven-dash line; (3) commitment to abiding by the principles of international maritime law, including UNCLOS; (4) emphasis on its role as a peacemaker in the region and concrete policy actions to support its rhetoric and proposals; (5) rejection of the international arbitration case initiated by the Philippines, in which Taipei was unable to formally participate; and (6) an increasingly vociferous push to demonstrate and publicize that, from both scientific and legal perspectives, Itu Aba (Taiping) Island is indeed an island in response to Manila's claims to the contrary and the Tribunal's conclusion on the matter in its Award.

Following her landslide victory on January 16, 2016, and inauguration on May 20, 2016, President Tsai Ing-wen has maintained major aspects of this successful policy approach, but the extent to which the content of the Award was detrimental to Taiwan's interests has forced ROC policymakers to reconsider key issues related to its maritime policy, the neutrality and influence of international organizations, and its engagement with other countries in the region. Nevertheless, the Tsai administration has attempted to remain steadfast about Taiwan's commitment to respecting international law, emphasized its support for shelving disputes and engaging in multilateral cooperation, and sought to position Taiwan as a worthwhile diplomatic partner for rival claimants and major stakeholders in the South China Sea.

Similar to all claimants, the ROC government has remained firm about its sovereignty claims both before and after the Award. It has also pur-

---

3　"United Nations Conference on the Law of the Sea, Official records, Volume VI: Fourth Committee, (Continental Shelf), Summary records of meetings and Annexes," February 24-April 27, 1958, <http://legal.un.org/diplomaticconferences/lawofthesea-1958/vol/english/4th_Cttee_vol_VI_e.pdf>.

sued a policy of non-acceptance and views it as having no legally binding force on the ROC because the Tribunal did not invite Taiwan to participate in the proceedings, solicit or take into account its views and evidence offered, or acquire first-hand evidence of the features upon which they made decisions despite having been invited by the ROC government to visit Itu Aba (Taiping) Island. On the day the Award was issued, the Ministry of Foreign Affairs (MOFA) released a statement calling it "unacceptable" and asserting that it has "no legally binding force" before reiterating its position that the disputes should "be settled peacefully through multilateral negotiations, in the spirit of setting aside differences and promoting joint development."[4]

opportunities. The four principles guiding the ROC government's policy approach are peaceful dispute resolution in accordance with international law, including UNCLOS; the inclusion of Taiwan in multilateral dispute settlement mechanisms; freedom of navigation and overflight; and shelving disagreements to pursue joint development and dispute resolution.[6]

Diplomatic Implications of the Award

For Taiwan, the diplomatic implications of the Award may be more profound than most observers had anticipated in the months leading up to its issuance on July 12, 2016. The content of the Award took many Taiwanese lawmakers by sur-

The Tsai administration has attempted to remain steadfast about Taiwan's commitment to respecting international law, emphasized its support for shelving disputes and engaging in multilateral cooperation, and sought to position Taiwan as a worthwhile diplomatic partner for rival claimants and major stakeholders in the South China Sea.

The following week, President Tsai convened her first National Security Council meeting, where she outlined the ROC government's "five actions and four principles" approach to the South China Sea in the post-arbitration context.[5] In brief, the five actions include increased maritime patrols, enhanced multilateral dialogue, strengthened international partnerships for scientific research cooperation, collaboration with international organizations on preparing to provide humanitarian aid, and improved maritime law educational

prise, not because it generally concurred with the Philippines' arguments but because of the extent to which the arbitrators offered legal conclusions that exceeded consideration of the fifteen submissions made by the Philippine government and its legal team. Taiwan has been put in an uncomfortable situation where it must not only maintain and safeguard its sovereignty claims as all other claimants do but also cope with the reality that the status of Itu Aba (Taiping) Island as an island, which it understands as based on historical, legal, geographical, and geological facts, has been undermined by the content of the Award. Moreover, the Tribunal's usage of the unfamiliar and particularly degrading term "Taiwan Author-

4 "ROC position on the South China Sea Arbitration," Public Diplomacy Coordination Council, Ministry of Foreign Affairs, Republic of China, July 12, 2016, <http://www.mofa.gov.tw/en/News_Content. aspx?n=1EADDCFD4C6EC567&s=5B5A9134709EB875>.

5 "Tsai holds 1st NSC meeting, unveils South China Sea approach," Taiwan Today, July 20, 2016, <http:// taiwantoday.tw/ct.asp?xItem=246353&ctNode=2175>.

6 "Tsai holds 1st NSC meeting, unveils South China Sea approach," Taiwan Today, July 20, 2016, <http:// taiwantoday.tw/ct.asp?xItem=246353&ctNode=2175>.

ity of China" throughout the Award has rekindled decades-old frustration regarding Taiwan's unique diplomatic status of *de facto* statehood without UN membership. This chapter argues that the major diplomatic implications for Taiwan in the post-arbitration context relate to its (1) capacity to participate in dispute management negotiations, (2) leverage in pushing for regional cooperation, (3) relations with mainland China, and (4) relations with countries and other actors that have sided with the Tribunal despite the controversy regarding some of its conclusions.

First, the content of the Award threatens to hinder Taiwan's capacity to participate in dispute management negotiations with rival claimants and major stakeholders. After nearly seventy years as a stable, established political entity on Taiwan, the ROC government still faces a difficult predicament in managing its relations with other countries because of its lack of representation

Similar to all claimants, the ROC government has remained firm about its sovereignty claims both before and after the Award.

at the UN, the precariousness of its ties with the PRC, and the resulting sensitivity of its diplomatic relations with other countries, which must often be presented as informal to outside observers. Taipei, despite its sovereignty claims and interests being directly affected by the proceedings, was not invited to participate or express its views in the arbitration case. Moreover, the content of the Award made legal conclusions about the ROC's occupied and claimed territories and further denigrated it by referring to it as "Taiwan Authority of China" – a term that is not used by

other countries or international organizations.[7] The ROC's capacity to engage in dispute management negotiations has thus been dealt another blow because of the decisions made by the arbitrators and the resulting increased difficulty it will have in participating in negotiations with other countries on an equal footing.

Second, largely due to the obstacles hindering its participation in negotiations, the Award may also reduce the ROC's leverage in pushing for regional cooperation. Under the previous and current administrations, Taiwan has emerged as one of the most vocal advocates of multilateral negotiations through its "shelve disputes, promote cooperation" framework. Indeed, the ROC has an unparalleled level of experience constructively navigating difficult sovereignty issues, and previous roadmaps for cooperation upon which its South China Sea initiatives are based have been effective in relevant scenarios, including cross-strait relations, the East China Sea, and the Luzon Strait. However, the Award threatens to damage the ROC's standing in regional and international affairs and reduce its leverage in its efforts to promote regional cooperation.

Third, the Award may alter the trajectory of Taiwan's relations with mainland China. The ROC and PRC have corresponding territorial claims in the South China Sea because the PRC's claims are derived directly

---

7   Government officials and statements from most countries around the world use the term "Taiwan" because it is factually accurate and avoids politicizing the issue. Taiwanese institutions abroad often use "Taipei" in their names (e.g., Taipei Economic and Cultural Office) while performing the same functions as the government-run institutions of other countries. Government officials from the PRC use the term "Taiwan authorities" without appending "of China" because of mutual understandings between the two sides that there remains disagreement on Taiwan's political status. International organizations often use Taiwan, "Chinese Taipei" in the case of international sporting events, or the "Separate Customs Territory of Taiwan, Penghu, Kinmen and Matsu" in the case of the World Trade Organization and Taiwan's bilateral free trade agreements with Singapore and New Zealand. The Tribunal's "Taiwan Authority of China" nomenclature, which is unfamiliar to those familiar with Taiwan issues, has provoked renewed frustrations among ROC policymakers who already had reason to question the legitimacy or legal effect of the Award.

from earlier ones made by the ROC.[8] Before and during the arbitral proceedings, Taiwan had reasserted it territorial claims but maintained strategic ambiguity in terms of its entitlements within the eleven-dash line featured on its "South China Sea Islands Location Map" published by the Ministry of the Interior's Department of Territory (now the Department of Land Management) in 1947. By remaining ambiguous and demonstrating patience during the proceedings, ROC policymakers could maintain greater flexibility in responding to the Award, and it appeared that the ROC government was keeping its options open in terms of clarifying its eleven-dash line claims to be in accordance with international law. Although doing so would provoke discontent in

extent of the damage done to Taiwan's interests by the conclusions outlined in the Award have decreased the feasibility of that option, at least in the near-term. Although the ROC government has long sought to be fully supportive of international law, the Award may have the effect of forcing Taiwan to defend its claims in a way that appears more in line with the policies of the PRC. As a result, Taiwan's relations with mainland China may not be as influenced by South China Sea issues as they would have been had Taipei been encouraged by the Award to clarify its claims to be in accordance with the Tribunal's interpretations international law.

Fourth, the Award may disrupt or otherwise alter the trajectory of Taiwan's relations with

> The Tribunal's usage of the unfamiliar and particularly degrading term "Taiwan Authority of China" throughout the Award has rekindled decades-old frustration regarding Taiwan's unique diplomatic status of *de facto* statehood without UN membership.

Beijing, the benefits of further promoting itself as an advocate of international maritime law and a rules-based order may have outweighed the risks of retaliation from Beijing for undermining its policies. However, the Tribunal's determination that Itu Aba (Taiping) Island is a rock not entitled to an exclusive economic zone (EEZ) – despite Taiwanese institutions having provided evidence that they assert qualifies it as an island from historical, legal, geographic, and geological perspectives – and its perceived disregard for Taiwan's interests has forced Taiwanese government officials across the spectrum to rethink Taiwan's policy approach and recalibrate its diplomatic posture in the post-arbitration context. Whereas clarifying the meaning of the eleven-dash line and thus breaking its tacit agreement with Beijing once seemed like a distinct possibility, the

countries and other actors that have sided with the Tribunal despite the controversy regarding some of its conclusions. Because of the extent to which the conclusions outlined in the Award are detrimental to Taiwan's interests, the ROC government's policy options have been severely limited, and many policymakers see that the only feasible option is to continue to reject the conclusions in the Award that are perceived as disregarding the evidence and views presented by the ROC government and Taiwanese institutions. Had the Tribunal taken the historical, legal, geographic, and geological evidence offered into account, accepted offers to visit Itu Aba (Taiping) Island first-hand, and also used a more standard, less disparaging term for Taiwan in its Award, ROC policymakers would have been able to make the case for clarifying its eleven-dash line claims to be in accordance with international law. By effectively forcing the ROC to more broadly reject the Award, relations between the ROC and other

---

8   Although Taipei and Beijing have corresponding territorial claims, their approaches to the South China Sea greatly differ.

countries may also be affected as a result. Countries such as Australia, Japan, the Philippines, the US, and Vietnam have explicitly supported the Award, although other countries and institutions such as the Association of Southeast Asian Nations (ASEAN) and the European Union have been more reserved in their statements on the issue. The ROC government's non-acceptance of the Award may emerge as a thorny issue in the relations between Taiwan and other countries, particularly the US, which has long been its most important ally and guarantor of security through the Taiwan Relations Act of 1979 and other agreements.

> Taiwan has emerged as one of the most vocal advocates of multilateral negotiations through its "shelve disputes, promote cooperation" framework.

Diplomatic Policy Options

Taiwan, as a vocal advocate of shelving disputes and cooperating on resource exploration and other issues of mutual interest, has framed itself as a potential partner for other actors interested in moving forward with cooperative measures. As a result of the Award, however, Taiwan's diplomatic policy options have become more limited, less feasible in terms of near-term implementation, and will require greater domestic and international commitment to accomplish in the long term. Despite its restricted space for diplomatic maneuvering, the ROC government still has various policy options available to it, and it needs to make several key choices regarding whether or not – and if so, how – to implement them. Each of these represents a continuation of preexisting policies, significant adjustments to these policies, or entirely new directions for Taiwan.

This chapter considers three of Taiwan's diplomatic policy options for which it must make important choices in the post-arbitration context. The three policy options include (1) whether the ROC government should maintain hardline or flexible positions on issues of territorial sovereignty, entitlements, and the inclusivity of international legal and diplomatic mechanisms; (2) whether or not it should continue its vociferous advocacy of the "shelve disputes, promote cooperation" framework; and (3) whether or not it should clarify its territorial claims as relate to the eleven-dash line to be in accordance with the Tribunal's interpretations of international law. This chapter attempts, in the limited space permitted, to assess the positive and negative impacts that these three policy options could have on the ROC's key interests, which include national security, territorial sovereignty claims, its role as a responsible stakeholder and regional peacemaker, domestic politics, cross-strait relations, relations with other claimants, relations with the US, regional stability, and its diplomatic status in international fora. Taiwan's policy options should clearly align with and support its key interests, but as with most foreign policy choices, there is rarely a clear-cut approach that is beneficial by all measures and avoids potentially detrimental impacts entirely.

Diplomatic Posture on Sovereignty, Entitlements, and Inclusivity

The ROC's first major policy option relates to whether it should maintain hardline or flexible positions on issues of territorial sovereignty, entitlements, and the inclusivity of international legal and diplomatic mechanisms. In terms of territorial sovereignty, the ROC government has maintained that, "[w]hether from the perspectives of history, geography, or international law, the [South China Sea islands and] their surrounding waters, are an inherent part of ROC territory and waters."[9] That said, it has also made an effort to be explicit about its commitment to abiding by international law. The above statement continues by noting that "the ROC enjoys all rights to these island groups and their surrounding waters in accordance with international law," also stating that "the ROC government does not recognize any claim to sovereignty over, or occupation of, these areas by other countries, irrespective of the reasons put forward or methods used for such claim or occupation."[10] The historical evidence for sovereignty in the context of international mari-

The Tribunal's determination that Itu Aba (Taiping) Island is a rock not entitled to an exclusive economic zone (EEZ) – despite Taiwanese institutions having provided evidence that they assert qualifies it as an island from historical, legal, geographic, and geological perspectives – and its perceived disregard for Taiwan's interests has forced Taiwanese government officials across the spectrum to rethink Taiwan's policy approach and recalibrate its diplomatic posture in the post-arbitration context.

9   "Statement on the South China Sea," Public Diplomacy Coordination Council, Ministry of Foreign Affairs, Republic of China, July 7, 2015, <http://www.mofa.gov.tw/en/News_Content.aspx?n=1EADDCFD4C6EC567&s=F5170FE043DADE98>.

10   "Statement on the South China Sea," Public Diplomacy Coordination Council, Ministry of Foreign Affairs, Republic of China, July 7, 2015, <http://www.mofa.gov.tw/en/News_Content.aspx?n=1EADDCFD4C6EC567&s=F5170FE043DADE98>.

time law today is admittedly stronger regarding the features that the ROC currently administers, which include Itu Aba (Taiping) Island, the adjacent Zhongzhou Reef patrolled by ROC forces, and the Pratas (Dongsha) Islands, than it is for features that it claims but does not occupy.

Remaining firm on issues of territorial sovereignty has the obvious benefit of not forfeiting any of its territorial sovereignty claims. It also benefits domestic politics by not introducing new variables that would cause partisan discord, cross-strait relations by tacitly maintaining alignment with PRC claims, and national security by historical rights or claims. The ROC's stance on territorial sovereignty is already widely known and consistent. Overemphasis on reasserting its claims risks disrupting relations between Taipei and other countries, making the government's proposals to shelve disputes seem less genuine, and distracting potential partners and outside observers from the more crucial issues of multilateral negotiations on cooperation and joint development. While a firm position on territorial sovereignty has its benefits, diplomatic finesse and caution should be also exercised in order to ensure that the ROC's foreign relations remain

Although the ROC government has long sought to be fully supportive of international law, the Award may have the effect of forcing Taiwan to defend its claims in a way that appears more in line with the policies of the PRC.

deterring incursions into ROC-occupied territory. However, the advantages or disadvantages of a hardline stance on territorial sovereignty in terms of the ROC's role as a responsible stakeholder and regional peacemaker, its relations with other claimants, its relations with the US, and its diplomatic status in international fora are less clear. They depend less on whether or not it maintains the claims and more on how vocal it is in making such assertions.

In light of these impacts, this analysis finds that the ROC government should remain firm on issues of territorial sovereignty but with certain caveats. In particular, it should not waver on sovereignty issues regarding its occupied features – particularly Itu Aba (Taiping) Island and the Pratas (Dongsha) Islands – because it has more than sufficient historical evidence and legal grounds to support these claims. However, the ROC government should refrain from making reassertions of its claims the central feature in all of its official statements, especially the broader claims that will be more difficult to argue that it has sovereignty over in the contemporary international maritime legal context that gives little weight to

positive and its initiatives for cooperation remain feasible.

In terms of its entitlements, Taipei has, as noted above, stressed that they are in accordance with international law, including UNCLOS. However, disagreement with the Tribunal's interpretation of UNCLOS and its treatment of Taiwan as more of an afterthought than a key claimant deserving of the opportunity to express its views has introduced new challenges. Given that Taiwanese lawmakers are not alone in viewing the Award's content regarding Itu Aba (Taiping) Island as beyond the scope of the conclusions that the Tribunal was expected to issue and in contradiction to the evidence presented, it would be difficult for the government to alter course on its view that the feature qualifies as an island under international law and is therefore entitled to a 200-nm EEZ. As for the Pratas (Dongsha) Islands, the land area of the main feature exceeds that of Itu Aba (Taiping) Island, so there would also be little reason for the government to suggest that it is not EEZ-entitled.

A hardline stance regarding EEZ and territorial waters entitlements in reference to its currently occupied features has the benefit of maintaining its territorial sovereignty claims, promoting bipartisan agreement domestically, avoiding confrontation with Beijing, and safeguarding national security on the features. Its effects on its role as a responsible stakeholder and regional peacemaker, its relations with other countries, regional stability, and its diplomatic status in international fora would be minimal assuming that the ROC government keeps them simply as policy and does not make them a central focus of diplomatic relations or securitization efforts. Assertions of entitlements beyond those currently occupied features, however, risk having detrimental impacts on all of these key interests because they could give the misimpression that Taiwan is not committed to being a responsible stakeholder, regional peacemaker, and law-abiding member of the international system. Therefore, in terms of entitlements beyond those related to Itu Aba (Taiping) Island and the Pratas (Dongsha) Islands, the ROC government should ensure that adaptability is central to all of its official statements, political rhetoric, and policies. In the distant future, there may come a time when settling for sovereignty over only these features is in its national interest.

> Taiwan's diplomatic policy options have become more limited, less feasible in terms of near-term implementation, and will require greater domestic and international commitment to accomplish in the long term.

In terms of the inclusivity of international legal and diplomatic mechanisms, the ROC government pushed before the Award for "consultations conducted on an equal footing"[11] and "ensur[ing] that all parties concerned are included in mechanisms or measures that enhance peace and prosperity in the South China Sea"[12] and after the Award for "negotiations conducted on the basis of equality."[13] Given the view of the current administration that the ROC is a sovereign country – albeit without UN member state status due to the 1971 shift to Beijing – being recognized as an equal and included in negotiations should indeed be a primary aim. However, the longstanding reality for Taiwan and its engagement with the world is that it often has had to settle for less. This is the case with its membership in the World Trade Organization and free trade agreements with Singapore (ASTEP) and New Zealand (ANZTEC) as the "Separate Customs Territory of Taiwan, Penghu, Kinmen and Matsu," its

---

11   "Statement on the South China Sea," Public Diplomacy Coordination Council, Ministry of Foreign Affairs, Republic of China, July 7, 2015, <http://www.mofa.gov.tw/en/News_Content.aspx?n=1EADDCFD4C6EC567&s=F5170FE043DADE98>.

12   "South China Sea Peace Initiative," Ministry of Foreign Affairs, Republic of China, May 26, 2016, <http://www.mofa.gov.tw/News_Content.aspx?n=604CBAA3DB3DDA11&sms=69594088D2AB9C50&s=4589151C339E71C5>.

13   "ROC government position on the South China Sea arbitration," Office of the President, Republic of China, July 12, 2016, <http://english.president.gov.tw/Default.aspx?tabid=491&itemid=37703&rmid=2355>.

use of "Chinese Taipei" in international sporting events, and the naming of its *de facto* embassies around the world. Thus, while the ROC can still cautiously demand equality in its official statements, it may be both necessary and in its best interests to engage in South China Sea negotiations by whatever means are deemed acceptable to its counterparts. The benefits of joining in negotiations will most likely outweigh the costs of doing so on a superficially unequal basis.

Advocacy of the "Shelve Disputes, Promote Cooperation" Framework

The ROC's second major policy option relates to whether or not it should continue to be a vocal advocate of its "shelve disputes, promote cooperation" framework and, if so, how it should do so. In light of the Award's negative impacts on Taiwan's interests, the government must decide the extent to which it will invest resources and political capital in promoting its proposed framework for shelving disputes and engaging in multilateral cooperation on resource exploitation, scientific research, maritime law enforcement, environmental protection, and other issues of mutual interest among claimants. The Ma administration made this a central component of its maritime policy approach and formalized it in the South China Sea Peace Initiative modeled off of its approach to the East China Sea.[14] Although the Tsai administration

> The historical evidence for sovereignty in the context of international maritime law today is admittedly stronger regarding the features that the ROC currently administers than it is for those it claims but does not occupy.

has refrained from adopting the previous initiative in name, its approach has been similar in concept. On the day the Award was issued, the MOFA statement in response reiterated the government's position that the disputes should "be settled peacefully through multilateral negotiations, in the spirit of setting aside differences and promoting joint development."[15] The following week, at her first National Security Council meeting, President Tsai announced the ROC government's "five actions and four principles" regarding the arbitration.[16] As outlined above, the five actions involve increased maritime patrols, enhanced multilateral dialogue, strengthened international partnerships

---

14 "South China Sea Peace Initiative," Ministry of Foreign Affairs, Republic of China, May 26, 2016, <http://www.mofa.gov.tw/News_Content.aspx?n=604CBAA3DB3DDA11&sms=69594088D2AB9C50&s=4589151C339E71C5>.

15 "ROC position on the South China Sea Arbitration," Public Diplomacy Coordination Council, Ministry of Foreign Affairs, Republic of China, July 12, 2016, <http://www.mofa.gov.tw/en/News_Content.aspx?n=1EADDCFD4C6EC567&s=5B5A9134709EB875>.

16 "Tsai holds 1st NSC meeting, unveils South China Sea approach," Taiwan Today, July 20, 2016, <http://taiwantoday.tw/ct.asp?xItem=246353&ctNode=2175>.

for scientific research cooperation, collaboration with international organizations on preparing to provide humanitarian aid, and improved maritime law educational opportunities. Therefore, it can be said that three of the five actions (i.e., two, three, and four) are clearly in line with the government's "shelve disputes, promote cooperation" framework. As for the four principles (i.e., peaceful dispute resolution in accordance with international law, including UNCLOS; the inclusion of Taiwan in multilateral dispute settlement mechanisms; freedom of navigation and overflight; and shelving disagreements to pursue joint development and dispute resolution), all four demonstrate Taiwan's continued commitment to the framework.

Vociferous advocacy of the "shelve disputes, promote cooperation" framework could have a positive impact on several of its key interests. It emphasizes Taiwan's role as a responsible stakeholder and regional peacemaker and backs up its rhetoric with concrete actions. Moreover, domestic politics could benefit because the approach represents bipartisan agreement on a key foreign policy issue. The framework is widely recognized as having emerged under the previous KMT administration under the leadership of President Ma, and for President Tsai and the majority-DPP legislature to carry on the torch – even if not in name but only in concept – would lend credence to the notion that cooperation between the major political parties is possible. It would also be beneficial for its diplomatic status in international fora and its relations with other claimants and major stakeholders, such as Australia and the US, that have expressed their commitment to ensuring a rules-based regional and international order. On the other hand, advocating the framework could have negative impacts on relations with Beijing if its leadership views the initiatives as representing incongruity with PRC policy or hinting at assertions of ROC sovereignty. As for its territorial sovereignty claims, there would be minimal impact because the nature of shelving disputes would effectively shift the focus away from sovereignty issues, at least in the near-term.

Thus, the ROC government should continue

The ROC government should refrain from making reassertions of its claims the central feature in all of its official statements, especially the broader claims that will be more difficult to argue that it has sovereignty over in the contemporary international maritime legal context.

down the path it has chosen as a vocal advocate of the "shelve disputes, promote cooperation" framework in the South China Sea. It should also be prepared to invest significant financial and political capital in these efforts if it intends for them to succeed. The potential long-term benefits of doing so far outweigh the short-term costs. Moreover, it should be flexible regarding its partnerships and the issues covered. Limited bilateral agreements on individual issues, such as scientific cooperation or maritime law enforcement, may be more immediately feasible and could serve as foundations for more comprehensive agreements involving more parties. Because of the many decades that the ROC government has spent cautiously managing its relationship with the PRC and diplomatic interactions with other countries, it could be argued that Taipei has more experience navigating sensitive sovereignty issues than any other claimant. Cross-strait relations deeply affect every aspect of Taiwan's foreign policy, yet it has demonstrated that it has the diplomatic finesse to make the best of even the most precarious situations. Its relations with the US, successful engagement with Japan in the

East China Sea, and agreement with the Philippines in 2015 also lend credence to the notion that, when it comes to territorial sovereignty disputes, Taipei's political leadership has the capacity to set the stage for step-by-step diplomatic engagement and the improvement of bilateral and multilateral relations.

Clarification of Claims

The ROC's third major policy option relates to whether or not it should clarify its territorial claims as relate to the eleven-dash line to be in accordance with the Tribunal's interpretations of international law. In the Award, which was focused not on Taiwan but on the PRC's claims derived from the earlier claims made by the ROC, the Tribunal concluded that China's claims regarding "historic rights, or other sovereign rights or jurisdiction, [within] the 'nine-dash line' are contrary to [UNCLOS and have no] lawful effect [where] they exceed the geographic and substantive limits of China's maritime entitlements under [UNCLOS]".[17] In doing so, it implicitly determined that the ROC's eleven-dash line claims also "exceed the geographic and substantive limits" of its entitlements under UNCLOS if they indicate either claims to historical rights or other rights or jurisdiction over the waters of the South China Sea and "may not extend beyond the limits imposed" in UNCLOS.[18] On the other hand, because issues of territorial sovereignty were beyond the Tribunal's jurisdiction, the text of the Award does not explicitly state or implicitly suggest that the eleven-dash line claim would contradict international law if it were to represent only a sovereignty claim to the land features that it encompasses.

Official ROC statements on the matter issued by MOFA and the Office of the President have maintained a position of strategic ambiguity and emphasized Taiwan's commitment to abiding by international law. The MOFA statement in response to the Award, for example, reiterated that "the ROC is entitled to all rights over the South China Sea Islands and their relevant waters in accordance with international law and the law of the sea."[19] Now, in the post-arbitration context, in which ROC policymakers view the Tribunal as having exceeded its authority by providing legal conclusions on issues beyond the scope of the Philippines' fifteen submissions, the ROC government faces a daunting task in deciding on an issue that, by any standard, will damage its interests no matter what it decides. As detailed above, it should remain firm about its positions regarding territorial sovereignty and entitlements as relate to its occupied features. That said, the ROC

> Taiwanese lawmakers are not alone in viewing the Award's content regarding Itu Aba (Taiping) Island as beyond the scope of the conclusions that the Tribunal was expected to issue and in contradiction to the evidence presented.

government should ensure that it takes a flexible approach in regards to the eleven-dash line claim for the time being and should conduct further research and policy analysis to determine the best approach to dealing with the issue in the post-arbitration context. It should also understand that, while its policy of ambiguity may serve its interests in the near term, it will be unsustainable in the long term as actors may forcefully call upon Taipei, as they have done in the past, to clarify its

---

17 Award, PCA Case No. 2013-19, July 12, 2016, X, 1203, B, 1, p. 473, <http://www.pcacases.com/pcadocs/PH-CN%20-%2020160712%20-%20Award.pdf>.

18 Award, PCA Case No. 2013-19, July 12, 2016, X, 1203, B, 2, p. 473, <http://www.pcacases.com/pcadocs/PH-CN%20-%2020160712%20-%20Award.pdf>.

19 "ROC government position on the South China Sea arbitration," Office of the President, Republic of China, July 12, 2016, <http://english.president.gov.tw/Default.aspx?tabid=491&itemid=37703&rmid=2355>.

claims. In essence, there are three options for the ROC regarding the clarification of its eleven-dash line claim in the post-arbitration context: maintain ambiguity (i.e., the status quo policy), clarify in accordance with the Tribunal's interpretation of international law, or clarify in contradiction with this interpretation. The ROC government should form a disappearing task force that includes policymakers as well as local and international policy analysts, legal experts, and scholars to further assess the potential advantages and disadvantages of these three policy options.

Apart from the three broad policy options discussed in detail above, there is at least one other action that ROC government officials should avoid. Despite the challenges presented by and frustration over what many understandably view

torical presence and role as claimant in the South China Sea, currently occupied features, unique legal status and relations with China, pivotal role in regional relations, and democratic political system. Due in part to these contextual factors, the Ma administration's multifaceted approach in the pre-Award context included (1) a reassertion of ROC claims based on the map issued by the government in 1947; (2) strategic ambiguity in terms of its entitlements within the map's eleven-dash line; (3) commitment to abiding by the principles of international maritime law, including UNCLOS; (4) emphasis on its role as a peacemaker in the region and concrete policy actions to support its rhetoric and proposals; (5) rejection of the international arbitration case initiated by the Philippines, in which Taipei was unable to formally par-

In terms of entitlements beyond those related to Itu Aba (Taiping) Island and the Pratas (Dongsha) Islands, the ROC government should ensure that adaptability is central to all of its official statements, political rhetoric, and policies.

as an unjust legal outcome for Taiwan, officials should refrain from making the perceived biases of the Tribunal or illegitimacy of the PCA as a private, non-UN institution a primary issue in their criticism of the Award. Although there may be reason to hold such views, the denigration of respected lawyers and organizations is not well received by the international community and may have damaging impacts on Taiwan's image internationally. Indeed, given its delicate diplomatic status internationally, being well received and supported by the international community is a core interest for Taiwan that should be seen as of the utmost importance.

Conclusion and Future Prospects

This chapter has suggested that Taiwan's policy approach to the Philippines v. China arbitration case and the South China Sea more broadly is influenced by several key factors including its his-

ticipate; and (6) an increasingly vociferous push to demonstrate and publicize that, from both scientific and legal perspectives, Itu Aba (Taiping) Island is indeed an island in response to Manila's claims to the contrary and the Tribunal's conclusion on the matter in its Award.

The Tsai administration has maintained major aspects of this successful policy approach, but the extent to which the content of the Award was detrimental to Taiwan's interests has forced ROC policymakers to reconsider key issues related to its maritime policy, the neutrality and influence of international organizations, and its engagement with other countries in the region. Since the Award, the ROC government has outlined its "five actions and four principles" approach to the South China Sea in the post-arbitration context.[20] The five actions include increased maritime pa-

---

20 "Tsai holds 1st NSC meeting, unveils South China Sea approach," Taiwan Today, July 20, 2016, <http://taiwantoday.tw/ct.asp?xItem=246353&ctNode=2175>.

trols, enhanced multilateral dialogue, strengthened international partnerships for scientific research cooperation, collaboration with international organizations on preparing to provide humanitarian aid, and improved maritime law educational opportunities. The four principles guiding the ROC government's policy approach can be summarized as peaceful dispute resolution in accordance with international law, including UNCLOS; the inclusion of Taiwan in multilateral dispute settlement mechanisms; freedom of navigation and overflight; and shelving disagreements to pursue joint development and dispute resolution.[21] The major diplomatic implications for Taiwan in the post-arbitration context relate to its capacity to participate in dispute management negotiations, leverage in pushing for regional cooperation, relations with mainland China, and relations with countries and other actors that have sided with the Tribunal despite the controversy regarding some of its conclusions.

The chapter then considered three of Taiwan's diplomatic policy options for which it must make important choices in the post-arbitration context, including (1) whether the ROC government should maintain hardline or flexible positions on issues of territorial sovereignty, entitlements, and the inclusivity of international legal and diplomatic mechanisms; (2) whether or not it should continue its vociferous advocacy of the "shelve disputes, promote cooperation" framework; and (3) whether or not it should clarify its territorial claims

> The ROC government should remain firm regarding territorial sovereignty over its occupied features but refrain from making its assertions the central feature of its official statements and engagement with other claimants.

as relate to the eleven-dash line to be in accordance with the Tribunal's interpretations of international law. In regards to these options, it concluded that the ROC government should remain firm regarding territorial sovereignty over its occupied features but refrain from making its assertions the central feature of its official statements and engagement with other claimants. In terms of entitlements, it should be more flexible when they relate to waters beyond the extent of the entitlements accorded to it based on its two major occupied features. Moreover, it should maintain flexibility regarding the inclusivity of international legal and diplomatic mechanisms and seek out opportunities for cooperation that may be bilateral and issue-specific at first in order to set the foundation for its involvement in more comprehensive

---

21 "Tsai holds 1st NSC meeting, unveils South China Sea approach," Taiwan Today, July 20, 2016, <http://taiwantoday.tw/ct.asp?xItem=246353&ctNode=2175>.

agreements. As for its advocacy of the "shelve disputes, promote cooperation" framework, the ROC government should continue to pursue this policy approach and should ensure that sufficient resources are invested accordingly. In terms of the clarification of its eleven-dash line claims, the status quo policy approach of strategic ambiguity may serve its interests in the near term, but a disappearing task force that includes policymakers as well as local and inter-

> As for its advocacy of the "shelve disputes, promote cooperation" framework, the ROC government should continue to pursue this policy approach and should ensure that sufficient resources are invested accordingly.

national policy analysts, legal experts, and scholars should be formed to further assess the potential advantages and disadvantages of the three options associated with policy clarification. Although Taiwan has been dealt a major blow by the content of the Award, there are still feasible policy options available to it, and the ROC government must make clear decisions and play its cards right in order to best take advantage of the opportunities that exist in the post-arbitration context.

Jonathan Spangler is the Director of the South China Sea Think Tank. His research focuses on Asia-Pacific regional security, maritime territorial disputes, and cross-strait relations. His publications, projects, and contact information can be found at jspangler.org.

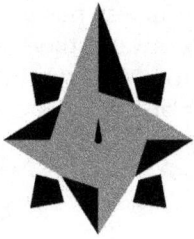

Post-Arbitration South China Sea:

Taiwan's Security Policy Options and Future Prospects

Fu-Kuo Liu

Abstract

In the South China Sea arbitration case initiated by the Philippines against China, Taiwan was not allowed to participate in the proceedings due to its unique political status with regards to the mainland. Nevertheless, the Award issued by the Arbitral Tribunal on July 12, 2016, which fell overwhelmingly in favor of the Philippines, has major political and security implications for Taiwan. This chapter first outlines Taiwan's response to the Award and its political and security policy approach regarding the South China Sea disputes. It then assesses the political and security implications of the Award for Taiwan, which include aggravating regional tensions, emboldening rival claimants, weakening international law, limiting the scope of and options for negotiations, stoking nationalism, aligning cross-strait interests, encouraging domestic political interest and opposition, and complicating the disputes. Following this, the chapter highlights some of the major political and security policy options that Taiwan's government must consider, which relate to national and regional security, Taiwan–US relations, and domestic politics and cross-strait relations.

Introduction

The Award issued on July 12, 2016, in the South China Sea arbitration case ruled overwhelmingly in favor of the Philippines. It was an unusual result that surprised many, and many policy makers and analyst believe that it reflects a strong political influence in the arbitration process. Although the Tribunal attempted to avoid making explicit legal conclusions on sovereignty and delimitation, issues that the arbitrators were aware was beyond their jurisdiction, the Award walks a fine line in this regard, with its content implicitly deciding the rights to the ownership and status of land features, rocks, reefs, and low-tide elevations in the Spratly Islands. Taiwanese lawmakers maintain that this clearly exceeds the scope of the Tribunal's jurisdiction under the United Nations Convention on the Law of the Sea (UNCLOS) by ruling on national sovereignty issues and that was confined to issuing an award related to the interpretation of international law as relevant to the disputes in question and parties involved. The function of an arbitral tribunal's award should be to provide parties concerned with legal guidelines that contribute to achieving a final resolution to the dispute. It would then depend on those parties involved to engage in diplomatic negotiations within the framework of the terms decided by the Tribunal to reach an agreement.

> The function of an arbitral tribunal's award should be to provide parties concerned with legal guidelines that contribute to achieving a final resolution to the dispute. It would then depend on those parties involved to engage in diplomatic negotiations.

The Tribunal emphasized that the two awards were legally binding, no matter what position was taken by the other party – in this case, China. Realistically, after the final award was given, the most critical step would be to urge China and the Philippines to go through the diplomatic negotiation process for dispute settlement. As China has firmly rejected the arbitration, it is not feasible for the two parties to reach an agreement concerning the terms of implementation, so the Award can only be considered a superfluous legal exercise. By toning down the Philippine government's criticism of China, President Rodrigo Duterte has taken a pragmatic approach by circumventing direct confrontation with China. In reality, the situation on the ground has not changed much at all following the Award. A big question that remains is whether or not this arbitration case will have any meaningful legal impacts and be referred to any future cases.

The Arbitral Tribunal's controversial conclusions in the Award have given rise to new challenges for the international legal system and regional politics and security. Taiwan and other countries view the Award as not conducive to peaceful settlement of the maritime disputes. Rather, it has served to disrupt the existing legal, diplomatic, and security structure of the South China Sea, which has existed for centuries. Although the arbitral proceedings were supposedly relevant only to Chinese and Philippine claims and conduct in the South China Sea, Taiwanese claims were also directly referred to in and affected by the Award. For Taiwan, there are clear political and security implications resulting from the Award and the entire arbitration process. The following sections discuss Taiwan's political and security policy approach, the political and security implications of the Award, and Taiwan's policy options related to national security and the political challenges for Taiwan's current government that have arisen as a result of the Award.

Political and Security Policy Approach

Immediately after the Award was announced, the DPP government released a strong statement rejecting it. The statement emphasized that Taiwan does not accept the Award and that it does not have any legally binding effect on Taiwan. The main reasons Taiwan was given no option but to issue such a strong statement against the Arbitral Tribunal's conclusions are based on at least three key political considerations.[1] First, throughout the arbitration process, the Tribunal did not consult or make any attempt whatsoever to engage with Taiwan. Second, the Tribunal referred to Taiwan as "Taiwan authority of China", which clearly defined Taiwan as a part of China. From legal standpoint, the arbitrators' unexpected decision to denigrate Taiwan by using this term – one that is not even used by foreign countries or international organizations – made it absolutely impossible for Taiwan's government to stand on the side of Arbitral Tribunal. Third, the Tribunal misguidedly determined that Itu Aba (Taiping) Island was defined as a "rock" instead of an "island" under the provisions set forth in UNCLOS. Accordingly, under the Tribunal's interpretation of international maritime law, Taiping Island does not generate an entitlement to an exclusive economic zone (EEZ) or continental shelf. If the government were to accept it, the Award is seriously detrimental to Taiwan's national interests.

> The Tribunal did not consult or make any attempt whatsoever to engage with Taiwan.

With its strong statement in response to the Award, the Democratic Progressive Party (DPP) government won a surprisingly high degree of popular support both from Taiwanese society and across the Taiwan Strait, even though being forced to do so happened to be against its original wishes. There are several profound implications of this outcome scenario. First, it has given President Tsai no option but to follow the traditional course of protecting sovereignty based on Taiwan's eleven-dash line claim that has been official government policy for seventy years. By insisting on basing Taiwan's claims on this traditional line of sovereignty, she may not be regarded as drifting away from the

---

1   "ROC position on the South China Sea Arbitration," Ministry of Foreign Affairs, Republic of China, July 12, 2016, <http://www.mofa.gov.tw/en/News_Content.aspx?n=1EADDCFD4C6EC567&s=5B5A9134709EB875>.

constitution of the Republic of China.

Secondly, from an international perspective, it may seem that Taiwan is echoing China's stance on South China Sea issues and agreeing to take the same policy line as China as far as sovereignty claims are concerned. Quite surprisingly, President Tsai was applauded by the public in mainland China as well. In fact, President Tsai wanted neither to align Taiwan with the Chinese policy in the South China Sea nor accept international legal conclusions so detrimental to Taiwan's national interests. For a few weeks afterwards, the rejection of the Award seemed to send out a hopeful political signal to Beijing as a possible political opportunity to link Taiwan with China without the latter directly affirming the "1992 consensus".

Nevertheless, later on, a review from within the DPP suggested that Taiwan's policy stance should not be in line with that of China.[2] According to an open survey, mismanagement of the response to the Award, the arbitral proceedings, and South China Sea issues overall was one of the main factors causing the decline in President Tsai's approval rating.[3] As the popularity of the Tsai administration continuously and dramatically drops, the hardliners inside the ruling party have tried to shift away from a hopeful course for cross-strait relations and differentiate Taiwan's policy stance from the Chinese one. On her first National Day address, President Tsai affirmed that she would not provoke China. However, she only elaborated on relations with China by referring to the historic fact that a meeting took place in 1992 without using the term "1992 consensus" that had previously served as the basis for cross-strait dialogue. Politically, it has diminished Taiwan's flexibility for engaging with China and weakened China's expectations that direct dialogue would continue. In terms of security, the tendency to drift away from rapprochement with China increases diplomatic uncertainty and security risks in the Taiwan Strait. This has come to be a critical issue for the administration as it continues to cope with the potential for tougher responses from Beijing and the lack of common understanding between the two governments.

> According to an open survey, mismanagement of the response to the Award, the arbitral proceedings, and South China Sea issues overall was one of the main factors causing the decline in President Tsai's approval rating.

Political and Security Implications of the Award

The Award's surprising and controversial conclusions that were detrimental to Chinese and Taiwanese interests on almost every key issue has aroused debate throughout the regional and international legal and political communities. The Arbitral Tribunal claimed that it was independent, offered objective legal perspectives, and considered only on legal issues that would affect the parties concerned. However, the whole arbitration process was seriously influenced by political factors, the arbitrators took it upon themselves to not simply offer legal arguments on the issues submitted by the Philippines but to make legal conclusions beyond what was requested of it and on issues that implicitly affect territorial sovereignty. Because of the resulting political and security implications, the arbitral proceedings did not serve to make progress towards the ultimate goal of peaceful dispute settlement. Instead, the Award was counterproductive to regional peace

---

2   "Taiwan Thinktank July Public Survey Press Conference," Taiwan Thinktank, July 30, 2016, <http://www.taiwanthinktank.org/chinese/page/5/61/3149/0>.

3   "Blue Survey: Tsai Ing-wen has been Too Moderate on South China Sea," Apple Daily / Radio France Internationale, September 7, 2016, <http://www.appledaily.com.tw/realtimenews/article/new/20160907/944356/>.

and stability and has since increased tensions among the related parties. For Taiwan, the Award has major political and security implications, which include aggravating regional tensions, emboldening rival claimants, weakening international law, limiting the scope of and options for negotiations, stoking nationalism, aligning cross-strait interests, encouraging domestic political interest and opposition, and complicating the disputes.

Aggravating Regional Tensions

Throughout the arbitration process, diplomatic battles between the Philippines and China and between the US and China have been further aggravated. With the arbitral proceedings ongoing, the bilateral relationship between the Philippines and China reached its lowest point in recent history. Most regional tensions are derived from the bilateral antagonism on the ground. Policy makers from Taiwan, China, and elsewhere are concerned that, as a result of the Philippines legal accusations, the whole region has been brought to the brink of confrontation. Moreover, as a result of the arbitration, most regional countries were pushed by the US into supporting the Philippines' arbitration case and were thus forced to either take sides regarding its lawfare approach or cautiously navigate a fine line in an attempt to find a middle ground for their South China Sea policies. The US has taken advantage of the arbitration case against China and placed further emphasis on its Asia-Pacific rebalancing strategy that has increased its involvement in regional security affairs.

Emboldening Rival Claimants

As the Award denied the legality of Chinese historical entitlements within its nine-dash line claims in the South China Sea and ruled on the status of land features, suggesting that many features in the Spratly Islands only receive the legal entitlements of rocks and low-tide or fully submerged features under UNCLOS, the surprising outcome of the arbitration case may have shifted the fundamental power structure of the South China Sea. It gives other claimants the legal basis to challenge Chinese claims by declaring them as not in accordance with international law and preventing features in the Spratly Islands from receiving the legal entitlements of an "island" under international law. In effect, it may have paved a way for further struggle among claimants and non-claimants rather than offering any clear guidelines for long-term peaceful settlement of the disputes. In terms of the goal of seeking regional peace, the Award has been counterproductive.

Furthermore, as the Award challenged the legality of China's nine-dash line claims and therefore sought to implicitly invalidate Taiwan's eleven-dash line claims that were the foundation for these, it may have unfortunately sent a wrong message to the region by encouraging other claimants and non-claimants to challenge the long-standing sovereignty claims of China and Taiwan in the South China Sea. This may even encourage other rival claimants to initiate more legal proceedings against China in the future. Following the Award, some voices in Japan and Indonesia have expressed their strong desire for presenting new arbitration cases against China. If this became a trend, it could have even grav-

> The US has taken advantage of the arbitration case against China and placed further emphasis on its Asia-Pacific rebalancing strategy that has increased its involvement in regional security affairs.

er security consequences for Taiwan as it would continue to be sidelined while third parties make legal decisions that directly affect its rights.

Weakening International Law

In part because of the Philippines' unilateral initiation of the arbitral proceedings, China's resulting decision to not participate, and the prohibition of Taiwan from participating, the legal conclusions set forth in the Award are primarily based on the provisions of UNCLOS and partial

(Taiping) Island that provided ample evidence that the feature qualifies as an island under UNCLOS, nor did it accept formal invitations by the Taiwanese government to visit the island or send relevant experts on its behalf. The arbitrators' unusually narrow interpretation of international law regarding the status of features, their tendency to make legal conclusions beyond what was requested of them, their unnecessary denigration of Taiwan, and their eagerness to make legal decisions based on incomplete evidence has led many observers in Taiwan, China, and elsewhere to lose faith in the potentially beneficial international arbitration process.

> The arbitrators' unusually narrow interpretation of international law regarding the status of features, their tendency to make legal conclusions beyond what was requested of them, their unnecessary denigration of Taiwan, and their eagerness to make legal decisions based on incomplete evidence has led many observers in Taiwan, China, and elsewhere to lose faith in the potentially beneficial international arbitration process.

information supplied by the Philippines. It did not accept the Chinese position on historic entitlements in the South China Sea but did accept that the Philippines had certain historic rights. Where the Tribunal did accept China's position on key issues, it used it in a way that was detrimental to Chinese interests. This was the case with the arbitrators' acceptance of China's argument that its infrastructural developments were for civilian purposes, which it then took to mean that, because they were not military installations, they could not be excluded from jurisdiction. Moreover, the Tribunal did not consider Taiwan's submission of a careful scientific survey of Itu Aba

Limiting the Scope of and Options for Negotiations

Now, the big question is how to implement the Award. If China rejects negotiations with the Philippines that are based on the Award, nobody will be able to force the parties concerned to negotiate. In terms of bilateral dialogue, China has emphasized that any possibility of negotiations with the Philippines would have to start from ground zero and could not make use of the content of the Award, while the Philippines faces external and internal political pressure to abide by the Award. In addition, the international community lacks a credible mechanism to help implement the Award issued by the Arbitral Tribunal. These factors have effectively limited the scope of and options for negotiations. If the Philippines does not make concessions, it will be difficult for the two parties to move forward with negotiations on dispute management and eventual dispute settlement.

Stoking Nationalism

Another security implication for Taiwan stems from the unfortunate reality that the arbitrators' decisions were overwhelmingly in favor of the Philippines and detrimental to Taiwanese and

Chinese national interests. The negative outcome of the Award has stirred up strong nationalism and absolutism in domestic politics in China and confusion in Taiwan. Acutely aware that accepting the Tribunal's conclusions would damage their national interests, China and Taiwan were clear in their respective rejections of the Award, and the public on both sides of the Taiwan Strait has been largely in support of their governments' decisions. Interestingly, nationalism in the Philippines has also been on the rise in the wake of the country's historic 'victory' in the unilaterally initiated arbitration case. In the future, these trends may have the unintended consequence of constraining the degree of policy flexibility that national decision makers have in negotiating with each other. In this regard, there is a marked difference between the pre-arbitration and post-arbitration South China Sea political environments.

alignment of these interests. Whether or not this partial policy alignment could pave the way for the two sides to consider South China Sea issues as new grounds for reconciliation is something that will be worth watching in the future.

Encouraging Domestic Political Interest and Opposition

In light of the arbitrators' denial of Taiwan's participation in the arbitration process and surprising decision to refer to the sovereign state as "Taiwan authority of China" throughout the Award, Taiwan's government under President Tsai responded that Taiwan would not accept

The negative impacts of the Award have alerted policy makers in Taipei and Beijing to the unfortunate reality that international legal mechanisms may not be as impartial as they had hoped and that they have the potential to threaten their national security interests.

Aligning Cross-Strait Interests

Since ambiguity about Taiwan's political relations with China remains and Taiwan's original claims serve as the basis for those of China, the Award has implicitly denied Taiwan's claims of historical entitlements based on its eleven-dash line, the source of China's nine-dash line claims. The negative impacts of the Award have alerted policy makers in Taipei and Beijing to the unfortunate reality that international legal mechanisms may not be as impartial as they had hoped and that they have the potential to threaten their national security interests. In the midst of the ongoing rivalry in the Taiwan Strait, both sides have nevertheless recognized that there may be common interests at stake on the South China Sea issues, and the Award may have led to an increasing

the Award and that it would not have any legally binding effect on Taiwan.[4] Taiwan's position that it rejects the Award has been clear and consistent. This led to a very interesting situation that Taiwan, by defending its national interests, has the appearance of siding with China in its response to the Award. This has catalyzed domestic political interest in and opposition to the Award and given rise to complicated feelings for the independence-oriented government at home and abroad.

Taiwan's new DPP government has made a surprisingly strong turn in responding to the Award. Traditionally, given its complicated political nature and lower priority relative to other more pressing policy issues, the South China Sea disputes were not high on the DPP agenda. When the Award seriously undercut Taiwan's national

---

4   "ROC rejects South China Sea arbitration award," *Taiwan Today*, July 12, 2016, <http://taiwantoday. tw/ct.asp?xItem=246168&ctNode=2175>.

interests by referring to the Republic of China government on Taiwan as "Taiwan authority of China" and stripping Itu Aba (Taiping) Island of the potential legal entitlements accorded to it as an island, Taiwan's government was forced to express its strong opposition to and rejection of the Award. To some extent, the government was surprised by the negative outcomes of the Award and was forced to change the original course of its policy, which has unintentionally given the impression that it is leaning toward China in the disputes. However, political concerns have increased as to whether or not Taiwan's government may seek to provide further clarification of its South China Sea policy and claims in order to distance itself from those of Beijing.

> Political concerns have increased as to whether or not Taiwan's government may seek to provide further clarification of its South China Sea policy and claims in order to distance itself from those of Beijing.

Complicating the Disputes

Finally, even though the Award has presented legal conclusions on certain aspects of disputes, offered legal bases for some sovereignty claims, and provided justifications for certain actions, the situation in the South China Sea has become an increasingly complicated aspect of the policy agendas of rival claimants and other major stakeholders. As a result, their national policies for the South China Sea may become further constrained by international and internal factors.

Political and Security Policy Options

As a result of the Award, security issues in the post-arbitration context have become increasingly difficult to manage for Taiwan and the region. The Award may have profound effects on China and Taiwan's policy approaches when dealing with other claimants in the future. Such a scenario will definitely increase security risks for Taiwan, as neighboring countries will naturally quote the awards vis-à-vis Taiwan as justification for their own actions and whenever touching upon the maritime territorial disputes. Furthermore, the arbitrators' references to Taiwan as the "Taiwan authority of China" have reinvigorated domestic political sentiment opposed to becoming closer to China. Should the Tsai administration drift further away from China, political tensions and security concerns will rise as a result. There remain questions as how much Taiwan can do to articulate its rejection of the Award and convey its message to the region and international community. Despite not being bound by the Award, Taiwan will still have to push to engage in some practical actions to strengthen its position and effectively deny the detrimental legal impacts of the Award. Consequently, there are three important dimensions of its security policy options that must be considered.

Regional Security and Marginalization

Regional security and stability are critical to Taiwan's national security interests. With the security environment in the South China Sea changing in the wake of the Award, other claimants and major stakeholders prepared to act according to the conclusions outlined in the Award. Although immediately after release of the Award there was no significant change to individual claims on the ground, there would be a tendency that regional countries would follow what the direction of the verdict gives. Taiwan is not the immediate party of the arbitration. However, based on the U-shaped line, its position and policy on territorial claims has the same base as China's. Regardless of the controversy surrounding the Award, Taiwan has to make a hard decision regarding how to engage in practical actions to show that it remains a key claimant and should be involved in any potential multilateral negotiations. Otherwise, Taiwan will be further marginalized to the extent of irrelevance in the South China Sea disputes. When regional order is going through a period of readjustment after the arbitral proceedings, it would serve Taiwan's national security interests to respond more actively by increasing military presence and strengthening its defense capabilities.

> The arbitrators' references to Taiwan as the "Taiwan authority of China" have reinvigorated domestic political sentiment opposed to becoming closer to China.

Taiwan–US Relations

The US has been a significant factor influencing the direction of Taiwan's South China Sea policy. Under former President Ma Ying-jeou, Taiwan would have liked to boost its strength in the South China Sea. However, because of US concerns that Taiwan's efforts could bolster China's position in the arbitration and disrupt its own South China Sea strategy, it attempted to dissuade Taiwan from becoming more actively engaged. Throughout the period of arbitration, Taiwan was constrained by US policy interests in the region and unbalanced domestic political preferences, so it could not freely pursue its own national interests.

In the wake of the arbitration case, Taiwan has been left with few legal and diplomatic policy options but to remain firm in its stance that the Award has no legal effect on Taiwan's claims in the South China

Sea. At the same time, Taipei must carefully calibrate its relations with Washington, particularly with US lawmakers calling upon China to accept and abide by the content of the Award. Although the Philippines' decreasing emphasis on the arbitration case and improving ties with China under President Rodrigo Duterte may alleviate US diplomatic pressure on all parties to abide by the Award, there will nevertheless remain some underlying incompatibility between Taiwan and US perspectives on the South China Sea. Nevertheless, Taiwan and the US have long maintained strong, albeit informal, diplomatic and security relations. The US remains a guarantor of Taiwanese security – although this would unlikely extend to its South China Sea claims – and a key supplier of defense technology and equipment. In the future, Taiwan will have to continue to demonstrate to US policymakers that supporting it is also in US

wan's South China Sea policy options have become increasingly constrained. As a result, the DPP government has taken a more indistinct position than its predecessor. By implicitly advocating Taiwan independence, the DPP government has reduced the possibility of working with China and actually undercut its own opportunities for engagement on relevant issues.

As previously discussed, the Tribunal's decisions in the arbitration case were overwhelmingly in favor of the Philippines and detrimental to China and Taiwan's interests, and this resulted in what has the appearance of legal policy alignment between Beijing and Taipei, even under the DPP administration. In terms of security, however, Taiwan is in a unique situation in that it must confront both the security challenges of cross-strait relations as well as those of the South China Sea. The government's reluctance to take

Taiwan will have to continue to demonstrate to US policymakers that supporting it is also in US interests, while simultaneously considering the feasibility and value of domestically developed defense programs.

interests, while simultaneously considering the feasibility and value of domestically developed defense programs.

Domestic Politics and Cross-Strait Relations

Internally, for two decades, Taiwan has been bogged down by domestic political struggle that has centered on different views of statehood, and these debates, in turn, affect its future as well as sovereignty claims in the South China Sea. Because the former KMT government was given greater leeway by Beijing in addressing international policy issues, it was active in asserting Taiwan's sovereignty claims in the South China Sea with its handicapped status in the international community being less of an obstacle. However, as cross-strait relations have soured due to the DPP government's rejection of the 1992 consensus, the common political basis for negotiations between the KMT government and Beijing, Tai-

more drastic actions to protect national sovereignty in the South China Sea is the result of the cross-strait dilemma, which presents a greater existential threat to its security than do its lesser maritime claims. The political dilemma is that increased efforts to protect its sovereignty claims could mean accepting the legitimacy of the "One China" concept, which the DPP is unable to swallow. In cross-strait relations, the DPP government now faces a tough choice in terms of its security policy. As it takes both internal and external pressures into consideration, its policy options are limited, and some fear that its actions are causing it to drift away from its national interests.

Conclusion and Future Prospects

The Award presents a great deal of security challenges for the incumbent government in Taipei, and many believe that President Tsai has not been doing enough to protect Taiwan's national interests. After rejecting the Award, the government has taken few actions in line with the tone of its legal stance and has seemingly backed down from its tough position. From a domestic political perspective, the government was not ready to take on the Award. While the cross-strait relations today are not stable and pathway for negotiations is unclear, any responses to South China Sea issues by Taipei could further complicate cross-strait relations depending on mainland China's interpretations of such actions. Although the strong rejection of the Award from a legal perspective may have been the right course of action, it does not seem to go along with the DPP's original desire to comply with the Award. Moreover, when the government destabilizes cross-strait relations and fails to back up its legal position with clear actions

> By its reluctance to take action, Taiwan puts its national security interests at risk on two fronts: it loses its edge in the South China Sea, and it causes a deterioration in cross-strait relations.

to protect its sovereignty, Taiwan may be further marginalized in future South China Sea negotiations. The great risk generated by the Award and Taipei's subsequent responses are that they may deepen Beijing's mistrust of the DPP government. When President Rodrigo Duterte of the Philippines visitied China in October 2016, it implied that a fundamental change in the South China Sea power struggle was taking place. By its reluctance to take action, Taiwan puts its national security interests at risk on two fronts: it loses its edge in the South China Sea, and it causes a deterioration in cross-strait relations. To show its determination, it is important for Taiwan to further strengthen its South China Sea claims while, at the same time, engage in bilateral dialogue with rival claimants including China.

Fu-Kuo Liu is the Executive Director of the Taiwan Center for Security Studies, a Research Fellow at the Institute of International Relations, and a Professor at National Chengchi University.

Post-Arbitration South China Sea:

Vietnam's Policy Options and Future Prospects

Truong-Minh Vu and Nguyen Thanh Trung

Abstract

The Award issued on July 12, 2016, by the Tribunal in the Philippines v. China arbitration case has had major legal implications and reshaped the geostrategic landscape in Southeast Asia. As a claimant nation with interests in the South China Sea, Vietnam's approach to the disputes as well as its relationships with other relevant nations have been affected by the Award. In light of the changing regional environment in the post-arbitration context, this chapter addresses four implications (both positive and negative) that the Tribunal's conclusions have for Vietnam, which relate to its shifting legal options, justification for maritime law enforcement operations, potential sovereignty disputes with the Philippines, and regional diplomatic relations. It then discusses Vietnam's policy options since the Award was issued as relate to its legal and diplomatic responses to the Award and relations with China, its diplomatic and military relations with non-claimant stakeholders, and its relations with rival claimants and role in ASEAN. The chapter concludes that, in formulating its policies, Vietnam must pursue a balanced approach that takes into account the benefits and risks of the various policy options available to it.

Introduction

The Award issued by the Tribunal on July 12, 2016, in the South China Sea arbitration case has had multiple legal implications for claimants and redefined the geostrategic landscape in Southeast Asia and even the Asia-Pacific. Even though the Tribunal has no enforcement powers, its conclusions will likely affect the maritime activities of rival claimants and major non-claimant stakeholders in areas of the South China Sea and compel countries to recalibrate their tactical and strategic approaches to the management of the disputes regardless of whether or not they agree with the Award.

As a South China Sea claimant nation, Vietnam's legal, diplomatic, and security approaches to the disputes have been affected by the Award. In the following section, we review Vietnam's policy approach since Award was issued while remaining aware of the fact that there are different approaches to analyzing Vietnam's post-arbitration South China Sea policies. In this chapter, we attempt to assess the current policy from the perspective of realpolitik. We then discuss the implications of the Award for Vietnam and the transformation of its policy options in the post-arbitration context.

Policy Approach

> Vietnam must consider the impacts of and lessons to be learned from the Philippines' case in reformulating its South China Sea policies.

The Award was not only a legal victory for the Philippines but also sent ripples throughout the region. In the post-arbitration context, Vietnam must consider the impacts of and lessons to be learned from the Philippines' case in reformulating its South China Sea policies. Considering the benefits, risks, and tradeoffs of its various options, Vietnam may opt for a stabilizing set of policy approaches to uphold its territorial integrity, maintain a good relationship with China, boost ASEAN unity, and appease Vietnamese nationalism. These policy approaches include four main components: support for the Award, reassertion of its sovereignty claims, maintenance of the status quo, and minimizing the extent of the disputed waters.

Support for the Award

On the same day that the Arbitral Tribunal issued its final award in the Philippines v. China arbitration case on July 12, 2016, Vietnamese Ministry of Foreign Affairs Spokesperson Le Hai Binh stated that Vietnam welcomed the Award and added that Vietnam confirmed its consistent stance on the arbitration case and support for the resolution of the South China Sea disputes through peaceful measures, including diplomatic and legal procedures without use or threat of force in accordance with the 1982 United Nations Convention on the Law of the Sea (UNCLOS) and relevant international law.[1]

---

1   "Remarks of the Spokesperson of the Ministry of Foreign Affairs of Viet Nam," Ministry of Foreign Affairs, Vietnam, July 12, 2016, <http://www.mofa.gov.vn/en/tt_baochi/pbnfn/ns160712211059>.

Reassertion of Sovereignty Claims

In the statement, the spokesperson reiterated that Vietnam would continue to assert its sovereignty over the Paracel and Spratly archipelagos as well as over its internal and territorial waters. He also emphasized that Vietnam would protect its sovereign rights and jurisdiction over its exclusive economic zone (EEZ) and continental shelf as well as the legal rights and interests of Vietnam related to the geographical structures on the Paracel and Spratly Islands.[2]

Indeed, the statement from the Ministry of Foreign Affairs did not come as a surprise. As a coastal state and claimant that must safeguard its maritime and territorial rights and interests in the South China Sea, Vietnam is highly alert to any changes that could lead to a disruption of the status quo in the region. Most importantly, the statement welcoming the Award demonstrated Vietnam's consistent policy of rejecting the Chinese imposition of its nine-dash line claims and endorsing the jurisdiction of an international tribunal.

On December 5, 2014, the Vietnamese Ministry of Foreign Affairs had already issued a position statement to the Arbitral Tribunal reasserting its claims in the Spratly Islands with three major points: Vietnam's support of the Philippines' case against China, Vietnam's rejection of China's nine-dash line, and Vietnam's request to the Tribunal to take note of its claims to the Paracel Islands.[3] Upon the conclusion of the arbitration case a year and a half later, Vietnam's positions on the issues remain consistent.

> Vietnam welcomed the Award and added that Vietnam confirmed its consistent stance on the arbitration case and support for the resolution of the South China Sea disputes through peaceful measures.

Maintenance of the Status Quo

From a realpolitik perspective, Vietnam has attempted to be prudent in asserting its national interests. The statement made it clear that Vietnam acknowledged that the Tribunal had jurisdiction in the arbitration case and hoped the Tribunal would take Vietnam's legal interests and

---

2 "Remarks of the Spokesperson of the Ministry of Foreign Affairs of Viet Nam," Ministry of Foreign Affairs, Vietnam, July 12, 2016, <http://www.mofa.gov.vn/en/tt_baochi/pbnfn/ns160712211059>.

3 "Statement of the Ministry of Foreign Affairs of the Socialist Republic of Viet Nam Transmitted to the Arbitral Tribunal in the Proceedings between the Republic of the Philippines and the People's Republic of China," Ministry of Foreign Affairs, Vietnam, December 5, 2014, <https://assets.documentcloud.org/documents/3011036/Statement-of-Vietnam.pdf>.

rights into consideration. It also reaffirmed Vietnam's position that Vietnam made clear when it made its joint submission with Malaysia to the UN Commission on the Limits of the Continental Shelf (CLCS) of information on the limits of their continental shelf beyond 200 nautical miles from the baselines in May 2009 in accordance with Article 76 of the United Nations Convention on the Law of the Sea.[4]

Minimizing the Extent of Disputed Waters

The Award could lead to some major clarifications from Vietnam. Firstly, Vietnam has taken the position that the islands they claim sovereignty over in the South China Sea will not enjoy more than a 12-nautical-mile territorial sea. Vietnam officially hinted at this hidden endorsement in its joint submission with Malaysia to the CLCS in 2009. Vietnam advocates maintaining the sta-

> Vietnam fears that any escalation leading to conflict with China might result in a change in the status quo unfavorable to Vietnam.

tus quo in the South China Sea even though it is obvious that it is increasingly worried about China's massive reclamation work on features in the Spratly Islands and its installation of a wide range of equipment that can serve both civilian and military purposes. Vietnam fears that any escalation leading to conflict with China might result in a change in the status quo unfavorable to Vietnam. Indeed, it has good reason for concern considering the loss of its occupied features in the Paracel Islands to Chinese forces in 1974. Secondly, Vietnam claims the area beyond the outer limits of its 200-nm EEZ as extended continental shelf. By juxtaposition, it can be seen that Vietnam's 2009 position does not contradict the Tribunal's con-

clusions in July 2016.

Implications of the Award

The implications of the Award go beyond the triangular relationship between Vietnam, China, and the Philippines, and what the award means for those claimants is entirely different from what it means for Vietnam. For Vietnam, there are four major implications of the Award, which relate to its shifting legal options, justification for maritime law enforcement operations, potential sovereignty disputes with the Philippines, and regional diplomatic relations.

Shifting Legal Options

From the perspective of international law as interpreted by the Tribunal, the Award significantly narrows down the scope of the maritime dispute between China and Vietnam because China's nine-dash line claim is not in accordance with international law as far as it represents claims to rights or entitlements beyond those which UNCLOS provides. Consequently, the nine-dash line cannot give China legal sovereignty over its maritime claims to the waters within Vietnam's EEZ. On this issue, Vietnam's perspective on China's excessive territorial claims has been vindicated as a result of the Tribunal's conclusions despite not having been a party to the arbitration case.

Furthermore, the Philippines' legal triumph against China in the South China Sea also suggests to rival claimants that such a lawfare approach to the disputes is a feasible policy option. This raises the possibility that Vietnamese leaders could seriously mull over potential legal measures against China over the legality of its occupation of features in the Paracel Islands, the status and entitlements of those features, or the legality of Chinese actions within Vietnamese-claimed maritime areas. If tensions with China increase and Vietnamese officials conclude that legal action is a viable approach to safeguarding the country's interests, Vietnam could follow in the Philippines'

---

4   "Submissions to the Commission: Joint submission by Malaysia and the Socialist Republic of Viet Nam," UN Commission on the Limits of the Continental Shelf, May 3, 2011, <http://www.un.org/depts/los/clcs_new/submissions_files/submission_mysvnm_33_2009.htm>.

footsteps in an effort to defend its South China Sea claims and entitlements under international law.

Justification for Maritime Law Enforcement Operations

The Award has also provided a legal avenue for Vietnam to protect its maritime interests and rights in the South China Sea. Vietnam now has a strong legal basis for engaging in maritime law enforcement operations to block future encroachments by Chinese vessels into its EEZ. The Tribunal effectively strengthened the legal

ed in 1998.[5]

Sovereignty Disputes with the Philippines

The Tribunal's conclusions regarding the status of all features in the Spratly Islands as "rocks" could increase tensions with the Philippines since some of the features that Vietnam claims in the area could become points of contention between Vietnam and the Philippines in the future. According to the Award, Second Thomas Shoal, Mischief Reef, and Reed Bank are submerged at high tide, forming part of the EEZ and continental shelf of the Philippines. In addition, Vietnam may

> The Award has provided a legal avenue for Vietnam to protect its maritime interests and rights in the South China Sea. Vietnam now has a strong legal basis for engaging in maritime law enforcement operations to block future encroachments by Chinese vessels into its EEZ.

foundation for Vietnam to protect its EEZ and continental shelf and justified its rejection other countries' claims that extend into its waters as accorded to it under international law. The Tribunal also invalidated the bidding offer of a series of nine oil blocks lying within Vietnam's EEZ and continental shelf that China National Offshore Oil Corporation (CNOOC) made to foreign investors in 1992. Given the content of the Award, other intimidating behaviors by Chinese vessels, such as cutting the sonar cables of PetroVietnam's vessels and chasing away Vietnamese fishermen from their traditional fishing grounds, can now more easily be protested legally and diplomatically and perhaps also deterred militarily by relevant Vietnamese agencies. Vietnam and other claimants also have the right to ask China to terminate its illegal unilateral fishing ban that start-

have to give up its claims to Boxall Reef, Alison Reef, Cornwallis South Reef, Ardasier Reef, Tennent Reef, and Dallas Reef or may lose its maritime rights in the waters around these features if the Philippines takes advantage of the Tribunal's

---

5   The Tribunal concluded that China violated the Philippines' rights in its EEZ accorded to it by UNCLOS by interfering with Philippine fishing and petroleum exploration, constructing man-made islands, and failing to deter Chinese fishermen from fishing in the zone. In the Award's accompanying press release, the arbitrators summarized their process of deliberation and conclusions as follows: "Lawfulness of Chinese Actions: The Tribunal next considered the lawfulness of Chinese actions in the South China Sea. Having found that certain areas are within the exclusive economic zone of the Philippines, the Tribunal found that China had violated the Philippines' sovereign rights in its exclusive economic zone by (a) interfering with Philippine fishing and petroleum exploration, (b) constructing artificial islands and (c) failing to prevent Chinese fishermen from fishing in the zone. The Tribunal also held that fishermen from the Philippines (like those from China) had traditional fishing rights at Scarborough Shoal and that China had interfered with these rights in restricting access. The Tribunal further held that Chinese law enforcement vessels had unlawfully created a serious risk of collision when they physically obstructed Philippine vessels." See "The Tribunal Renders Its Award," Press Release, Permanent Court of Arbitration, July 12, 2016, <http://www.pcacases.com/web/sendAttach/1801>.

interpretations of international law to declare these reefs as falling within its EEZ as extended from Palawan and Sabah or prevents Vietnamese fishermen from fishing in relevant waters.[6] Although the Award does not address these features directly, Vietnam could potentially be targeted by Philippine demands to give them up.[7] If this were to happen, the outcome scenario would depend on various factors including the way the Philippines asserted its claims and Vietnam's re-

Because the Tribunal declared that China had violated the Philippines' sovereign rights with its fishing, oil exploration, and artificial island construction activities, Vietnam may take it as a legal precedent to advance its own interests in the maritime area.

sponse to such assertions, but there is a distinct possibility that the interactions could increase diplomatic or military tensions between the two countries.

---

6   Danh Huy Duong, "Phán quyết Biển Đông: lợi, hại, và tương lai," BBC, July 19, 2016, <http://www.bbc.com/vietnamese/forum/2016/07/160719_forum_scs_duong_danh_huy_china_philippines_ruling>.

7   Vietnam is also expected to abandon its claims over Mischief Reef and Second Thomas Shoal, which the Tribunal declared to be low-tide elevations (LTEs) that belong to the Philippines' continental shelf. These features fall within the EEZ of the Philippines and outside the territorial waters of any nearby features. Under UNCLOS, they are not subject to sovereignty claims and the Philippines has sovereign rights over them. According to some analysts, Mischief Reef and Second Thomas Shoal now belonging to the Philippines' EEZ may affect Vietnam's sovereignty claims to the Spratly Islands, but they forget that Award did not deal directly with territorial sovereignty disputes. The possible sovereignty disputes over Mischief Reef and Second Thomas Shoal between the Philippines and Vietnam might need to be settled through another channel. See Tran Cong Truc, "Không dễ trả lời câu hỏi Việt Nam kiện Trung Quốc hay không, bao giờ kiện," Nhatbaovanhoa, July 25, 2016, <http://www.nhatbaovanhoa.com/a4333/ts-tran-cong-truc-noi-ve-ts-duong-danh-huy>.

Regional Diplomatic Relations

In addition to considering its relations with the Philippines, Vietnam may also have to recalibrate its relations with rival claimants and non-claimant stakeholders (e.g., ASEAN, Australia, India, Japan, and the US) as a result of the Award and other countries' responses to the Award. Generally speaking, it is likely that every South China Sea stakeholder benefits from the rule-of-law principle and freedom of navigation. Thus, it is crucial for Vietnam to pursue further engagement with them in order to maintain regional security and contribute to economic development and prosperity in the Asia-Pacific.

Policy Options

Although Vietnam was not a party to the arbitration case, the Award was cause for excitement for Vietnam and some other claimants. Most importantly, it invalidated China's all-encompassing nine-dash line claim, which extended over the vast majority of the South China Sea, where it was in excess of the rights entitled to China under the provisions of UNCLOS. The Award thus restricted the scope of waters over which the Chinese government could legally claim sovereignty. Vietnam, as one of the biggest stakeholders in the South China Sea and long at odds with China over its disputed nine-dash line claims, welcomed the Award, with many viewing it as likely to turn Vietnam into a beneficiary of the Philippines' lawfare strategy. Because the Tribunal declared that China had violated the Philippines' sovereign rights with its fishing, oil exploration, and artificial island construction activities, Vietnam may take it as a legal precedent to advance its own interests in the maritime area. However, contrary to some observers' predictions that it would take a new proactive approach to the disputes, Vietnam has opted for a relatively cautious and balanced approach in the post-arbitration context. In the aftermath of the Award, Vietnam's major policy options relate to its legal and diplomatic responses to the Award and relations with China, its diplomatic and military relations with non-claimant stakeholders, and its relations with rival claimants and role in ASEAN.

Contrary to some observers' predictions that it would take a new proactive approach to the disputes, Vietnam has opted for a relatively cautious and balanced approach in the post-arbitration context.

In formulating its policies, Vietnam must pursue a balanced approach that takes into account the benefits and risks of the various policy options available to it.

Legal and Diplomatic Responses and Vietnam–China Relations

Apart from the Philippines, Vietnam may be one of the nations that gains most from the conclusion of the arbitral proceedings, but the government has yet to provide a detailed opinion of the Award. The brief statement by the Vietnamese Ministry of Foreign Affairs spokesperson that Vietnam welcomed the Award demonstrated Vietnam's prudence in dealing with South China Sea issues. In the statement, he also added that "the ministry would issue a more detailed comment on the contents of the ruling at a later time". However, a second statement by the Ministry of Foreign Affairs in response to the Award has not come out yet, and no release date

has been confirmed.[8]

Another visible indication of a Vietnamese softened measure can be clearly seen from top Vietnamese leaders' visits. Immediately following the Award, there was a lull in Vietnam's foreign policy activity.[9] However, the scenario changed dramatically in September 2016 when Vietnam saw an uptick in high-level diplomatic activities, including frequent incoming and outgoing trips made by state leaders.

Because of Vietnam's deep economic dependency on China, its relatively soft, cautious approach might be expected. Two months after the Award, Vietnamese leaders attempted to deepen

---

8   Vietnam's delayed reaction to the Award has baffled numerous Vietnamese observers. Some analysts have even suggested Vietnam should follow suit by bringing the disputes over the Paracel Islands to an international court because Beijing seized some of the features there by force from the South Vietnamese government in 1974. Since then, China has consistently refused every single Vietnamese attempt at negotiation on the Paracel Islands issue. The ruling is a good precedent for Vietnam to take bolder steps. Another stream of ideas seem to be less daunting. Proponents of this approach opt for a non-disruptive approach of waiting until further scenarios unfold. The overwhelming victory by the Philippines motivates Vietnamese who are deeply concerned about the South China Sea disputes. There is a sentiment pushing the government to give an official assessment of the Award. It behooves Hanoi to figure out its stance on the Award soon. The Vietnamese government does not want conflict in the South China Sea. Its core objective in the Spratlys is to safeguard its jurisdiction and maritime rights. This objective overrides other concerns, and any unnecessary commotion might complicate its strategy.

9   An explanation for Vietnam's recent foreign policy of diversification is the current lack of active US involvement in the Asia-Pacific. The coming lame duck period of US politics before the November election has forced Hanoi to recalibrate its foreign policy. The prospects for the Trans-Pacific Partnership's ratification have greatly diminished since the election. Aware of the current US domestic political situation, Vietnamese leaders twice delayed passing the trade deal at the legislative body even though Vietnam is deemed to be the biggest beneficiary. The "wait and see" tactic might best characterize how Vietnam is dealing with the shifting US political landscape. When capitalizing on the US seems to be of little value, Vietnam must turn to other great powers for help.

engagement with China with an official visit to China by Prime Minister Nguyen Xuan Phuc from September 10–15, 2016. It was also his first trip to China since he assumed office in April 2016, and the first visit made by a Vietnamese Politburo member to China since the end of the 12th National Congress of the Communist Party of Vietnam held in January 2016. The trip reaffirmed the importance of the Sino–Vietnamese relationship with Vietnam having maintaining the status quo with China as its top priority. It is not difficult to understand why China is always on the top of Vietnam's agenda. According to the Chinese statistics, China was Vietnam's biggest trade partner with a total trade volume of approximately $96 billion USD in 2015, eclipsing all of Vietnam's other trade partners. The US was Vietnam's second largest trade partner with the total trade in goods reaching around $45 billion in 2015. On top of discussions on bilateral trade, Prime Minister Nguyen also talked with his Chinese counterpart about political and security cooperation, South China Sea issues, and other topics. The two countries vowed to maintain peace and stability in the South China Sea, but no concrete details about their evaluations of the Award were offered. [10]

> Deepening relations with powerful non-claimant stakeholders remains in Vietnam's national interest, and the government's actions suggest that it is still committed to developing ties with relevant countries.

Relations with Non-Claimant Stakeholders

However, maintaining good relations with China does not mean that Vietnam does not cultivate its relations with other countries. Deepening relations with powerful non-claimant stakeholders remains in its national interest, and the government's actions suggest that it is still committed to developing ties with relevant countries. Prime Minister Nguyen's trip to China came right after Indian Prime Minister Narendra Modi's visit to Vietnam from September 2–3, 2016. Significantly, Modi was only the fourth Indian prime minister to visit Hanoi in more than fifty years and the first in the last fifteen years. Vietnam and India signed twelve agreements including a $500 million USD line of credit to

---

10   "Việt Nam- Trung Quốc ra Thông Cáo chung", Viet Nam Government Portal, September 14, 2016, <http://thutuong.chinhphu.vn/Home/Viet-NamTrung-Quoc-ra-Thong-cao-chung/20169/25378.vgp>.

Vietnam on defense cooperation.[11] Specifically, the two leaders sealed a deal to build off-shore patrol boats for Vietnam.

On the heels of Modi's visit, French President Francois Hollande paid a visit to Hanoi from September 5–7, 2016. Hollande was the third French president, after Francois Mitterrand and Jacques Chirac, to visit Hanoi since Vietnam's adoption of economic reforms in 1986. France is considered to be a traditional partner for Vietnam in Europe. With respect to economic and trade deals, France is currently Vietnam's fifth largest European trade partner and the third largest European investor. Even though trade was the key focus of Hollande's visit, France and Vietnam expressed their agreement on the need for respecting the law of the sea as well as freedom of navigation and overflight.[12]

Deepening ties with India may serve the best interests of both countries. Vietnam is increasingly worried about China's assertiveness in the South China Sea, while India is on high alert regarding China's bold thrust into India's sphere of influence in South Asia. India's $500 million line of credit to Vietnam, Modi noted, aimed to "facilitate deeper defense cooperation".[13] Compared to the credit line of $100 million two years ago, this signing was a giant step towards greater bilateral cooperation. Both sides refrained from providing details on the contents of the $500 million credit, but the best arms shopping list for Vietnam might include fast patrol vessels and missile systems to guard its long coast and vast EEZ. India is the country that Vietnam could approach for Brahmos missiles as well as training services for its six Kilo-class submarine crews. In addition, closer defense cooperation with India might be a viable alternative to cooperation with Russia in case the latter stops its sale of advanced weapons to Vietnam to be in favor of China.

> Deepening ties with India may serve the best interests of both countries. Vietnam is increasingly worried about China's assertiveness in the South China Sea, while India is on high alert regarding China's bold thrust into India's sphere of influence in South Asia.

11 "India & Vietnam sign 12 agreements; Modi offers US $500 Mn credit line for defence cooperation," DNA, September 3, 2016, <http://www.dnaindia.com/india/live-pm-modi-in-vietnam-hanoi-nguyen-xuan-phuc-defence-tran-dai-quang-trade-oil-exploration-bilateral-talks-2251440>.

12 "France to support Vietnam's sovereignty over waters, airspace: Hollande," Tuoi Tre News, September 7, 2016, <http://tuoitrenews.vn/politics/36898/france-supports-vietnams-sovereignty-over-waters-airspace>.

13 Sanghamitra Sarma "India-Vietnam Relations After Modi's Visit," The Diplomat, September 5, 2016, <http://thediplomat.com/2016/09/india-vietnam-relations-after-modis-visit/>.

Relations with Rival Claimants and ASEAN

It is also a time for Vietnam to boost relationships with other regional claimants and encourage ASEAN centrality. The Philippines would be the key nation in ASEAN for Vietnam to deepen ties with. The two countries have had some promising achievements in maritime cooperation with the establishment of the Joint Committee on Sea and Ocean Cooperation at the deputy foreign ministerial level, which convened its first meeting in February 2012 and second one in September 2015. During the two-day trip to Hanoi by Philippine President Rodrigo Duterte from September 29–30, 2016, the two sides affirmed the need to boost solidarity in ASEAN in addition to stressing maritime cooperation.[14]

This move came as no surprise since Vietnam

resolving the South China Sea disputes.[15] In the coming months and years, Vietnam will have to carefully consider how deeper diplomatic engagement with other Southeast Asian claimants and pushing for ASEAN unity on South China Sea issues may be in its best interests.

Finding a Balance

Given the interdependent nature of international politics, Vietnamese leaders have to weigh the available policy options in the post-arbitration context, striking a delicate balance between China and the US, between a hard and soft approach, between patience and haste, and between legal clarity and ambiguity. Above all, it is imperative that Vietnam should pursue active diplomacy.

> Vietnam has repeatedly expressed its frustration over ASEAN disunity over the South China Sea issue.

has repeatedly expressed its frustration over ASEAN disunity over the South China Sea issue. Earlier in August 2016, addressing the 38th Singapore Lecture organized by the Institute of Southeast Asian Studies (ISEAS), Vietnamese President Tran Dai Quang called for a united ASEAN to tackle serious challenges, including the South China Sea disputes. He even hinted at another formula to replace the consensus principle within ASEAN but still acknowledges the centrality of ASEAN in

Against the backdrop of the rapprochement between the Philippines and China after Duterte's historic visit to Beijing, Standing Secretary of the Central Committee Secretariat of the Communist Party of Vietnam Dinh The Huynh made a three-day visit to China from October 19–21, 2016.[16] Some analysts have interpreted this as a sign that Hanoi continues to place greater emphasis on maintaining stable, if not cordial, ties with its giant

15 Tran Dai Quang, "38th Singapore Lecture 'Strengthening Partnership for Regional Sustainable Development'," ISEAS / Yusof Ishak Institute, August 30, 2016, <https://www.iseas.edu.sg/medias/event-highlights/item/3859-38th-singapore-lecture-strengthening-partnership-for-regional-sustainable-development-by-he-tran-dai-quang>.

14 Alexis Romero, "Duterte flies to Vietnam for a working visit," Philippine Star, September 28, 2016, <http://www.philstar.com/headlines/2016/09/28/1628333/duterte-flies-vietnam-working-visit>.

16 "Chủ tịch Trung Quốc Tập Cận Bình tiếp đồng chí Đinh Thế Huynh," VOV, October 20, 2016, <http://vov.vn/chinh-tri/chu-tich-trung-quoc-tap-can-binh-tiep-dong-chi-dinh-the-huynh-561889.vov>.

neighbor, despite their intensified jostling in the South China Sea.[17] Upon closer inspection, however, it becomes clear that the trip to Beijing was largely designed as a "shock absorber" to offset the strategic fallout of Huynh's visit to Washington. If Huynh made substantial concessions to China on the South China Sea, he would definitely isolate himself, especially with the mid-term National Party Congress set to take place. Right after that, he visited the US from October 23–30, 2016, more than double the length of his trip to China. It is puzzling that Huynh's visit came right before the US presidential election in November as it would certainly be eclipsed by American attention to domestic politics. However, the trip was significant in the sense that it was indicative of Vietnam's efforts to strike a balance between China and the US.

> Vietnam continues to follow a "legally murky" strategy by not explicitly stating its legal stance on the Tribunal's decisions. This silent strategy was widely believed to be "safe" for Vietnam prior to the Award because Vietnam did not know whether the Tribunal would favor the Philippines or to what extent its decisions might affect Vietnam's interests in the South China Sea.

Additionally, a bold suggestion is that the Vietnamese cabinet should not delay publicly stating their legal stance on the Award any longer. They are expected to quickly take advantage of the Tribunal's conclusions that are unfavorable to China's claims or the government might miss a chance to garner public support while the cake is still hot. Other countries with shared interests have also been waiting for Vietnam's reactions to the Award. The more delayed Vietnam's response is, the shorter their menu of policy options becomes. Based on these assessments, we recommend that Vietnam should swiftly opt for any of the following three policy plans or embrace them as a whole.

Firstly, Vietnam continues to follow a "legally murky" strat-

---

17 "Ngoại trưởng Kerry: Việt Nam là đối tác quan trọng trong khu vực," Vietnam+, October 26, 2016, <http://www.vietnamplus.vn/ngoai-truong-kerry-viet-nam-la-doi-tac-quan-trong-trong-khu-vuc/412747.vnp>; Nguyen Manh Hung, "Why the Washington Visit of the Vietnam Communist Party Permanent Secretary is Critical," cogitAsia, Center for Strategic and International Studies, October 21, 2016, <http://cogitasia.com/why-the-washington-visit-of-the-vietnam-communist-party-permanent-secretary-is-critical/>.

egy by not explicitly stating its legal stance on the Tribunal's decisions. This silent strategy was widely believed to be "safe" for Vietnam prior to the Award because Vietnam did not know whether the Tribunal would favor the Philippines or to what extent its decisions might affect Vietnam's interests in the South China Sea. The muted attitude could enable Vietnam to avoid making blunders if the decision went against Vietnam's interests. Since the Award, Vietnam's continued silence has prompted two major hypotheses about the lack of an official statement on the content of the Award. The first hypothesis is that the Vietnamese government needs more time to fully assess and thoroughly analyze its potential impacts. The formulation of Vietnam's position requires careful examination by various agencies and ministries before the final draft lands on the Politburo's table for endorsement. The second hypothesis is the Vietnamese government is being pressured by China, either directly or indirectly, not to make public its position. Vietnam's cautious approach and responses to it serve as a gentle reminder that, although silence is not always golden, it can be used to avert disaster.

> For Vietnam, combining its voice with those of other countries on selected aspects of the Tribunal's decisions would certainly increase its leverage and perhaps reduce the risks of publicly denouncing China's excessive maritime claims in the South China Sea.

Secondly, Vietnam can selectively support the Tribunal's decisions if it does decide to offer its positions. Among the key points in the Award, the conclusions that the nine-dash line is invalid and China has done harm to the marine environment and aggravated the disputes might serve Vietnam's interests better than the decision on the status of features, which did not grant Taiwan-occupied Itu Aba (Taiping) Island an entitlement to a 200-nm EEZ. Itu Aba's status as a rock implies that all other features in the Spratly Islands, including those controlled by Vietnam, would not be entitled to EEZs either. Supporting only certain aspects of the Award that would be beneficial to Vietnam could be a pragmatic choice for the country, but it could also provoke reactions from interested parties. Either way, Vietnam should speed up its calculations of what it should and should not advocate in the post-arbitration context.

The third option for Vietnam is a combination of approaches and selective transparency. Vietnam actively cooperates with other multilateral institutions (notably ASEAN-led arrangements) and with other regional powers through bilateral mechanisms and could use such cooperative fora to come out with a joint communique on the Award. Specifically, Vietnam could work with Indonesia, the Philippines, and Malaysia to issue a joint statement, emphasizing the invalid nature of the nine-dash line since these nations have similar interests to Vietnam in terms of wanting China to abandon its claims to historic rights within the nine-dash line, which was deemed to not be in accordance with international law. For Vietnam, combining its voice with those of other countries on selected aspects of the Tribunal's decisions would certainly increase its leverage and perhaps reduce the risks of publicly denouncing China's excessive maritime claims in the South China Sea. Vietnam could also enlist the help of other major stakeholders, such as Australia, India, Japan, and the US, and engage them more on the South China Sea issues. Mutual benefits could begin with joint communiques on ensuring freedom of navigation and overflight and protecting the marine environment. These areas of cooperation are safe for Vietnam to kick off its external balancing strategy.

> Vietnam could also enlist the help of other major stakeholders, such as Australia, India, Japan, and the US, and engage them more on the South China Sea issues. Mutual benefits could begin with joint communiques on ensuring freedom of navigation and overflight and protecting the marine environment.

Recently, a rising wave of local scholars' opinions, especially those voiced at two international conferences on the South China Sea held in Vietnam, have called for legal and diplomatic measures to lead the way. Several notable views have been raised. (1) The Award will serve as a legal precedent regardless of whether one agrees or disagrees with the arbitrators' conclusions, and EEZ and continental shelf entitlements are already defined under international law. Hence, Vietnam does not need to issue a statement concerning the Award. (2) Vietnam must be prepared to initiate legal procedures in case China engages in more assertive behavior in the South China Sea. If China opts for a conciliatory post-arbitration approach, Vietnam could simply refrain from using legal means and deepen ties with China to maintain peace and security in the region. (3) Vietnam needs to capture the international media's attention in the post-arbitration context so that the potential benefits of the Tribunal's conclusions for Vietnam are clear. It must be prepared for China to use international summits like the G-20 Summit in Hangzhou and other events in an effort downplay the South China Sea disputes and divert the world's attention towards other issues, such as trade deals, that benefit China.

A close examination of recent Vietnam's foreign policy moves suggests that the legal-diplomatic approach seems to be domi-

Although Vietnam has remained cautious since the arbitration case, it has systematically engaged in a set of policies to protect its national interests in the South China Sea.

nant. It is clear that this approach has attempted to take all of the pros and cons of the Award for Vietnam into account. The current cautious policy approach primarily comes from top Vietnamese policymakers' doubt that there is little chance the Award could dramatically alter the status quo in the South China Sea. From a broader view, Vietnam's approaches to the South China Sea, like those of rival claimants, are based the pursuit of its national interests. The top priority is to protect Vietnam's territorial integrity and entitlements in the maritime areas that it claims. Ensuring the success of its delicate balancing strategy that involves engagement with rival claimants, including China, and major stakeholders is also crucial to Vietnam's foreign policy. These two major objectives are believed to help Vietnam protect its national interests while avoiding points of contention with China.

Conclusion and Future Prospects

All things considered, the Award issued by the Tribunal has offered a chance for Vietnam to reassess its policy options in order to respond to opportunities and challenges arising in the post-arbitration context. Although Vietnam has remained cautious since the arbitration case, it has systematically engaged in a set of policies to protect its national interests in the South China Sea. The Vietnamese government has sought to strengthen relations with China, with major non-claimant stakeholders, and with other rival claimants and ASEAN countries in an ongoing attempt to strike a balance that promotes its national interests. However, it is still too early to come up with a comprehensive evaluation of Vietnam's responses to the Award because less than a year has passed and Vietnam's political tradition encourages continuity with the past. Nevertheless, it is obvious that Vietnam is moving to deepen its relations with foreign countries across the board and proactively participate in multilateral arrangements and international organizations. Since the Award, Vietnam has seen its relations with India, France, and the Philippines reach new levels of cooperation with many new commitments and agreements being signed over the past months. Yet it would be premature to conclude that Vietnam has shed its reliance

Striking a delicate balance between China and the US, between a hard and soft approach, between patience and haste, and between legal clarity and ambiguity is the defining characteristic of Vietnam's policy approach in the post-arbitration context.

on great powers in defining its foreign policy. It will take time to see how effective Vietnam's recent moves are, but it can be clearly seen that Vietnam has been more active in its foreign policy. Striking a delicate balance between China and the US, between a hard and soft approach, between patience and haste, and between legal clarity and ambiguity is the defining characteristic of Vietnam's policy approach in the post-arbitration context.

Truong-Minh Vu is a visiting fellow at the ISEAS-Yusof Ishak Institute, Singapore, and Director of the Center for International Studies (SCIS) at the University of Social Sciences and Humanities in Ho Chi Minh City. He is co-editor of the book *Power Politics in Asia's Contested Waters – Territorial Disputes in the South China Sea* (Springer, 2016).

Nguyen Thanh Trung earned his PhD at the Hong Kong Baptist University Department of Government and International Studies and is now the Dean of Faculty of International Relations at the University of Social Sciences in Ho Chi Minh City.

Part III:
Major Stakeholders

Post-Arbitration South China Sea:

ASEAN's Policy Options and Future Prospects

Siew Mun Tang

Abstract

The Association of Southeast Asian Nations' (ASEAN) engagement with China on the South China Sea disputes long predates the Philippines v. China arbitration case. Since issuing its first joint statement on the disputes in 1992, ASEAN has consistently maintained the position of not taking sides on merits of the disputes and kept its involvement within the remit of protecting and affirming regional peace and security, freedom of navigation and overflight, peaceful resolution of the disputes, and adherence to the principles of international law and the United Nations Convention on the Law of the Sea (UNCLOS). The Award issued by the Arbitral Tribunal on July 12, 2016, was a good test of ASEAN's ability to measure up its capacity for advocating these principles. While ASEAN was successful in differentiating between national and regional interests, its member states' divided support for the collective interest after the arbitration case has been disconcerting. Their failure to affirm the primacy of international law in international affairs can be seen as a sign of the regional organisation's fraying unity. At the same time, China's "Trojan Horse" tactics to break ASEAN consensus on the South China Sea is evidence of Beijing's disregard for ASEAN centrality in managing Southeast Asian diplomatic and security issues. The South China Sea disputes are instructive for ASEAN and provide insights into China's approach to and management of regional affairs. The Award has provided some impetus for China to agree to some compromises such as committing to a framework for completion of a Code of Conduct (COC) in the South China Sea and the Code for Unplanned Encounters at Sea (CUES). In the post-arbitration context, ASEAN's policy options relate to strengthening internal cohesion and unity, supporting and reaffiring the role of the ASEAN–China coordinator, and working towards an expeditious conclusion of a legally binding COC.

Introduction

The Award of July 12, 2016, in the Philippines v. China arbitration case was a game changer in the long-running South China Sea dispute pitting China against four ASEAN claimants – Brunei, Malaysia, the Philippines, and Vietnam. Right from the beginning, when the Philippines initiated legal proceedings against China through the Permanent Court of Arbitration (PCA) to clarify the two countries' rights and entitlements related to their conflicting claims, Beijing declared its adherence to what would become known as the "four noes" policy – no acceptance, no participation, no recognition, and no implementation.[1] Following the arbitration case, analysts from ASEAN and around the world have observed that the immense international pressure to acknowledge and implement the Award has failed to convince China of the sanctity of international law. In fact, the pressure brought to bear by the international community has only served to reinforce China's steadfast belief in the justness of its position and traditional rights in the South China Sea.

> ASEAN made known its position on the South China Sea disputes as early as 1992, with the adoption of the Declaration on the South China Sea.

ASEAN is not a claimant to the disputes, and has long maintained that it holds no position on the merits of the claims. Although four of its members are party to the disputes, ASEAN operates on the basis of impartiality. However, not taking sides does not mean that ASEAN does not have a position on the disputes. ASEAN made known its position on the South China Sea disputes as early as 1992, with the adoption of the Declaration on the South China Sea. The declaration emphasized the direct link between the disputes and regional security by noting that "any adverse developments in the South China Sea directly affect peace and stability in the region."[2] A decade later, ASEAN and China inked the Declaration on the Conduct of Parties in the South China Sea (DOC). Signed in Phnom Penh in November 2002, the ten-point declaration established the basis for ASEAN and

---

1   Xiao Jianguo, "China Doesn't Accept or Recognize the South China Sea Arbitration," China-US Focus, April 20, 2016, <http://www.chinausfocus.com/peace-security/china-doesnt-accept-or-recognize-the-south-china-sea-arbitration>.

2   "ASEAN Declaration on the South China Sea," Association of Southeast Asian Nations, July 22, 1992, <https://cil.nus.edu.sg/rp/pdf/1992%20ASEAN%20Declaration%20on%20the%20South%20China%20Sea-pdf.pdf>.

China to address the South China Sea conflict.[3] The implementation of the DOC, which contains a provision on the establishment of a Code of Conduct (COC), has been slow and haphazard.

The important point here is that South China Sea issues has been on ASEAN's official agenda since 1992. Contrary to China's narrative, it was not an agenda "introduced" by the US to contain China. Nevertheless, it is true that US Secretary of State Hillary Clinton's speech at the 2010 ASEAN Regional Forum in Hanoi, Vietnam, which declared that the US "has a national interest in freedom of navigation, open access to Asia's maritime commons, and respect for international law in the South China Sea," elevated public scrutiny on the issue.[4] In raising the South China Sea issue at the region's premier multilateral security meeting, Clinton astutely tapped into the region's growing unease with China's growing assertiveness in the South China Sea. This chapter analyses ASEAN's responses to the Award and provides a perspective on what the South China Sea means for ASEAN.

Policy Approach

ASEAN does not take a position on the merits of the South China Sea claims, notwithstanding the fact that the four of the key claimants are members of the regional organisation. This is a point of confusion and contestation between ASEAN and China as Beijing would prefer that the South China Sea be removed from ASEAN's agenda. The contention arises from China's preference for dealing with South China Sea issues bilaterally and view that ASEAN involvement implies "internationalising" the disputes. Also anathema to China is the perception that ASEAN discussions on the South China Sea frame the disputes as a confrontational "ASEAN v. China" issue. ASEAN's approach to the South China Sea disputes is premised on four key interests – regional stability and peace, freedom of navigation and overflight, peaceful dispute resolution, and respect for international law – and maintaining a delicate balance between national and regional imperatives.

> Anathema to China is the perception that ASEAN discussions on the South China Sea frame the disputes as a confrontational "ASEAN v. China" issue.

---

3   "Declaration on the Conduct of Parties in the South China Sea," Foreign Ministers of ASEAN and the People's Republic of China, November 4, 2002, <https://cil.nus.edu. sg/rp/pdf/2002%20Declaration%20on%20the%20Conduct%20of%20Parties%20in%20 the%20South%20China%20Sea-pdf.pdf>.

4   "Remarks at Press Availability," US Department of State, July 23, 2010, <http://www. state.gov/secretary/20092013clinton/rm/2010/07/145095.htm>.

Interests in the South China Sea Disputes

ASEAN has indeed been active in the South China Sea disputes, even if only in the context of playing a role in managing the conflict as opposed to resolving the disputes. It understands that a solution to the complex, overlapping claims of ASEAN claimants and China will only come about

> ASEAN understands that its role is one of supporting and creating an environment conducive to making progress toward an eventual resolution. The Declaration on the Conduct of Parties in the South China Sea (DOC) and the Code of Conduct in the South China Sea (COC) are two ASEAN initiatives that aim to put a check on rising tensions and offer a clear roadmap for negotiations among claimants.

through direct negotiations among the claimants. ASEAN understands that its role is one of supporting and creating an environment conducive to making progress toward an eventual resolution. The Declaration on the Conduct of Parties in the South China Sea (DOC) and the Code of Conduct in the South China Sea (COC) are two ASEAN initiatives that aim to put a check on rising tensions and offer a clear roadmap for negotiations among claimants. ASEAN has four key interests in the South China Sea disputes.

First, ASEAN's primary concern is regional stability and peace. Escalation in the South China Sea would inevitably draw in interested parties from near and far, including major powers such as the US and Japan, which would, in turn, serve to ratchet up the already-intensified major power rivalry in the region. ASEAN understands that such a scenario would not be conducive to regional stability, the security of its member states, or fulfilling its role as a mediator in the disputes.

Second, ASEAN has an abiding interest in maintaining and safeguarding freedom and safety of navigation and overflight in the region, including in the South China Sea. Threats to this strategic waterway – which carries some US$5 trillion annually in seaborne trade – would have a direct negative impact on the economies and well-being of ASEAN member states and also jeopardize the security of energy-dependent states such as China and Japan, countries for which large proportions of the energy resources they consume are transported through the South China Sea.

Third, ASEAN holds the disputing parties accountable for abiding by the Treaty of Amity and Cooperation in Southeast Asia (TAC) first signed in Indonesia in 1976. Among other issues, the TAC, which has since been acceded to by over a dozen non-ASEAN countries including China in 2003 and the US in 2009, formalizes signatories' agreement to "refrain from the threat or use of force" and, in the event of escalation, commitment to "at all times settle such disputes among themselves through friendly negotiations."[5]

Fourth, ASEAN promotes and advocates respect for and application of international law, including the United Nations Convention on the Law of the Sea (UNCLOS) as the basis for "governing state-to-state relations" and managing and resolving the South China Sea disputes.[6]

These four interests form the basis of ASEAN's approach toward the South China Sea disputes and are reflected in relevant ASEAN declarations,

---

5   Treaty of Amity and Cooperation in Southeast Asia, Association of Southeast Asian Nations, February 24, 1976, <http://asean.org/treaty-amity-cooperation-southeast-asia-indonesia-24-february-1976/>.

6   "Declaration on the Conduct of Parties in the South China Sea," Foreign Ministers of ASEAN and the People's Republic of China, November 4, 2002, <https://cil.nus.edu.sg/rp/pdf/2002%20Declaration%20on%20the%20Conduct%20of%20Parties%20in%20the%20South%20China%20Sea-pdf.pdf>.

statements, and communiqués. The principle of "full respect for legal and diplomatic processes" was recently emphasized at the Special U.S.-ASEAN Leaders' Summit in Sunnylands, California, in February 2016.[7] This was also later affirmed by the foreign ministers of ASEAN member states in the joint communiqué issued at the conclusion of the 49th ASEAN Foreign Ministers' Meeting in Vientiane on 24 July 2016.[8]

Differentiating National and Regional Interests

The extent of the Philippines' "victory" in the arbitration case caught many in ASEAN by surprise. The Arbitral Tribunal handed Manila a resounding victory that all but put any remaining doubts

states went was to urge both China and the Philippines to respect and uphold international law. Even then, this commonly held ASEAN position was not uniformly applied. Only five of the eight ASEAN member states that issued a statement before or after the Award mentioned international law, and critics took ASEAN to task for not even mentioning the arbitration case at the ASEAN Foreign Ministers' Meeting (AMM) held in Vientiane in July 2016. For many, the analysis was that ASEAN had caved to Chinese pressure.

However, ASEAN's silence at the Vientiane AMM was not a case of Chinese meddling. On the contrary, it was at Manila's behest that the Award was left out of the joint communiqué. Philippine Foreign Secretary Perfecto Yasay made it clear that "the arbitral award is a matter between Chi-

> There were positions within ASEAN against taking "ownership" of the Award since Manila initiated the legal proceedings without prior consultation with or agreement from other member states.

about whether or not China's nine-dash line claim was in accordance with international law to rest. Also among the most important conclusions was the pronouncement that all the features in the Spratly Islands, including Taiwan-occupied Itu Aba (Taiping) Island, the largest feature in the archipelago, were legally "rocks" that were not entitled to an exclusive economic zone (EEZ) or continental shelf claim. Diplomatically, none of the other ASEAN member states explicitly called upon China to abide by the conclusions of the Arbitral Tribunal. The furthest ASEAN member

na and the Philippines."[9] In fact, the Philippines' stance on keeping the Award a bilateral matter may have saved ASEAN the embarrassment of putting out yet another display of disunity as China's allies within ASEAN would not have allowed its inclusion in the joint communiqué if the matter had been brought to a decision at the foreign ministers' meeting. Although ASEAN member states did have extensive discussions on forging a common position prior to the announcement of the Award, they ultimately decided to leave the matter in the hands of individual member states.

There were also positions within ASEAN against taking "ownership" of the Award since Manila initiated the legal proceedings without prior consultation with or agreement from other member states. Thus, Manila's suggestion of keeping the Award as strictly a bilateral is-

---

7   "Joint Statement of the U.S.-ASEAN Special Leaders' Summit: Sunnylands Declaration," Heads of State/ Government of the Member States of the Association of Southeast Asian Nations and the United States, February 16, 2016, <https://obamawhitehouse.archives.gov/ the-press-office/2016/02/16/joint-statement-us-asean-special-leaders-summit-sunnylands-declaration>.

8   "Joint Communiqué of the 49th ASEAN Foreign Ministers' Meeting," Association of Southeast Asian Nations, July 24, 2016, <http://asean.org/storage/2016/07/Joint-Communique-of-the-49th-AMM-ADOPTED.pdf>.

9   Lesley Wroughton and Martin Petty, "Philippines says ASEAN omission of arbitration case not a Chinese victory," Reuters, July 27, 2916, <http://uk.reuters.com/article/uk-southchinasea-ruling-philippines-idUKKCN107068>.

sue between the Philippines and China was one that suited the ASEAN member states as well as Manila's rapprochement with Beijing following the inauguration of President Rodrigo Duterte in June 2016, just weeks before the conclusion of the arbitration case. In essence, ASEAN's response to the Award was in keeping with the long-held position of differentiating national and regional interests in the matter of the South China Sea disputes. In hindsight, this approach has been vindicated by the Duterte administration's downplaying of the Award in its effort to reset relations with Beijing.

> The varied official responses across Southeast Asia were a testimony to both the lack of unity within ASEAN and the degree of self-censorship applied by some of the ASEAN member states for fear of antagonising China.

Implications of the Award

The Award did not have any official or explicit impact on ASEAN's position on the South China Sea, which remains unchanged and centred on the four points of (a) regional peace and stability, (b) freedom of navigation and overflight, (c) peaceful dispute resolution, and (d) adherence to the principles of international law, including UNCLOS. The Philippines' pronouncement that the Award was a bilateral matter between Manila and Beijing has absolved ASEAN of having to take a formal position, which would have been very unlikely to materialise given Cambodia's strong objections. However, this did not stop individual ASEAN member states from making known their positions. The implications of the Award have been different for each ASEAN member state, but five aspects stand out and merit closer examination: (a) international law, (b) confidence-build-ing measures, (c) ASEAN–China relations, (d) ASEAN centrality, and (e) the Philippines' relations with China and the US.

Lack of Consensus on Affirming International Law

All ASEAN member states, with the exception of Brunei and Laos, issued a statement or press release either before or after the announcement of the Award. The Cambodian statement did not mention international law while the Thai statement made no reference to the Arbitral Tribunal or international law. The varied official responses across Southeast Asia were a testimony to both the lack of unity within ASEAN and the degree of self-censorship applied by some of the ASEAN member states for fear of antagonising China.

ASEAN's failure to affirm the importance of international law is jarring. Four member states – Brunei, Cambodia, Laos, and Thailand – failed to support the majority of the ASEAN member states in highlighting the importance of the rule of law in regional affairs. This point is telling and could be taken as yet another sign of ASEAN's fraying political unity. Adherence to the rule of law has been an long-standing ASEAN principle, but four ASEAN member states failed to stand up for this principle in the absence of a convenient "regional cover."

This is a worrisome development given that international law functions as small states' first and last line of defence in international affairs. Without international law providing a level playing field for all states, both weak and powerful, the international system could degenerate into a chaotic mess governed by the old adage that "might makes right." Granted that the Arbitral Tribunal has no enforcement mechanism other than relying on the dignity and concurrence of the parties in respecting and upholding international law, it still falls on the ASEAN member states to take the position that international law matters.

Progress on Confidence-Building Measures

The Award's larger impact lies in the political sphere. In an apparent attempt at damage control, China had pledged to finalize the "framework" for the Code of Conduct by the middle of 2017. The announcement by Chinese Foreign Minister Wang Yi is a welcome respite from the tense run-up to the ASEAN Foreign Ministers' Meeting in July 2016. The Award may have provided the impetus for China to engage ASEAN in a meaningful way to work toward stabilising the South China Sea disputes. In addition, ASEAN and China agreed to abide by the Code for Unplanned Encounters at Sea (CUES) in regards to encounters in the South China Sea during the 28th and

the South China Sea should not be underestimated. It shows that China is not averse to making compromises when facing strong international pressure. While the Award has not had any material impact on the South China Sea claims, it has contributed to advancing ASEAN's efforts to de-escalate tensions in these strategic waters.

The agreement to abide by CUES in the South China Sea underscores the value of ASEAN to China by providing China with an avenue to alleviate international pressure resulting from the Award. At the same time, China has implicitly recognized ASEAN's role in managing the South China Sea disputes by agreeing to the ASEAN-proposed South China Sea CUES and committing to the completion of a COC "framework."

> The agreement to abide by CUES in the South China Sea underscores the value of ASEAN to China by providing China with an avenue to alleviate international pressure resulting from the Award. At the same time, China has implicitly recognized ASEAN's role in managing the South China Sea disputes by agreeing to the ASEAN-proposed South China Sea CUES and committing to the completion of a COC "framework."

29th ASEAN Summits held in September 2016.[10] Another confidence-building measure signed is the establishment of hotlines among the ministries of foreign affairs to deal with "maritime emergencies." These are positive overtures, but China's track record has been poor in terms of implementing its pledges. CUES, for example, may not be effective, as an "incident at sea" would most likely involve the Chinese Coast Guard, which is not part of the agreement.

Despite its inherent weaknesses, the value of the agreement to abide by CUES in the context of

ASEAN–China Relations

The South China Sea disputes go beyond the determination of the claimants' sovereignty and entitlements. The stakes for ASEAN are increasing as the unfolding of events in the South China Sea sheds light on its relations with China. China has been ASEAN's largest trade partner since 2009 and has had deep, longstanding, and multifaceted engagement with the regional grouping and its member states. China's rising economic fortunes have been both a boon and a bane for ASEAN. On one hand, it has provided ASEAN with a new market to lessen its dependence on traditional partners such as the US, Japan, and Europe. On the other hand, China's rise has also transformed Beijing into a political-military powerhouse that is eager to regain its pride and reas-

---

10 "Joint Statement on the Application of the Code for Unplanned Encounters at Sea in the South China Sea," Heads of State/Government of ASEAN Member States and the People's Republic of China, September 7, 2016, <http://asean.org/storage/2016/09/Joint-Statement-on-the-Application-of-CUES-in-the-SCS-Final.pdf>.

sert its place in regional affairs. China's rise is a reality that ASEAN has to live with. To a large extent, the state of affairs has been a "win-win" situation and based on a productive partnership. However, China's behaviour and unbending assertion of its position on the South China Sea disputes show a different side of China that is worrisome for ASEAN. China's liberal use of its military might, in the form of the Chinese Coast Guard, in support of its fishing fleet in Malaysian and Vietnamese exclusive economic zones (EEZ) is proof that Beijing is increasingly willing to use force in the South China Sea in pursuit of its interests.

At another level of analysis, China's behaviour in the South China Sea disputes provides crucial insights into how it deals with its less powerful neighbours. Beijing's actions contradict its frequent assertions about its peaceful rise and respect for international law. ASEAN's concerns were compounded by its impotence in responding to China's land reclamation efforts in the South China Sea in recent years. These developments are a wake-up call for ASEAN and serve as a reminder that it is dealing with a major power on the other side of the table who knows very well the limits of ASEAN member states' collective and individual power and influence. The question for ASEAN is how it should recalibrate its relations with China in light of these new realities of *realpolitik*. Questions about the extent to which hedging will continue to be the preferred strategy for many ASEAN states as China grows increasingly impatient with their "strategic promiscuity" remain unanswered.

> These developments are a wake-up call for ASEAN and serve as a reminder that it is dealing with a major power on the other side of the table who knows very well the limits of ASEAN member states' collective and individual power and influence.

ASEAN Centrality under Threat

The other lesson for ASEAN relates to the challenge for China in managing relations with the regional organisation. Beijing's rhetoric of respecting ASEAN centrality rings hollow throughout the region. In at least three instances, China has used its considerable influence to stymie ASEAN internal discussions on the South China Sea. In the first instance, Cambodia blocked discussions on the South China Sea whilst holding the ASEAN chairmanship in 2012, resulting in the regional organisation's failure to issue a joint communiqué for the first time in history. In the second instance, it broke an existing consensus among ASEAN member states to issue a standalone statement at the conclusion of the Special ASEAN-China Foreign Ministers' Meeting in Kunming in June 2016. More recently, China gained the support of its allies in the Non-Aligned Movement (NAM) Summit to block an update on Southeast Asia in the Final Document of the NAM Summit, with Venezuela as the NAM Chair taking the lead to sweep aside the ASEAN consensus on the update.

ASEAN had fatalistically accepted the fact that China will continue to pressure its allies within the regional organisation to dilute discussions and whitewash its members' positions on the South China Sea. However, events at the NAM Summit marked a new low for ASEAN–China relations, as it was the most visible attempt in one of the world's biggest multilateral forums to constrict ASEAN's diplomatic space in international affairs. Beijing's astute manipulation of ASEAN's consensus rule means that it could literally control ASEAN from the outside through "friendly" parties.

China's "Trojan Horse" tactics pose an existential threat to ASEAN, which was originally founded in 1967 to band five small Southeast Asian states together to ward off major power interference and dominance. However, ASEAN has since re-calibrated its strategy of engaging the major powers in an effort to maintain and enhance its autonomy. Its open and inclusive strategy has turned ASEAN's logic on its head, at least when it comes to its relations with China. Beijing's influence over Cambodia and Laos has had a detrimental effect on ASEAN unity. Above all, the South China Sea disputes have shown how fragile and susceptible ASEAN is to external interference through indirect machinations.

> The South China Sea disputes are a test of ASEAN unity and its viability as a political entity. The value and relevance of the regional organisation greatly diminish if it is unable to articulate a common approach to the single most important regional security issue in its own backyard.

At the strategic level, the South China Sea disputes are a test of ASEAN unity and its viability as a political entity. The value and relevance of the regional organisation greatly diminish if it is unable to articulate a common approach to the single most important regional security issue in its own backyard. The challenge for ASEAN is to find new modalities to get around the detrimental effect of consensus decision-making.

Changing Dynamics of the Philippines' Relations with China and the US

The Award put China on the defensive, and Beijing made sure that it would not be embarrassed by a united ASEAN front in support of the Philippines. The stakes were particularly high for Beijing as 2016 marked the 25th anniversary of ASEAN–China relations. The commemorative summit attended by Premier Li Keqiang in Vientiane following the ASEAN Summit proceeded without incident. ASEAN dealt with the Award by largely ignoring it and not using it as leverage to exact concessions from China. Having survived the announcement of the award without any significant fallout, ASEAN now has to deal with the Philippines' volte-face of appearing to disown the Award under the Duterte administration. Duterte shelving the Award and initiating direct talks with Beijing is a positive development as the easing of tensions between China and the Philippines brings an element of stability to the South China Sea. On the other hand, shelving the Award may send the wrong signal that international law can be summarily side-lined for political expediency. More importantly, the Philippines' eagerness to "make deals" with China, coupled with Duterte's

Sea disputes, it has also kept above the fray of the simmering rivalry between China and the US. In appearing to be terminating the Philippines' strategic relations with the US and cosying up to China, the Duterte administration has opted to take sides and, in turn, complicated ASEAN's efforts to serve a constructive role in managing the disputes.

To be sure, individual ASEAN member states have been known to have closer relations with certain major powers over others in their bilateral ties, but none have taken such an explicit and high-profile approach to declaring their strategic inclinations. Duterte's actions have undermined ASEAN's neutrality and called into question the Philippines' effectiveness as ASEAN chair, a position it formally assumed in 2017. The Philippines' realignment and its president's open disdain for

ASEAN will keep to its old playbook of not taking sides in the South China Sea disputes. Being neutral means two things: not taking a position on the merits of the claims and not siding with any party or parties, including China or the Philippines.

announcement of "separation" with the US will continue to shake up the regional strategic balance.

Speaking at the Philippines-China Trade and Investment Forum in Beijing on October 20, 2016, Duterte declared, "I've realigned myself in your [China] ideological flow and maybe I will also go to Russia to talk to (President Vladimir) Putin and tell him that there are three of us against the world – China, Philippines and Russia. It's the only way."[11] This puts ASEAN in a delicate position and could potentially compromise ASEAN's "no choosing sides" policy. Not only has ASEAN maintained a neutral stance on the South China

the US will also put one of ASEAN's most important dialogue partner relationships under strain.

Policy Options

ASEAN will keep to its old playbook of not taking sides in the South China Sea disputes. Being neutral means two things: not taking a position on the merits of the claims and not siding with any party or parties, including China or the Philippines. This is a position that ASEAN claimant states and China have to accept and respect as the alternative would do irreparable damage to ASEAN–China relations or relations between member states. Taking sides with any ASEAN claimant state would effectively cast the disputes as an ASEAN versus China confrontation. It would be equally untenable for ASEAN to side with Chi-

---

11 "Duterte: It's Russia, China, PH 'against the world'," ABS-CBN News, October 20, 2016, <http://news.abs-cbn.com/news/10/20/16/duterte-its-russia-china-ph-against-the-world>.

na against any its members. Thus, ASEAN is not being disingenuous when it claims to play a neutral role as its policy is based on solid strategic and political rationales. Beyond maintaining its policy of neutrality, the post-arbitration context has necessitated several ASEAN policy responses that relate to strengthening unity, supporting the ASEAN–China dialogue relations coordinator, and moving forward towards the conclusion of the COC.

Strengthening Unity

China's strong arm tactics have forced ASEAN to re-examine its approach to the South China Sea disputes and its role in the region more broadly. The adherence to the neutrality principle will be maintained. However, ASEAN is growing increasingly frustrated at China's interference in its internal discussions and affairs, which calls for a tactical reorientation to bolster ASEAN unity and political cohesion. The focus is on bringing Brunei, Cambodia, Laos, and Thailand – member states that have taken an anodyne perspective on international law and UNCLOS since the Award – around to the imperative of regional cohesion. If reason fails, what institutional restructuring can be made to separate ASEAN from the debilitating effects of China's Trojan Horse tactics? At the same time, ASEAN has to do a better job of convincing China that using its allies to silence ASEAN when it encounters disagreements with ASEAN does Beijing more harm than good. Silencing ASEAN effectively cuts off lines of communication with the members of the regional organisation. The simmering dissatisfaction with China's proxy-based meddling in ASEAN and regional affairs has led to calls for a re-examination of the consensus-based decision-making model in favour of alternatives such as an "ASEAN minus X" formula. The unintended consequence of China's actions aimed at containing ASEAN's response to the Award has been the opening of this discourse on the ASEAN consensus model.

ASEAN had appeared to lack unity of late, especially in its dealings with China. It has a tradition of conducting internal discussions prior to meeting with dialogue partners, and this mechanism can and should be used more frequently and effectively to build a bottom-line consensus. Although the South China Sea disputes directly involve four ASEAN claimants, a number of other states, including but not limited to Indonesia and Singapore, are major stakeholders in the stability of the maritime domain in the South China Sea. Therefore, wider regional interests should be taken into account when forging a bottom-line consensus.

Supporting the ASEAN–China Coordinator

The ASEAN dialogue coordinatorship mechanism is an important aspect of ASEAN's external relations. The coordinators, which serve three-year terms, serve as the primary interlocutor with their designated dialogue partners. Singapore took on the responsibility of managing some aspects of ASEAN's engagement with China on the South China Sea as part of its duties as the coordinator for ASEAN–China dialogue relations. Unfortunately, Singapore has come under fire by China for "taking sides" and panned for its alleged interference as not in keeping with its status as a non-claimant state. Singapore's challenging experience is collateral damage in China's efforts to keep ASEAN from organising a united approach on the South China Sea.

The attacks on Singapore are disconcerting for two reasons. First, while Singapore has indeed been more active in facilitating discussions on the South China Sea since it took over as the coordinator for ASEAN–China dialogue relations in August 2015, it cannot be faulted for performing its duties. It is Singapore's responsibility to endeavour toward positive movement on the long-standing disputes. Second, the media attacks on Singapore are, in fact, targeting ASEAN and aimed at neutralising the function of the dialogue coordinator. At a time when leadership is needed in ASEAN, the dialogue coordinator plays an oversized role in keeping ASEAN–China relations on track. In the absence of an active and effective interlocutor, ASEAN will surrender the initiative on the South China Sea disputes to China. In addition, a

disinterested or constrained coordinator will deprive China of a focal point upon which to engage ASEAN on this issue. In any case, for Singapore to perform these functions effectively, it needs the support and cooperation of other member states. A major aspect of ASEAN unity involves providing political and moral support to member states being put under pressure while in the line of ASEAN duty.

Moving Forward with the Code of Conduct

ASEAN's primary focus and priority on South China Sea issues remains the conclusion of a legally binding COC. In practical terms, this is the only recourse open to ASEAN for engaging China in a manner that is consistent with the regional or-

> The COC is the only recourse open to ASEAN for engaging China in a manner that is consistent with the regional organisation's principle of neutrality on the South China Sea. This is also the only mechanism under which China is willing – albeit grudgingly – to hold discussions on a multilateral basis with ASEAN.

ganisation's principle of neutrality on the South China Sea. This is also the only mechanism under which China is willing – albeit grudgingly – to hold discussions on a multilateral basis with ASEAN.

Beyond the COC, ASEAN should broaden the South China Sea discourse to include security institutions. Confidence-building measures such as hotlines between senior diplomats are a good and perhaps important gesture, but they may not yield practical payoffs as the protagonists on the ground are military and law enforcement agencies. It is thus important to bring the regional navies, coast guards, and para-military agencies into the policy mix and ongoing discussions. Expanding the line of communication between local and regional commanders with direct operational command over maritime assets would be an enhanced step toward conflict management and preventing escalation.

Conclusion and Future Prospects

The Award in the South China Sea arbitration case has not changed ASEAN's approach to the South China Sea in any discernible manner. ASEAN continues to uphold its policy of "not taking sides" while affirming the importance of safeguarding regional peace and security, protecting freedom of navigation and overflight, calling for the peaceful resolution of the disputes, and upholding respect for and application of international law including UNCLOS. At the same

China's responses to the Award threaten ASEAN centrality in managing regional affairs. At the same time, the Philippines' strategic pivot towards China and away from the US has also complicated ASEAN's position of neutrality on South China Sea issues.

time, ASEAN has not been unaffected by the new legal environment handed down by the Arbitral Tribunal.

Most glaringly, the Award has amplified divisions within ASEAN as evidenced by the varied responses of individual member states, which ranged from "no response" to calls for respect for and implementation of the Award. The failure of member states to affirm the sanctity of international law puts into perspective the member states' different levels of support for this basic principle of global governance. On the positive side, the Award has provided an impetus for ASEAN and China to put into place confidence-building measures such as the foreign ministry hotlines and CUES. Nevertheless, the negative implications outweigh these positive developments. China's responses to the Award, especially its outright dismissal of international law and the arbitration process and its efforts to constrain ASEAN's diplomatic space, remind ASEAN that the current and future power asymmetry that overwhelmingly favours China will give the latter enormous advantages to dictate the course of regional affairs.

In addition, China's responses to the Award threaten ASEAN centrality in managing regional affairs. At the same time, the Philippines' strategic pivot towards China and away from the US has also complicated ASEAN's position of neutrality on South China Sea issues. Questions will be asked of the Philippines' effectiveness as ASEAN Chair and Coordinator for ASEAN-China dialogue relations, positions Manila will assume in 2017 and mid-2018, respectively. Since the Award, ASEAN has shown its frailty in responding to political, legal, and strategic developments in the South China Sea. Among the policy options available to ASEAN, it could endeavour to strengthen internal cohesion

Political will be needed to maintain forward momentum on a binding COC, despite its limitations, as China is very unlikely to be in favour of a regional legal regime that will bind its hands and constrain its strategic options.

and unity to formulate baseline positions on the South China Sea and to support an active role for the ASEAN-China dialogue relations coordinator. Political will also be needed to maintain forward momentum on a binding COC, despite its limitations, as China is very unlikely to be in favour of a regional legal regime that will bind its hands and constrain its strategic options. Unfortunately, ASEAN is left with no other choice but to move forward with these few policy options available to it in the post-arbitration context.

Siew Mun Tang is Head of the ASEAN Studies Centre at ISEAS-Yusof Ishak Institute.

Post-Arbitration South China Sea:

Australia's Policy Options and Future Prospects

Sam Bateman

Abstract

Australia's policy options for responding to the situation in the South China Sea are influenced by four major factors: its interest in the stability of Southeast Asia, its dependence on seaborne trade and freedoms of navigation, its commitment to a rules-based global order, and the need to maintain a careful balance in its relations with China and the United States. The Award of July 12, 2016, in the arbitration case between China and the Philippines has highlighted anomalies in Australia's position with regard to compulsory arbitration on maritime boundaries, its position on the rules-based global order, and possible questions regarding the status of some of Australia's offshore insular features as 'fully entitled' islands. Australia's official responses calling for all parties to abide by the ruling have created tensions in its relations with China. Generally, the Award has not helped Australia's regional interests. While calling upon all parties to exercise restraint in the South China Sea, Australia has several possible policy options for contributing to resolving the situation following the Award. These relate to how to pursue a carefully balanced and sensitive diplomatic approach with China, the United States and Southeast Asian countries to help promote cooperation and build trust and whether or not Australia should increase its current military efforts in the South China Sea, which is unlikely given the current situation. There is scope, however, for Australia to contribute its expertise to help develop regimes for the effective management of the South China Sea, particularly with the management of its fish stocks and the protection of its marine environment. Working through ASEAN and its associated institutions will be an important part of Australia's response.

Introduction

Australia has a range of strategic, political and economic interests in the South China Sea.[1] These complicate its position when developing policy options following the Award in the Philippines v. China arbitration case and for dealing with the situation in the South China Sea. Following the Award, the Australian Government called on the Philippines and China to abide by the ruling as final and binding on both parties.[2] It went on to state that Australia will continue to exercise its international legal rights to freedom of navigation and overflight, and to support the right of others to do so.[3]

> Australia is caught in a difficult balancing act between its relations with the United States, as its major security partner, and with China, as its major trading partner. The United States wants Australian support for its position in the South China while China is warning Australia to keep out of the South China Sea.

In calling on parties to abide by the Award, Australia became one of only seven countries that have formally called for the Award to be respected – the other six being Canada, Japan, New Zealand, the Philippines, the United States and Vietnam.[4] Adding further to Australia's response, the Australian Foreign Minister later joined with her counterparts in Japan and the United States to express their serious concerns over the maritime disputes in the South China Sea and to voice their strong opposition to any coercive unilateral actions that could alter the status quo and increase tensions.[5] These responses by Australia created tensions in Australia's relations with China with a strong warning from China for Australia to stay out of the South China Sea or risk damaging bilateral relations.[6]

These developments since the arbitration case demonstrate

---

1   These were discussed in Sam Bateman, "Australia's Diplomatic and Security Responses," in Fu-Kuo Liu and Jonathan Spangler (eds.), *South China Sea Lawfare: Legal Perspectives and International Responses to the Philippines v. China Arbitration Case*, South China Sea Think Tank and Taiwan Center for Security Studies, January 29, 2016, pp. 75–82, <http://scstt.org/reports/2016/525/>.

2   Julie Bishop, "Australia supports peaceful dispute resolution in the South China Sea," Media Release, Minister for Foreign Affairs, July 12, 2016, <http://foreignminister.gov.au/releases/Pages/2016/jb_mr_160712a.aspx>.

3   Julie Bishop, "Australia supports peaceful dispute resolution in the South China Sea," Media Release, Minister for Foreign Affairs, July 12, 2016.

4   "Who Is Taking Sides After the South China Sea Ruling?," Asia Maritime Transparency Initiative, Center for Strategic and International Studies, August 15, 2016, <https://amti.csis.org/sides-in-south-china-sea/>.

5   "Joint Statement of the Japan-United States-Australia Trilateral Strategic Dialogue," Office of the Spokesperson, US Department of State, July 25, 2016, <http://www.state.gov/r/pa/prs/ps/2016/07/260442.htm>.

6   Matthew Carney, "China warns Australia to stay out of the South China Sea or risk damage to bilateral relations," ABC News, July 15, 2016, <http://www.abc.net.au/news/2016-07-15/china-tells-australia-stay-out-of-the-south-china-sea/7631492>.

how Australia is caught in a difficult balancing act between its relations with the United States, as its major security partner, and with China, as its major trading partner. The United States wants Australian support for its position in the South China while China is warning Australia to keep out of the South China Sea. These conflicting pressures fundamentally underpin the legal, diplomatic, and security implications of the Final Award for Australia and the policy options available for it to respond to the situation in the South China Sea.

Policy Approach

There are four major aspects of Australia's policy approach to the South China Sea and to the arbitration case. Firstly, Australia has vested interests in the stability of Southeast Asia and the avoidance of conflict in the region. Secondly, as a major exporting and trading nation, Australia is heavily dependent on freedom of navigation and the security of the sea lines of communication (SLOCs) that link it to its main trading partners in East Asia. Thirdly, Australia faces a difficult balancing act in its bilateral relations with China and the United States, and the South China Sea has become a key element in this aspect. Lastly, Australia is firmly committed to a rules-based global order that supports Australia's interests. To some extent, these four aspects are all related.

Regional Stability

Australia's interest in regional stability is a matter of its geographical proximity to Southeast Asia and the belief that any major threat to Australia's security can only emerge from that region. Policy issues associated with the maintenance of regional stability are not new for Australia with its long history of military presence in the region and involvement in the provision of regional maritime security, including in the South China Sea. Forward defence based on the security of Southeast Asia was the central element of Australian strategic thinking from the early 1950s to the mid-1970s. This period saw Australian engagement in the Malayan Emergency, Indonesian Confrontation and the Vietnam War. Associated naval operations were largely

> Forward defence based on the security of Southeast Asia was the central element of Australian strategic thinking from the early 1950s to the mid-1970s. This period saw Australian engagement in the Malayan Emergency, Indonesian Confrontation and the Vietnam War. Associated naval operations were largely focused in and around the South China Sea.

focused in and around the South China Sea.

Australia was an active member of the Southeast Asia Treaty Organization (SEATO) that existed from 1954 until 1977 to prevent communism from gaining ground in the region.[7] The Australian navy was always a major participant in the very large SEATO naval exercises held regularly in the South China Sea. Concurrently, Australia contributed two destroyers or frigates and an occasional aircraft carrier to the British Commonwealth Far East Strategic Reserve (FESR), a joint military force of the British, Australian, and New Zealand armed forces based in Singapore and Malaya (Malaysia after 1963) that was established

larly conducts surveillance flights over the South China Sea from the Malaysian air base at Butterworth.[9] During the Cold War, these flights were mainly aimed at detecting and tracking Soviet ships and submarines in the region, but subsequently, they have been focussed more generally on regional maritime security, including people smuggling and piracy.

Major policy pronouncements on Australia's position with regard to the South China Sea are included in the periodic defence white papers issued by the Australian Government. The *2016 Defence White Paper* released in February 2016 said a lot about the South China Sea. It noted that territorial disputes between claimants in the East China Sea and South China Sea have created uncertainty and tension in Australia's region.[10] It said that Australia does not take sides on competing territorial claims in the South China Sea but expressed concern about land reclamation and construction activities by claimants

> The risk here is that while Australia claims it does not sides in the South China Sea disputes, comments such as those in the White Paper suggest that it is siding against China.

to provide security for the former British colonies in that part of Southeast Asia. The organisation existed from the mid-1950s to the early 1970s when the still functioning Five Power Defence Arrangements (FPDA) were set up.

The FPDA linked the military forces of the three countries forming the FESR with the armed forces of newly independent Singapore and Malaysia. FPDA has always had a significant maritime dimension.[8] Its main area of operations has been the Malacca Strait and the South China Sea with maritime exercises regularly conducted in these waters. Initially these exercises were focussed on the defence of Malaysia and Singapore, but since the early 2000s their focus has been on countering maritime terrorism and piracy. Under the umbrella of FPDA, the Australian air force regu-

in the sea and about the possible use of artificial island infrastructure for military purposes.[11] While China was not explicitly named as the offender in this regard, it was clearly in the mind of the paper's authors. Not unexpectedly, China assumed that this was the case and expressed its displeasure with the document, particularly its comments regarding the South China Sea, claiming that Australia had misinterpreted its policies in the region.[12] The risk here is that while Australia claims it does not sides in the South China Sea disputes, comments such as those in the White

---

7   "Southeast Asia Treaty Organization (SEATO), 1954," Office of the Historian, US Department of State, <https://history.state.gov/milestones/1953-1960/seato>.

8   Sam Bateman, "The FPDA's Contribution to Regional Security: The Maritime Dimension," in Ian Storey, Ralf Emmers, and Daljit Singh (eds.), *Five Power Defence Arrangements at Forty*, Singapore: Institute of Southeast Asian Studies, 2012, pp. 68–84.

9   "Operation Gateway," Department of Defence, Australian Government, <http://www.defence.gov.au/operations/SouthChinaSeaIndianOcean/>.

10 *2016 Defence White Paper*, Department of Defence, Australian Government, 2016, paragraph 1.6, <http://www.defence.gov.au/whitepaper/Docs/2016-Defence-White-Paper.pdf>.

11 *2016 Defence White Paper*, paragraph 2.77.

12 Shalailah Medhora, "China expresses 'dissatisfaction' at Australia's defence white paper", *The Guardian*, February 26, 2016, <https://www.theguardian.com/world/2016/feb/26/china-expresses-dissatisfaction-at-australias-defence-white-paper>.

Paper suggest that it is siding against China.

The *2016 Defence White Paper* maintained a focus on regional stability. It identified three key strategic defence interests for Australia, all of which are factors in determining major aspects of Australia's policy approach to the South China Sea. The second of these was identified as '[a] secure nearer region, encompassing maritime South East Asia and the South Pacific'.[13] With regard to Southeast Asia, the Defence White Paper states:

> Instability or conflict in South East Asia would threaten Australia's security and our vital and growing economic relationships in that region. Stability in South East Asia is important to countering other threats including transnational crime and terrorism. Australia's reliance on maritime trade with and through South East Asia, including energy supplies, means the security of our maritime approaches and trade routes within South East Asia must be protected, as must freedom of navigation, which provides for the free flow of maritime trade in international waters.[14]

Freedoms of Navigation

With regard to the free flow of trade through the South China Sea, the *2016 Defence White Paper* claimed that 'nearly two-thirds of Australia's exports pass through the South China Sea, including our major coal, iron ore and liquefied natural gas exports'.[15] However, this figure was an exaggeration.[16] The accurate figure, based on recent data for Australia's overseas trade,[17] is a little over twenty per cent, and most of this is trade with China.[18] The White Paper actually disproves its own estimate with its map in Figure 2 showing that most of Australia's sea freight does not pass through the South China Sea.[19] Nor does the map show the busy trade route between eastern Australia, Japan and South Korea that passes to the east of the Philippines, rather than the South China Sea. Australian policymakers need to be cautious of the White Paper's exaggerations about how much China threatens Australian trade and security interests in the South China Sea.

By making a big play of the South China Sea, the *2016 Defence White Paper* falls into line with what Greg Austin has called 'The Pentagon's Big Lie about the South China Sea'.[20] For Austin, the lie is the claim that China's actions in the South China Sea threaten commercial shipping. How-

Australian policymakers need to be cautious of the White Paper's exaggerations about how much China threatens Australian trade and security interests in the South China Sea.

---

13 The first key defence strategic interest is 'a secure, resilient Australia, with secure northern approaches and proximate sea lines of communication.' *2016 Defence White Paper*, paragraph 3.5.

14 *2016 Defence White Paper*, paragraph 3.8.

15 *2016 Defence White Paper*, paragraph 2.72.

16 Sam Bateman, "What are Australia's interests in the South China Sea?," *The Strategist*, May 28, 2015, <http://www.aspistrategist.org.au/what-are-australias-interests-in-the-south-china-sea/>.

17 Composition of Trade Australia 2013-14, Table 7, Department of Foreign Affairs and Trade, 2014, <http://dfat.gov.au/about-us/publications/Documents/cot-fy-2013-14.pdf>.

18 Sam Bateman, "Australia's flawed position on the South China Sea," *East Asia Forum*, March 10, 2016, <http://www.eastasiaforum.org/2016/03/10/australias-flawed-position-on-the-south-china-sea/#more-49860>.

19 *2016 Defence White Paper*, Figure 2, p. 70.

20 Greg Austin, "'Mountains out of Molehills:' The Pentagon's Big Lie About the South China Sea," *The Diplomat*, February 24, 2016, <http://thediplomat.com/2016/02/mountains-out-of-molehills-the-pentagons-big-lie-about-the-south-china-sea/>.

ever, China has repeatedly denied it poses such a threat, and with so much of China's own trade passing through the sea, it is most unlikely that it would. American commentators also invariably overstate the value of US trade passing through the South China Sea. They fail to recognize that the majority of American trade with East Asia either does not go through the area or is trade with China.

While the United States is protesting a general threat by China to freedoms of navigation in the South China Sea,[21] at the heart of its protests are peculiarly American concerns that relatively few regional countries share. In particular, these include the right to conduct hydrographic surveys

> All the major powers in the South China Sea are trying to achieve an advantageous outcome by pushing dangerous events to the edge of active conflict.

and so-called 'military surveys' in the exclusive economic zone (EEZ) of another country without the permission of that country.[22] The United States argues that these activities, and military activities more generally, are an exercise of the high seas freedoms of navigation and overflight available in an EEZ.[23] Conversely, China argues that some of these activities do not have such rights in its EEZ and that military surveys in par-

ticular are a form of intelligence collection.[24] Australia shares the American position that military activities generally may be conducted in an EEZ without the permission of the coastal state, but in practice with hydrographic surveys, it does not conduct these in the EEZ of another state without the permission of that state.[25]

Bilateral Relations

There is much to fault in the actions of the two major powers in the South China Sea. China's actions have been assertive and, as found by the arbitration tribunal, contrary to customary views of the international law of the sea. Meanwhile, the United States with its freedom of navigation operations and its defence assistance to Vietnam and the Philippines has been fueling the security dilemma in the region and adding to the strategic distrust that currently exists. All this is looking like dangerous brinkmanship.[26] All the major powers in the South China Sea are trying to achieve an advantageous outcome by pushing dangerous events to the edge of active conflict. This situation poses a difficult challenge for Australia with its need to maintain a careful balance in its relations with China and the United States, as well as with Japan with whom Australia also shares an important economic and strategic relationship.[27]

Major power rivalries are the big problem throughout the region and for Australia. Following the freedom of navigation operations con-

21 Sam Bateman, "What is the US protesting in the South China Sea?," *East Asia Forum*, October 20, 2015, <http://www.eastasiaforum.org/2015/10/20/what-is-the-us-protesting-in-the-south-china-sea/>.

22 James Kraska, *Maritime Power and the Law of the Sea*, New York: Oxford University Press, 2011, p. 275.

23 Raul (Pete) Pedrozo, "Preserving Navigational Rights and Freedoms: The Right to Conduct Military Activities in China's Exclusive Economic Zone," *Chinese Journal of International Law*, 9(1), March 2010, pp. 9–30.

24 Zhang Haiwen, "Is It Safeguarding the Freedom of Navigation or Maritime Hegemony of the United States?—Comments on Raul (Pete) Pedrozo's Article on Military Activities in the EEZ," *Chinese Journal of International Law*, 9(1), March 2010, pp. 31–48.

25 Sam Bateman, "Hydrographic surveying in the EEZ: differences and overlaps with marine scientific research," *Marine Policy*, 29 (2), 2005, p. 170.

26 Sam Bateman, "Brinkmanship in the South China Sea helps nobody," *East Asia Forum*, June 7, 2016, <http://www.eastasiaforum.org/2016/06/07/brinkmanship-in-the-south-china-sea-helps-nobody/>.

27 *2016 Defence White Paper*, paragraph 5.59.

ducted by the US Navy in the South China Sea, this rivalry has come to the forefront of long simmering South China Sea tensions. It does not help that both countries tend to hold worst-case beliefs of each other. First, Beijing views Washington as imperialist and attempting to undermine its growth. At the same time, Washington views itself as a guardian of the existing "rules-based" international order, which Beijing allegedly seeks to reconfigure and expel the United States from the Asia-Pacific. This perception drives the evolution of the United States' policy towards Asia, which includes building the economic and military capacities of its allies and partners in the region. As Hugh White has noted, both major powers are competing for influence in the region and the rules.[30]

Community attitudes towards China are another consideration in the bilateral relationship. A recent survey found that 69 percent of Australians are comfortable with the idea that China could be or is the world's leading superpower.[31] Australia also has a large (over four percent of the total population) and politically active Chinese community who hold widely differing views on the current regime in Beijing ranging from strongly supportive to highly critical.[32]

Rules-based Global Order

Australia's 2016 Defence White Paper identified

> A recent survey found that 69 percent of Australians are comfortable with the idea that China could be or is the world's leading superpower.

the only chance for a happy ending is for both sides to make major concessions, which would leave a stronger China, and weaker American role in Asia.[28]

Australia's relations with China are the subject of much spirited debate in Australia. This debate covers everything from Chinese 'hand-outs' to Australian politicians, to Chinese purchase of key infrastructure in Australia, and to the pros and cons of Australia becoming more actively involved in the South China Sea. There is emerging tension between those who take a generally positive view of the Australia-China relationship, including Prime Minister Malcolm Turnbull and his conservative predecessors, Tony Abbott and John Howard, and those who hold a negative view, including some leading Australian academics.[29] Rather than making any kinds of threats, Australia has preferred to remind China that its interests are overwhelmingly served by obeying

Australia's third key Defence Strategic Interest as a stable Indo-Pacific region and rules-based global order that supports Australia's interests.[33] The White Paper made much of the importance of a rules-based global order to Australia's security. The term 'rules-based' was mentioned 56 times in the paper, suggesting that the phrase was short-form for an Australian preference for the status quo.[34] There is a clear message in the White Paper that some countries are not following these rules. As one telling statement reads,

While it is natural for newly powerful coun-

28   Hugh White, "Wishful thinking dominates 'failed' White Paper," *Australian Naval Institute Analysis*, March 1, 2016, <http://navalinstitute.com.au/wishful-thinking-dominates-failed-white-paper>.

29   Bob Carr, "Abbott injects Dose of Realism on Australia's relationship with China," *The Australian*, October 4, 2016, p. 10.

30   David Wroe, "Chinese checkers – After this week's ruling, the world waits on Beijing's next step," *The Sydney Morning Herald*, July 16–17, 2016, p. 23.

31   Natalie Sambhi, "The Puzzles of the Pivot: America in the Asia-Pacific," War on the Rocks, October 4, 2016, <http://Warontherocks.Com/2016/10/The-Puzzles-Of-The-Pivot-America-In-The-Asia-Pacific/>.

32   Rowan Callick, "Inscrutable ties to another China", *The Weekend Australian*, August 22–28, 2016, p. 27.

33   *2016 Defence White Paper*, paragraph 3.9.

34   Crispin Rovere, "Defence White Paper 2016: Eight strategic observations," *The Interpreter*, February 29, 2016, <http://www.lowyinterpreter.org/post/2016/02/29/Defence-White-Paper-2016-Eight-strategic-observations.aspx>.

tries to seek greater influence, they also have a responsibility to act in a way that constructively contributes to global stability, security and prosperity. However, some countries and non-state actors have sought to challenge the rules that govern actions in the global commons such as the high seas, cyberspace and space in some unhelpful ways, leading to uncertainty and tension.[35]

This statement did not mention China specifically, but most commentators have interpreted such comments as referring to China. This reflects the concern that, in the South China Sea, China is not showing respect for widely respected interpretations of international law, particularly the law of the sea as embodied in the 1982 UN Convention on the Law of the Sea (UNCLOS).[36] It also reflects the fundamental struggle between preserving the status quo world order, which some claim disproportionately benefits the developed world, and altering the system to the benefit of China and other developing countries.[37]

> The United States and other major powers have a long tradition of ignoring decisions when they lose cases.

Despite the 2016 Defence White Paper's references to a rule-based global order, the reality is not that simple. For one, other countries besides China do not follow the rules either. Australia's major security partner, the United States, is not party to many important international conventions, including UNCLOS. Also, the United States and other major powers have a long tradition of ignoring decisions when they lose cases.[38]

Implications of the Award

In the light of Australia's strategic interests in Southeast Asia, the Award in the arbitration case has several implications that can be identified. Firstly, there are legal implications, particularly regarding the ruling about distinguishing 'islands' and 'rocks'. Secondly, there are diplomatic implications, especially for Australia's relations both with China and with Timor-Leste. Thirdly, there are security implications following China's 'hard line' resistance to abiding by the ruling. Lastly, there are risks that Australia's influence in the region could be diminished by its

---

35 *2016 Defence White Paper*, paragraph 2.24.

36 Rory Medcalf, "Rules, Balance and Lifelines: An Australian Perspective on the South China Sea," *Asia Policy*, January 21, 2016, p. 9.

37 Mark Valencia, "Can of Worms", *South China Morning Post*, September 7, 2016, p. A11.

38 Graham Allison, "Of Course China, Like All Great Powers, Will Ignore an International Legal Verdict," *The Diplomat*, July 11, 2016, <http://thediplomat.com/2016/07/of-course-china-like-all-great-powers-will-ignore-an-international-legal-verdict/>.

apparent ambivalence in relations with China.

Legal Implications

One surprising feature of the Award was the judgment that there are no 'fully entitled' islands in the Spratly group. That is, the Tribunal concluded that none of the features are entitled to an EEZ or continental shelf under UNCLOS.[39] The arbitrators took a narrow interpretation of an insular feature's ability to 'sustain human habitation or an economic life of [its] own'. Their criteria rested on a feature's ability to provide a naturally occurring supply of food, water, or shelter in quantities sufficient to enable a group of persons to live for an indeterminate period of time. They considered that any past economic activity was purely extractive in nature and were unimpressed by any past history of habitation.

> The arbitrators took a narrow interpretation of an insular feature's ability to 'sustain human habitation or an economic life of [its] own'.

The ruling has far-reaching implications. It presents challenges for other countries, including Australia, Japan and the United States, which have claimed a full set of maritime zones from small, isolated features. Those countries are all likely to ignore the precedent established by the ruling on 'rocks' and 'islands'. Japan has already reasserted that the small feature of Okinotorishima in the Pacific Ocean, from which it claims both an EEZ and an extended continental shelf, is a true island rather than a rock.[40]

The United States recently announced expansion of the Papahānaumokuākea Marine National Monument around the Northwest Hawaiian Islands to create the world's largest marine protected area (MPA).[41] In doing so, it ignored the possibility that, under the precedent established by the Award, most of the islands and atolls comprising the Northwest Hawaiian Islands would not be accepted as 'fully enti-

---

39   Sam Bateman, "The South China Sea arbitration: challenges and opportunities," *The Strategist*, August 2, 2016, <http://www.aspistrategist.org.au/south-china-sea-arbitration-challenges-opportunities/>.

40   Ayako Mie, "Japan steps up rhetoric over Okinotorishima in wake of Hague ruling," *Japan Times*, July 15, 2016, <http://www.japantimes.co.jp/news/2016/07/15/national/politics-diplomacy/japan-steps-rhetoric-okinotorishima-wake-hague-ruling/>.

41   "Fact Sheet: President Obama to Create the World's Largest Marine Protected Area", Media Release, Office of the Press Secretary, The White House, August 26, 2016, <https://www.whitehouse.gov/the-press-office/2016/08/26/fact-sheet-president-obama-create-worlds-largest-marine-protected-area>.

tled' islands and not entitled to an EEZ that would justify the MPA.[42] However, the United States is unlikely to be too concerned about these implications. The EEZ around the Northwest Hawaiian Islands has been in place for many years without any protest from another nation. This is different to the situation in the Spratlys, which attract controversy due to the conflicting sovereignty claims and the impact of their status on maritime jurisdiction in the area.

Similar considerations apply to Australian islands, such as Heard and McDonald islands in the southern Indian Ocean and Mellish Reef in the Coral Sea, whose status might be questioned in the light of the arbitral ruling. However, these islands have all been used as basepoints in maritime boundary agreements with neighboring countries, and even to support an outer conti-

Diplomatic Implications

The most important diplomatic implication for Australia is that it is hard for Australia to criticize China in deciding not to participate in the arbitration when Australia itself has opted out of mandatory dispute settlement under Article 298 of UNCLOS.[44] It risks allegations of hypocrisy if it were to do so. As a former senior Australian diplomat has observed, Australia is not well placed to suggest that China should stop bullying smaller countries on boundary issues.[45]

Australia, like China, is one of the relatively few countries that have made declarations regarding optional exceptions to compulsory dispute settlement under Article 298.[46] Timor-Leste would like to take Australia to arbitration over maritime boundaries, but has been frustrated

> It is hard for Australia to criticize China in deciding not to participate in the arbitration when Australia itself has opted out of mandatory dispute settlement under Article 298 of UNCLOS.

nental shelf that has been approved by the Commission on Limits of the Continental Shelf.[43] This helps substantiate the status of these features as 'fully entitled' islands. Despite the precedent established by the ruling on 'islands' and 'rocks', Australia is unlikely to adjust its legal position on the status of some of its insular features.

in this by Australia opting out of compulsory dispute resolution in respect of maritime boundaries. Nevertheless, in April 2016, Timor-Leste launched compulsory, though non-binding conciliation with Australia to try to get Australia to agree permanent maritime boundaries in the Timor Sea. Australia's Foreign Minister and At-

44   Anne Sheehan, "Dispute Settlement under UNCLOS: The Exclusion of Maritime Delimitation Disputes," *University of Queensland Law Journal*, 24(1), p. 165.

45   John McCarthy, "Australia and the South China Sea," *The Strategist*, March 17, 2016, <http://www.aspistrategist. org.au/australia-and-the-south-china-sea/>.

46   Twenty-nine countries have made such declarations relating to maritime boundaries and historic title. Saiful Karim, "Litigating law of the sea disputes using the UNCLOS dispute settlement system," in Natalie Klein (ed.), *Litigating International Law Disputes: Weighing the Options*, Cambridge: Cambridge University Press, 2014, p. 272, Table 12.1.

42   This part of the chapter draws on Sam Bateman, "Obama at Midway: Picking and choosing the law of the sea," *The Interpreter*, September 2, 2016, <http://www. lowyinterpreter.org/post/2016/09/02/Obama-at-Midway-Picking-and-choosing-the-law-of-the-sea.aspx>.

43   Sam Bateman and Clive Schofield, "Australia's outer continental shelf regime," *Australian Journal of Maritime and Ocean Affairs*, 4(4), 2012, pp. 131–140.

torney-General have declared in respect of this conciliation that, while 'Australia will abide by the Commission's finding as to whether it has jurisdiction to hear matters on maritime boundaries', if the commission finds that it does have jurisdiction 'then its final report on that matter is not binding'.[47]

Timor-Leste was quick to note that Australian Foreign Minister Julie Bishop's call for China to respect an international rules-based order was at odds with Australia's persistent refusal to negotiate maritime boundaries with it.[48] However, Timor-Leste may have missed an opportunity to make its point by not taking any public position on the recent arbitral ruling. Its position in its dispute with Australia might have supported a statement from Dili critical of China for not abiding by the rules, but that could have jeopardized its own relations with China, which is a major source of its overseas aid.[49]

> The apparent anomaly in Australia's position whereby it has refused compulsory dispute resolution with Timor-Leste while regularly committing itself to the rules-based global order, including criticizing China's position in the South China Sea has become a 'hot' political issue in Australia.

The apparent anomaly in Australia's position whereby it has refused compulsory dispute resolution with Timor-Leste while regularly committing itself to the rules-based global order, including criticizing China's position in the South China Sea has become a 'hot' political issue in Australia. Pointing to this apparent anomaly in Australia's position, the opposition party in Australia has committed itself to reaching a binding international resolution with Timor-Leste, whether it be through bilateral negotiation or international arbitration.[50]

---

47   Julie Bishop and George Brandis, "Conciliation between Australia and Timor-Leste," Joint media release, Minister for Foreign Affairs, Australia, August 29, 2016, <http://foreignminister.gov.au/releases/Pages/2016/jb_mr_160829c.aspx>.

48   Michael Leach, "The PCA ruling, Australia and Timor-Leste," *The Interpreter*, July 20, 2016, <http://www.lowyinterpreter.org/post/2016/07/20/The-PCA-ruling-Australia-and-Timor-Leste.aspx>.

49   Lora Horta, "The Dragon and the Sleeping Crocodile – China and Timor-Leste," *Macauhub*, February 8, 2014, <http://www.macauhub.com.mo/en/2014/02/08/the-dragon-and-the-sleeping-crocodile-china-and-timor-leste/>.

50   Penny Wong, "Australia should commit to dispute resolution with Timor-Leste," *The Interpreter*, September 1, 2016, <http://www.lowyinterpreter.org/post/2016/09/01/Australia-should-commit-to-dispute-resolution-with-Timor-Leste.aspx>.

Security Implications

The main security implications of the ruling for Australia are its possible impacts on regional stability and on Australia's bilateral relations with China. As one commentator has claimed, 'The Tribunal ruling makes it painfully clear that there's a stark incompatibility between Australia and China's approach'.[51] There are different interpretations of what constitutes the rules-based global order and a belief that, by rejecting the ruling, China is laying claim to a large part of the region in which Australia has asserted a critical national security interest.

As was noted earlier, the Australian Government's formal statements on the ruling met an angry response from China. As a *Global Times* article observed, 'Australia has unexpectedly made itself a pioneer of hurting China's interest with a fiercer attitude than countries directly involved in the South China Sea dispute'.[52] This article included the view that Australia is a "paper cat' – all talk and no action' – and a relatively insignificant regional player. This perception suggests that Beijing believes Canberra will not risk the economic relationship by pushing back too strongly against China's assertive actions in the South China Sea.[53]

If other regional countries share this perception that Australia, despite its rhetoric, is unwilling to push back too strongly against China's assertive behaviour in the South China Sea, this could lead to Australia's diminished influence in the region. Australia thus faces a dilemma between on the one hand being seen as a 'paper cat' if it does not take firmer action, but if it does and for example, follows the United States' lead into more active military operations in the South China Sea, including freedom of navigation operations, it risks criticism of being the 'deputy sheriff' of Washington in the region. Australia's closeness to Washington has previously caused fears among some of its Asian neighbours, particularly Indonesia, that Australia is 'alien' to the region.[54] These fears re-sur-

> If other regional countries share this perception that Australia, despite its rhetoric, is unwilling to push back too strongly against China's assertive behaviour in the South China Sea, this could lead to Australia's diminished influence in the region.

---

51 Peter Jennings, "The South China Sea: how will this end?," *The Strategist*, July 13, 2016, <http://www.aspistrategist.org.au/south-china-sea-will-end/>.

52 "'Paper cat' Australia will learn its lesson," *Global Times*, July 20, 2016, <http://www.globaltimes.cn/content/997320.shtml>.

53 Alan Dupont, "China wants what we have, so it won't want a spat," *The Australian*, August 30, 2016, p. 12.

54 David Fickling, "Australia seen as 'America's deputy sheriff'," *The Guardian*, September 10, 2004, <https://www.theguardian.com/world/2004/sep/10/indonesia.australia>.

faced in 2011 when Australia announced it would host deployments of US marines in Darwin.[55]

Policy Options

There are two opposing views in Australia as to what policy options to adopt following the Award. The first and that supported in the main by the Australian Government is to continue providing strong support for American primacy in the region and to follow Washington in the policies it adopts. Proponents of this view consider that not only is the United States essential to balance the rise of China in the region but also in a global

Washington's lead.[57] In essence, the White Paper assumes that peace will be maintained by China backing down, leaving America dominant. Despite this official view, there is increasing appreciation in Australia that American primacy in East Asia cannot be maintained forever.

Diplomatic Responses

The situation in the South China Sea is fluid. It requires clever diplomacy from countries such as Australia that need to balance carefully the strategic costs and benefits of their prospective diplomatic responses. Australia faces a dilemma

> The White Paper assumes that peace will be maintained by China backing down, leaving America dominant.

sense to maintain the rules-based global order. As the *2016 Defence White Paper* states, 'The global strategic and economic weight of the United States will be essential to the continued stability of the rules-based global order'.[56]

The alternative view believes that Australia's responses to the arbitration ruling should appreciate the rate of strategic change in the region and look to the future. This view recognises that the continued rise of China's economic and maritime power is the leading influence on the future maritime security environment of Asia and that the United States is declining in strategic and political influence. It is reflected in the criticism of the *2016 Defence White Paper* that it simply assumes that Australia has no choice but to follow

about whether it should adopt a more active diplomatic position on the South China Sea, which could have an adverse impact on its strong economic relationship with China.

Australia has a clear strategic interest in the situation in the South China Sea not deteriorating further. However, the situation there is complicated, and Australia should have an eye on its broader regional relations. As Peter Drysdale pointed out, Asia takes Australia seriously as a 'crucial element in Asia's security in terms of strategic resource and energy supply'.[58] That is where the bigger picture and Australia's interests in the South China Sea lie. The South China Sea itself is not that important to Australia. Rather, it

55   Tom Allard, "Indonesia wary of strengthened Australia-US defence ties in Darwin," *The Sydney Morning Herald*, November 19, 2011, <http://www.smh.com.au/national/indonesia-wary-of-strengthened-australiaus-defence-ties-in-darwin-20111118-1nnfd.htm>.

56   *2016 Defence White Paper*, paragraph 2.8.

57   Hugh White, "Wishful thinking dominates 'failed' White Paper."

58   Peter Drysdale, "The importance of reliable resource markets to Australian and Asian security," *East Asia Forum*, May 25, 2015, <http://www.eastasiaforum. org/2015/05/25/the-importance-of-reliable-resource-markets-to-australian-and-asian-security/>.

is Australia's broader regional role. This broader role and interests suggest that while Australia has called for relevant parties to abide by the Tribunal's award, it will not be more vocal than it has been already.

A prospective diplomatic option now for Australia is to work with Southeast Asian countries to promote cooperation and trust in the South China Sea. It could use its good offices to play a role in de-escalating the current situation, including by supporting the role of ASEAN and its associated institutions, such as the ASEAN Regional Forum, the East Asia Summit, and the Expanded ASEAN Maritime Forum, in building cooperation and dialogue to improve the situation. Australia has committed much diplomatic energy in the past to helping these institutions work.

Security Policy Options

Security policy options concern Australia's relations with the major powers. With the United States, Washington's policy approach will critically define what happens next, including with Canberra's policies.[59] Australia is under pressure from the United States to engage in stronger military operations in the South China Sea, but consideration of its own interests suggests a more cautious approach, consisting of political rhetoric rather than a greater military role.

> Washington's policy approach will critically define what happens next, including with Canberra's policies. Australia is under pressure from the United States to engage in stronger military operations in the South China Sea, but consideration of its own interests suggests a more cautious approach, consisting of political rhetoric rather than a greater military role.

With China, there may be scope for Australia to use the positive aspects of its bilateral relationship to explore 'creative, oblique ways to point out to China that island-building and coercion are harmful to its own interests'.[60] Skilful diplomacy and sensitivity here is important at a time when all parties need to work their way through the issue with much at stake.[61]

Australia also needs to develop a better understanding of China, including a more balanced and methodical approach to the relationship. For many in Australia, it is difficult to see China other than through

---

59   Jennings, "The South China Sea: how will this end?."

60   Medcalf, "Rules, Balance and Lifelines," p. 12.

61   Glenda Korporaal, "Let's tread carefully on South China Sea ruling", *The Australian*, July 27, 2016, <http://www.theaustralian.com.au/business/opinion/lets-tread-carefully-on-south-china-sea-ruling/news-story/12769c0f95be73b9ea5f04c946455bfc>.

American eyes and Cold War instincts that China is a looming threat.[62] Yet it is clear that Australia has its own interests that are not necessarily the same as those of the United States. A former Australian Foreign Minister has noted the lack of a well-funded 'think tank' in Australia focused on relations with China whereas there are numerous well-funded 'think tanks' studying relations with the United States.[63]

Management of the South China Sea

Effective management of the South China Sea and activities within it is another common interest of all stakeholders in the South China Sea. This requires recognizing that the sea is a 'semi-enclosed sea' covered by Part IX of UNCLOS. Use of the words 'should co-operate' and 'shall endeavour"' in Article 123 of UNCLOS places a strong obligation on the littoral States to co-ordinate their activities as defined in the sub-paragraphs of that article. They should now recognise their legal obligation to cooperate in UNCLOS Part IX.

While resource management, the protection of the marine environment and marine scientific research are mentioned specifically as areas for cooperation, the opening sentence of Article 123 creates a more general obligation to cooperate. Article 123(d) also opens up the possibility of the littoral countries inviting other interested States or international organizations to cooperate with them in furtherance of the provisions of this article. Regional countries and external stakeholders in the South China Sea all have responsibilities under international law to protect the marine environment, including obligations to manage straddling and migratory fish stocks. However, these obligations are not being adhered to by the

> Australia also needs to develop a better understanding of China, including a more balanced and methodical approach to the relationship. For many in Australia, it is difficult to see China other than through American eyes and Cold War instincts that China is a looming threat. Yet it is clear that Australia has its own interests that are not necessarily the same as those of the United States.

---

62 Bob Carr, "Cut it out, Cold Warriors; the great China panic has gone too far already", *The Weekend Australian*, September 10–11, 2016, p. 18.

63 Bob Carr, "Think tank that sees hope in China needed', *The Sydney Morning Herald*, September 12, 2016, p. 16.

various parties involved.

On the credit side, the Award provides possible opportunities to go back to basics and start with 'a clean sheet of paper' in managing the South China Sea. The ruling provides opportunities, particularly by providing a basis for negotiations between the parties involved.[64] Constructive dialogue is required instead of destructive sniping. As the editors of East Asia Forum have rightly pointed out, 'It is not a time for grandstanding, adding insult to injury or taking action that could be construed as provocative'.[65] The focus of the negotiations should now be functional cooperation for activities, such as marine scientific research, fisheries management, protecting and preserving the marine environment, maritime law enforcement, and search and rescue. Unfortunately, the need for those forms of cooperation has been lost in recent rhetoric on the South China Sea.[66]

There is an opportunity here for Australia. Australia has a very large area of maritime jurisdiction, including important World Heritage sites, such as the Great Barrier Reef, with considerable expertise in the management of maritime areas, including fisheries management and arrangements for the preservation and protection of the marine environment. This expertise could possibly be turned to good use in the South China Sea under the provisions of UNCLOS Article 123 (d).

Conclusion and Future Prospects

Overall, the arbitration case and the Award have not helped Australia's interests. Australia's strong public reaction to the award has created tensions in its bilateral relations with China. The

> Australia has a very large area of maritime jurisdiction, including important World Heritage sites, such as the Great Barrier Reef, with considerable expertise in the management of maritime areas, including fisheries management and arrangements for the preservation and protection of the marine environment. This expertise could possibly be turned to good use in the South China Sea.

64 Yanmei Xie, "Landmark South China Sea Ruling Could Revive Negotiations," *International Crisis Group Commentary*, July 12, 2016, <https://www.crisisgroup.org/asia/north-east-asia/china/landmark-south-china-sea-ruling-could-revive-negotiations>.

65 Editors, East Asia Forum, "Moment for compromise in the South China Sea," *East Asia Forum*, 18 July 2016, <http://www.eastasiaforum.org/2016/07/18/moment-for-compromise-in-the-south-china-sea/>.

66 Zha Daojiong, "What Now for China?," *RSIS Commentary*, July 18, 2016, <https://www.rsis.edu.sg/rsis-publication/rsis/co16181-what-now-for-china/>.

case has highlighted Australia's anomalous position regarding delimitation of its maritime boundaries with Timor-Leste. The Award has thrown doubts on the legitimacy of Australia's claimed EEZ around some of its offshore features. It has also introduced further regional instability and new tensions in the China–United States bilateral relationship, as well as new divisive pressures within ASEAN, including fresh doubts about the ability of the ASEAN-led regional security framework to deal with the situation in the South China Sea. Lastly, the case and the Award have opened up new questions about just what constitutes the 'rules-based global order'.

Although there is a tendency to exaggerate some of Australia's interests in the South China Sea, particularly its dependence on freedoms of navigation through the sea, Australia does have legitimate interests in the region, including a strong interest in the avoidance of conflict. These provide the basis and justification for Australia to play an active role in efforts and initiatives to address issues in the South China Sea, including the effective management of the sea and activities within it.

The main limitation on Australia's policy options is the difficult foreign and defence policy balancing act it faces between China as its main trading partner and the United States as its major security partner. Any sign of wavering by Canberra towards China is viewed with concern by Washington. Nevertheless, Australia has forged a defence relationship with China through senior-level dialogue, educational exchanges, reciprocal naval ship visits, and humanitarian assistance and disaster relief exercises, involving the military forces of the two countries.

The case and the Award have opened up new questions about just what constitutes the 'rules-based global order'.

While Australia does not face a direct choice between China and the United States, it needs to be cognizant of where present trends are heading and of the geographical reality of its proximity to Southeast Asia. Its economic and security future is dependent on Southeast Asia. For these reasons, the main consideration in Australia's policy options should be the stability of the region, including peaceful resolution of the situation in the South China Sea. It can assist in this regard by promoting cooperation between the various stakeholders that can help build the necessary strategic trust between them. The need for restraint on all sides should continue to be the basic theme of Australia's policy.[67]

China and ASEAN should now be given space to work out their differences and explore cooperation for managing the South China Sea without pressure or provocation from extra-regional/non-litto-

---

67   Medcalf, "Rules, Balance and Lifelines," p. 11.

ral powers. There is no strategic imperative for these powers to take any action, including no extant threat to freedoms of navigation and overflight that warrant confrontational assertions of these freedoms. Dialogue between ASEAN and China should now

China and ASEAN should now be given space to work out their differences and explore cooperation for managing the South China Sea without pressure or provocation from extra-regional/non-littoral powers. There is no strategic imperative for these powers to take any action, including no extant threat to freedoms of navigation and overflight that warrant confrontational assertions of these freedoms.

be given the chance to work. As Australia's Foreign Minister has noted, 'It is an opportunity for the region to come together, and for claimants to re-engage in dialogue with each other based on greater clarity around maritime rights.'[68]

Sam Bateman retired from the RAN as a Commodore (one-star) and is now a Professorial Research Fellow at the Australian National Centre for Ocean Resources and Security (ANCORS) at the University of Wollongong in Australia, and an Adviser to the Maritime Security Programme at the S. Rajaratnam School of International Studies (RSIS) at the Nanyang Technological University in Singapore. He was awarded his PhD from the University of NSW for a dissertation on "The Strategic and Political Aspects of the Law of the Sea in East Asian Seas". He is widely recognized as a regional maritime security expert and regularly provides comments for Australian and international media. His current research interests include regional maritime security, piracy and maritime terrorism, oceans policy, the strategic and political implications of the Law of the Sea, and maritime cooperation and confidence-building.

---

68   Julie Bishop, "Australia supports peaceful dispute resolution in the South China Sea," Media release, Minister for Foreign Affairs, July 12, 2016.

Post-Arbitration South China Sea:

United States' Policy Options and Future Prospects

Raul (Pete) Pedrozo

Abstract

The Award issued by the Arbitral Tribunal in the South China Sea arbitration case presents the United States with a number of legal, diplomatic and security opportunities, as well as challenges. The Tribunal's decision reaffirms the well-established principle of freedom of navigation in the South China Sea and clarifies the status of the features in the region, which can be exploited by the U.S. to legally support its freedom of navigation assertions and presence operations in the South China Sea. On the other hand, the Tribunal's decision that a number of low-tide elevations occupied by China form part of the Philippine exclusive economic zone (EEZ) and continental shelf increase the risk of U.S. involvement in regional maritime disputes if the Philippines elects to exercise and enforce its rights and jurisdiction as confirmed by the Tribunal. Moreover, the Tribunal's sweeping determination that none of the features in the Spratly archipelago are entitled to an EEZ and its positions regarding environmental degradation and the applicability of the military activities exemption in UN-CLOS Article 298 could undermine U.S. efforts to become a party to the Convention.

Introduction

The Award issued by the Arbitral Tribunal on July 12, 2016, soundly repudiates what the U.S. Government views as China's excessive maritime claims and coercive behavior in the South China Sea, and has direct legal, diplomatic and security implications for the United States.[1] The Tribunal's Award reaffirms the time-honored principle of freedom of navigation by specifically rejecting the validity of China's infamous "nine-dash line," as well as China's claim to historic rights to resources in the waters encompassed within the line.

The Tribunal also clarified the status of a number of low-tide elevations,

---

1   Award, PCA Case No. 2013-19, Permanent Court of Arbitration, July 12, 2016, <http://www.pcacases.com/web/sendAttach/2086>.

and concluded that all of the high-tide land features in the Spratly archipelago are legally "rocks" under UNCLOS, Article 121, and therefore do not generate an exclusive economic zone (EEZ) or continental shelf. This clarification can be used to inform U.S. freedom of navigation (FON) and other operations in the South China Sea.

The Tribunal further found that Mischief Reef, Second Thomas Shoal and Reed Bank are low-tide elevations that form part of the Philippine EEZ and continental shelf, and that the Philippines has sovereign rights with respect to the sea areas in its EEZ. Therefore, the Tribunal concluded that China had violated the Philippines' sovereign rights with respect to its EEZ and continental shelf. If the Philippines elects to enforce these rights, it could have security implications for the U.S. under its Mutual Defense Treaty with the Philippines.

> The Tribunal concluded that China had violated the Philippines' sovereign rights with respect to its EEZ and continental shelf. If the Philippines elects to enforce these rights, it could have security implications for the U.S. under its Mutual Defense Treaty with the Philippines.

The Tribunal additionally considered the lawfulness of various Chinese activities in the South China Sea. In doing so, the Tribunal determined that China's large-scale land reclamation projects and construction of artificial islands in the South China Sea, as well as its ecologically unsound fishing practices, violated China's obligations under UNCLOS Articles 192 and 194 to preserve and protect the marine environment, a position that has been advocated by the U.S. since 2014.

Finally, the Tribunal concluded that Chinese law enforcement vessels obstructing Philippine access to Scarborough Shoal had violated China's obligations under the Convention on the International Regulations for Preventing Collisions at Sea (COLREGS 1972) and Article 94 of UNCLOS. Application of the Tribunal's reasoning could be extended to Chinese interference with U.S. surveillance operations in the South China Sea, resulting in a similar conclusion.

Policy Approach

The United States has an abiding interest in maintaining peace and stability in the South China Sea and has repeatedly called on the South China Sea claimants to resolve their differences through diplomatic efforts. Unilateral actions that change the status quo and increase tensions in the region, such as China's massive land reclamation activities, are of serious concern to the U.S. Consequently, since the U.S. first expressed an official position on the South China Sea dispute in 1995, it has consistently maintained that it is opposed to the use or threat of force to resolve the competing claims, has urged the claimants to exercise restraint and to avoid destabilizing actions, and has called on the parties to settle their disputes in a way that contributes to peace and prosperity in the region.[2] Thus, the U.S. welcomed the Philippines' decision to submit the case to arbitration in 2013, and has repeatedly reaffirmed its opposition to the "use of intimidation, coercion or force to assert a territorial claim," calling on the claimants to settle their disputes peacefully, diplomatically and in accordance with international law, such as arbitration.[3]

Maintaining freedom of navigation is equally important to the U.S. Unimpeded navigation by all ships and aircraft through the strategic sea lines of communication of the South China Sea is essential for the peace and prosperity of the Asia-Pacific region, as well as the U.S.. Thus, while maintaining its neutrality on the underlying sovereignty claims to the various land features in the South China Sea, the U.S. is opposed to any excessive maritime claim or restriction on maritime activity that is inconsistent with international law, and routinely challenges such unlawful claims by exercising freedom of navigation assertions and other military operations in the South China Sea.

> The U.S. is opposed to any excessive maritime claim or restriction on maritime activity that is inconsistent with international law, and routinely challenges such unlawful claims by exercising freedom of navigation assertions and other military operations in the South China Sea.

Beginning in 2014, U.S. officials stepped-up their criticism of the "nine-dash line," arguing that China's lack of clarity with regard to its South China Sea claims was creating "uncertainty, insecurity and in-

---

2   Christine Shelly, "Daily Press Briefing," Office of the Spokesman, US Department of State, May 10, 1995, <http://dosfan.lib.uic.edu/ERC/briefing/daily_briefings/1995/9505/950510db.html>.

3   Daniel Russel, "Maritime Disputes in East Asia," Testimony Before the House Committee on Foreign Affairs Subcommittee on Asia and the Pacific [HCFA Testimony], Department of State, February 5, 2014, <http://www.state.gov/p/eap/rls/rm/2014/02/221293.htm>; Daniel Russel, "Maritime Issues in East Asia," Testimony Before the Senate Foreign Relations Committee [SFRC Testimony], May 13, 2015, <http://www.foreign.senate.gov/imo/media/doc/051315_REVISED_Russel_Testimony.pdf>; The Asia-Pacific Maritime Security Strategy: Achieving U.S. National Security Objectives in a Changing Environment, US Department of Defense, August 14, 2015, p. 6, <http://www.defense.gov/Portals/1/Documents/pubs/NDAA%20A-P_Maritime_SecuritY_Strategy-08142015-1300-FINALFORMAT.PDF>; John Kirby, "Daily Press Briefing," Office of Press Relations, Bureau of Public Affairs, US Department of State, October 29, 2015, <http://www.state.gov/r/pa/prs/dpb/2015/10/248963.htm>; John Kirby, "Decision in the Philippines-China Arbitration," Press Statement, Office of Press Relations, Bureau of Public Affairs, US Department of State, July 12, 2016, <http://www.state.gov/r/pa/prs/ps/2016/07/259587.htm>.

stability in the region."[4] U.S. officials further indicated that use of the "nine dash line" to "claim maritime rights not based on claimed land features would be inconsistent with international law," and called on China "to clarify or adjust..." its claim to bring it in line with international law.[5]

The Department of State also released a study in 2014 that analyzes China's maritime claims in the South China Sea. The study criticized China for not clarifying its claims associated with the "nine-dash line" in a manner consistent with international law.[6] The study concluded that, unless China clarifies that its claim is restricted only to islands within the line "and any maritime zones that are generated from those land features...," the "nine-dash line" claim "does not accord with the international law of the sea."[7]

Implications of the Award

Although the U.S. views the Tribunal's hallmark decision as strongly supporting the rule of law and directly contributing to the shared goal of peacefully resolving the South China Sea territorial and maritime disputes, the Award presents a number of important legal, diplomatic and security implications for the U.S., not all of which are consistent with U.S. interests.

Legal Implications

From a legal perspective, the Award could prove to be a double-edged sword for the U.S. On the one hand, it confirms the U.S. position that the "nine-dash line" and Chinese maritime claims in the South China Sea have no basis in international law, thus reinforcing the importance of freedom of navigation. The reasoning applied by the Tribunal to reach this conclusion supports U.S. opposition to similar spurious claims, such as Chile's Mar Presencial, Libya's line-of-death, and Canada's arctic claims. Additionally, the U.S. could leverage the Tribunal's determination that Chinese vessels violated COLREGS by engaging in unsafe maneuvers, arguing that Chinese law enforcement and non-state vessels have engaged in similar harassment of U.S. surveillance ships operating in the South China Sea.

On the other hand, the Tribunal's sweeping decision that none of the features in the Spratly Islands are entitled to claim an EEZ could be used by nations to challenge U.S. EEZ claims, particularly in the Aleutians and the Northwest Hawaiian Islands. In determining the status of the features in the South China Sea under Article 121, the Tribunal concluded "that the entitlements of a feature depend on (a) the objective capacity of a feature, (b) in its natural condition, to sustain either (c) a stable community of people or (d) economic activity that is neither dependent on outside resources nor purely extractive in nature."[8] It is questionable whether many of the outlying features in the Aleutians or Northwest Hawaiian Islands are capable of sustaining a stable community of people or economic activity that is not dependent on outside resources or purely ex-

> The Tribunal's sweeping decision that none of the features in the Spratly Islands are entitled to claim an EEZ could be used by nations to challenge U.S. EEZ claims, particularly in the Aleutians and the Northwest Hawaiian Islands.

4   Russel, HCFA Testimony.

5   Russel, HCFA Testimony; Russel, SFRC Testimony.

6   *Limits in the Seas No. 143: China: Maritime Claims in the South China Sea*, Bureau of Oceans and International Environmental and Scientific Affairs, US Department of State, December 5, 2014, p. 23, <https://www.state.gov/documents/organization/234936.pdf>.

7   *Limits in the Seas No. 143*, p. 24.

8   "The Tribunal Renders Its Award," Press Release, Permanent Court of Arbitration, July 12, 2016, p. 9, <http://www.pcacases.com/web/sendAttach/1801>; Award, paras. 539–553.

tractive in nature.

Diplomatic Implications

Diplomatically, the United States has been unable to garner widespread international support, including that of the other South China Sea claimants, to endorse the Award. Even the new Philippine government appears to have lost its appetite to enforce its newly affirmed maritime rights, thereby sending mixed signals on the enforceability of the Award. U.S. policy to engage cussions.[9] China's strident response to the Tribunal's decision and its continued destabilizing actions, coupled with the lackluster support for the ruling by the international community, are arguably more significant in terms of diplomatic implications than the Award itself. Some notable examples include:

1. China renewed its threat to declare an Air Defense Identification Zone over the South China Sea with minimal reaction from the international community, except from the U.S.[10]

> The United States has been unable to garner widespread international support, including that of the other South China Sea claimants, to endorse the Award.

in military-to-military relations with China has similarly sent mixed signals on holding China accountable for not complying with the ruling. More importantly, the Tribunal's decisions could have the unintended consequence of undermining U.S. efforts to become a party to UNCLOS. Opponents to the Convention could argue that the arbitration sets a precedent that will expose the U.S. to frivolous legal action in U.S. and international tribunals.

Ironically, China appears to have benefited most diplomatically from the arbitration. Following public release of the Award, China vehemently denounced the Tribunal's decision as "null and void" and has flagrantly failed to comply with the pronouncement with no apparent adverse reper-

2. Chief of Naval Operations Admiral John Richardson, making his first official visit to China two days after the release of the Award, was rebuked by his Chinese counterpart, Admiral Wu Shengli, regarding China's land reclamation activities, indicating that China would not stop con-

---

9   "With regard to the award rendered on 12 July 2016 by the Arbitral Tribunal in the South China Sea arbitration…, the Ministry of Foreign Affairs of the People's Republic of China solemnly declares that the award is null and void and has no binding force. China neither accepts nor recognizes it. … China's territorial sovereignty and maritime rights and interests in the South China Sea shall under no circumstances be affected by those awards. China opposes and will never accept any claim or action based on those awards." See "Statement of the Ministry of Foreign Affairs of the People's Republic of China on the Award of 12 July 2016 of the Arbitral Tribunal in the South China Sea Arbitration Established at the Request of the Republic of the Philippines," Xinhua / Ministry of Foreign Affairs, People's Republic of China, July 12, 2016, <http://news.xinhuanet.com/english/2016-07/12/c_135507744.htm>.

10 An Baijie, "Air defense zone called option," *China Daily*, July 14, 2016, <http://www.chinadaily.com.cn/world/2016-07/14/content_26080422.htm>; "South China Sea: China 'has right to set up air defence zone," BBC, July 13, 2016, <http://www.bbc.com/news/world-asia-china-36781138>; Andrew Tilghman, "Top U.S. admiral: Trip to China looked for ways to reduce friction between navies," *Military Times*, July 26, 2016, <http://www.militarytimes.com/story/military/pentagon/2016/07/26/cno-china/87569146/>.

struction on the Spratly Islands. Admiral Sun Jianguo, Deputy Chief of the Joint Staff Department of the Central Military Commission, further warned that U.S. FON operations in the South China Sea "could play out in a disastrous way."[11]

Following the ASEAN meeting in Laos, Secretary of State John Kerry encouraged the Philippines to engage in dialogue and negotiations with China over the South China Sea issue.

3. The People's Liberation Army Air Force (PLAAF) conducted combat air patrols over disputed areas in the South China Sea and Scarborough Shoal to increase "response capabilities to all kinds of security threats and [safeguard] national sovereignty, security and maritime interests" with no apparent reaction from the other claimants.[12]

4. PLA Navy ships successfully completed participation in the U.S.-hosted Rim of the Pacific exercise, enhancing their war fighting capabilities and scoring a major political and strategic communications coup, despite its repudiation of the Tri-

bunal's Award.[13]

5. ASEAN issued a watered-down joint communiqué following the 49th ASEAN Foreign Ministers' Meeting in Vientiane, Laos. Although the communiqué expresses concern over land reclamation activities and stresses the importance of freedom of navigation in and over the South China Sea, it fails to specifically mention China or the Arbitral Tribunal's Award.[14] Moreover, China secured a commitment from the Foreign Ministers agreeing to refrain from occupying any of the remaining uninhabited features in the South China Sea.[15]

6. Similarly, the European Union's declaration on recent developments in the South China Sea merely "acknowledge[s]" the Award, instead stressing the importance of freedom of navigation and calling on all claimants to refrain from militarizing the region.[16]

7. Following the ASEAN meeting in Laos, Secretary of State John Kerry encouraged the Philippines to engage in dialogue

---

11 Sam LaGrone, "PLAN's Wu to CNO Richardson: Beijing Won't Stop South China Sea Island Building," *USNI News*, July 18, 2016, <https://news.usni.org/2016/07/18/plans-wu-cno-richardson-beijing-wont-stop-south-china-sea-island-building>; Andrew Tilghman, "Top U.S. admiral: Trip to China looked for ways to reduce friction between navies," *Military Times*, July 26, 2016, <http://www.militarytimes.com/story/military/pentagon/2016/07/26/cno-china/87569146/>.

12 "China's air force flies combat patrol over disputed islands," Reuters, August 6, 2016, <http://www.reuters.com/article/us-southchinasea-china-patrols-idUSKCN10H091>; Anders Corr, "Chinese Bomber Buzzes Philippines' Scarborough Shoal In Latest Salvo Of U.S.-China Signalling War," *Forbes*, July 17, 2016, <http://www.forbes.com/sites/anderscorr/2016/07/17/chinese-bomber-buzzes-philippines-scarborough-shoal-in-latest-salvo-of-u-s-china-signalling-war/>.

13 "Our participation in the RIMPAC 2016 exercise is a trip for friendship, cooperation and exhibition, not only showcasing our strength, but also conveying our sincere goodwill for seeking peace. The Chinese Navy is willing to cooperate with the navies of all peace-loving countries, so as to jointly safeguard world peace and regional stability." Li Ruojun, "Chinese warships return after RIMPAC 2016 exercise," China Military Online, August 8, 2016, <http://english.chinamil.com.cn/news-channels/2016-08/08/content_7196509.htm>.

14 "Joint Communiqué of the 49th ASEAN Foreign Ministers' Meeting," Association of Southeast Asian Nations, July 24, 2016, <http://asean.org/storage/2016/07/Joint-Communique-of-the-49th-AMM-ADOPTED.pdf>.

15 "Joint Statement of the Foreign Ministers of ASEAN Member States and China on the Full and Effective Implementation of the Declaration on the Conduct of Parties in the South China Sea," Association of Southeast Asian Nations, July 25, 2016, <http://asean.org/storage/2016/07/Joint-Statement-on-the-full-and-effective-implementation-of-the-DOC-FINAL.pdf>.

16 "Declaration by the High Representative on behalf of the EU on the Award rendered in the Arbitration between the Republic of the Philippines and the People's Republic of China," Press Release, European Council, July 15, 2016, <http://www.consilium.europa.eu/en/press/press-releases/2016/07/15-south-china-sea-arbitration/>.

and negotiations with China over the South China Sea issue.[17]

8. Despite have decisively won the arbitration case, the Philippine government advised its fishermen to avoid fishing areas in the South China Sea, including Scarborough Shoal, to avoid harassment from Chinese authorities.[18]

industries,[21] the U.S. is not yet a party to the Convention. This lack of U.S. participation has been systematically criticized by China[22] and has been recognized by the administration as an obstacle to its ability to resolve problems in the South China Sea.[23] It is therefore understandable that the Tribunal's Award has resulted in a renewed call by supporters of UNCLOS to push for Senate advice and consent.[24] Although the Award provides

> Although the Award provides an impetus for U.S. accession to UNCLOS, it could also be used by opponents to the Convention to derail any efforts to obtain Senate action.

9. DoD did not conduct an FON operation in the South China Sea from May 2016 to October 2016,[19] even though U.S. defense officials stated that DoD would conduct at least two FON operations in the South China Sea per quarter to "regularly exercise our rights under international law and remind the Chinese and others about our view."[20]

The Tribunal's Award could also potentially undermine the efforts within the US government to become a party to UNCLOS. Despite widespread support within the U.S. government, non-governmental organizations and maritime

an impetus for U.S. accession, it could also be used by opponents to the Convention to derail any efforts to obtain Senate action.

One of the major criticisms of the Convention is that, if the U.S. were to accede to UNCLOS, the compulsory dispute settlement provisions could

17 John Kerry, "Press Availability in Vientiane, Laos," US Department of State, July 26, 2016, <http://www.state.gov/secretary/remarks/2016/07/260475.htm>; John Kerry, "Remarks With Philippines Foreign Secretary Perfecto Yasay," US Department of State, July 27, 2016, <http://www.state.gov/secretary/remarks/2016/07/260541.htm>.

18 "Philippines warns fishermen to steer clear of disputed South China Sea," AFP, August 3, 2016, <http://www.firstpost.com/world/philippines-warns-fishermen-to-steer-clear-of-disputed-south-china-sea-2932132.html>.

19 Zack Cooper and Bonnie Glaser, "How America Picks Its Next Move in the South China Sea," *The National Interest*, May 11, 2016, <http://nationalinterest.org/feature/how-america-picks-its-next-move-the-south-china-sea-16153>; Idrees Ali and Matt Spetalnick, "U.S. warship challenges China's claims in South China Sea," Reuters, October 21, 2016, <http://www.reuters.com/article/us-southchinasea-usa-exclusive-idUSKCN12L1O9>.

20 Andrea Shalal and Idrees Ali, "U.S. Navy plans two or more patrols in South China Sea per quarter," Reuters, November 2, 2015, <http://www.reuters.com/article/us-southchinasea-usa-navy-idUSKCN0SR28W20151103>.

21 See, for example, Center for Ocean Law and Policy website <http://www.virginia.edu/colp/los.html>, US Department of State website <http://www.state.gov/e/oes/lawofthesea/>, and Department of the Navy website <http://www.jag.navy.mil/organization/code_10_law_of_the_sea.htm.>

22 "Some Americans regard themselves as the defender of maritime governance, but the United States still refuses to ratify the United Nations Convention on the Law of the Sea, 34 years after the document was signed." See Lu Kang, "Foreign Ministry Spokesperson Lu Kang's Remarks on Statement by Spokesperson of the US State Department on South China Sea Arbitration," Ministry of Foreign Affairs, People's Republic of China July 13, 2016, <http://www.fmprc.gov.cn/mfa_eng/xwfw_665399/s2510_665401/t1380409.shtml>.

23 Barack Obama, "Remarks by the President at the United States Military Academy Commencement Ceremony," Speech, Office of the Press Secretary, The White House, May 28, 2014, <https://www.whitehouse.gov/the-press-office/2014/05/28/remarks-president-united-states-military-academy-commencement-ceremony>.

24 Sydney J. Freedberg, Jr., "Law Of The Sea: US In, China Out? Dems Push Ratification," Breaking Defense, July 12, 2016, <http://breakingdefense.com/2016/07/law-of-the-sea-us-in-china-out-dems-push-ratification/>; Dave Majumdar, "Why the United States Needs to Join UNCLOS," *The National Interest*, July 12, 2016, <http://nationalinterest.org/blog/the-buzz/why-the-united-states-needs-join-unclos-16948>; Ben Cardin, "The South China Sea Is the Reason the United States Must Ratify UNCLOS," *Foreign Policy*, July 13, 2016, <http://foreignpolicy.com/2016/07/13/the-south-china-sea-is-the-reason-the-united-states-must-ratify-unclos/>.

open the U.S. "to any number of specious allegations brought by opportunistic nations, including allegations of environmental degradation or polluting the ocean environment with carbon emissions or even from land-based sources."[25] Adverse judgments would be final and enforceable by U.S. courts.[26]

Proponents of the Convention argue that the U.S. can protect itself from spurious litigation by declaring under UNLCOS Article 298 that they do not accept compulsory dispute settlement with respect to, *inter alia*, military and law enforcement activities.[27] The Tribunal nonetheless noted that Article 298(1)(b) only applies to "disputes concerning military activities" and not to all "military activities" as such, focusing on "whether the dispute itself concerns military activities, rather than whether a party has employed its military in some manner in relation to the dispute."[28] The tribunal also decided that Article 298(1)(b) would not limit its "ancillary jurisdiction to prescribe provisional measures in respect to military activities taking place in relation to a dispute that does not, itself, concern military activities."[29] It is therefore unclear whether the U.S. could shield itself from frivolous allegations by invoking the military activities exemption.

> The Tribunal's decisions could increase the risk of U.S. military involvement in the dispute if Philippine units enforcing the Award were attacked by Chinese maritime and air forces.

Security Implications

The United States has treaty commitments to defend the Philippines if certain contingencies occur. Thus, the Tribunal's decisions could increase the risk of U.S. military involvement in the dispute if Philippine units enforcing the Award were attacked by Chinese maritime and air forces. These security implications are compounded by the fact that traditional U.S. allies, like Japan, have disavowed previous offers to

---

25 "U.N. Convention on the Law of the Sea: It's Still a Bad Idea," The Heritage Foundation, July 7, 2011, <http://www.heritage.org/research/factsheets/2011/07/un-convention-on-the-law-of-the-sea-its-still-a-bad-idea>.

26 Steven Groves, "The Law of the Sea: Costs of U.S. Accession to UNCLOS," Hearing before the United States Senate Committee on Foreign Relations, The Heritage Foundation, June 14, 2012, <http://www.heritage.org/research/testimony/2012/06/the-law-of-the-sea-convention-treaty-doc-103-39>.

27 "Message from the President of the United States," Senate Treaty Document 103-39, October 7, 1994, pp. X, 83–84, 86, <http://www.foreign.senate.gov/imo/media/doc/treaty_103-39.pdf>.

28 Award, para. 1158.

29 Award, para. 1158.

jointly patrol the South China Sea with the U.S. Navy.[30] Even the new Philippine government has indicated that it will not conduct joint patrols with the U.S., citing Chinese concerns.[31]

Nonetheless, as noted in the Tribunal's proceedings, China has routinely interfered with the Philippines exclusive resource rights in its EEZ in the vicinity of Mischief Reed, Second Thomas Shoal, Reed Bank and Scarborough Shoal.[32] In the past, the Philippines has not been reluctant to deploy military assets to support its resource exploration activities or respond to Chinese harassment. In March 2011, Manila deployed a Philippine Air Force OV-10 Bronco light attack/observation aircraft and a Navy reconnaissance aircraft to investigate reported harassment of the seismic survey vessel M/V *Veritas Voyager* by two Chinese patrol boats in the vicinity of Reed Bank.[33] In October 2011, the BRP *Rizal* (PS-74) collided with a Chinese fishing vessel after it was dispatched to Reed Bank to investigate illegal Chinese fishing activities 80 nm off Palawan.[34] In December 2011, the BRP *Gregorio del Pilar* (PF-15) deployed to the West Philippine Sea to protect ongoing energy projects in the Malampaya oil and gas field off Palawan.[35] In April 2012, the BRP *Gregorio Del Pilar* (PF-15) attempted to arrest 15 Chinese fishing vessels that were caught illegally fishing in the vicinity of Scarborough Shoal, but was prevented from doing so mission by two Chinese surveillance ships—*Zhonggou Haijian* 75 and 84.[36] In addition, the BRP *Sierra Madre* (LT-57), with a Philippine Marine detachment on board, remains aground on Second Thomas Shoal.

> The new Philippine government has indicated that it will not conduct joint patrols with the U.S., citing Chinese concerns.

---

30   "Japan's top admiral urges resumption of China port calls to ease tensions," Reuters, September 27, 2016, <http://www.japantimes.co.jp/news/2016/09/27/national/politics-diplomacy/msdf-top-brass-urges-resumption-china-port-calls-ease-tensions/>.

31   "Philippine President Says He'll Open Trade Alliances With China, Russia," NPR, September 26, 2016, <http://www.npr.org/sections/thetwo-way/2016/09/26/495490988/philippine-president-says-hell-open-trade-alliances-with-china-russia>.

32   Award, paras. 652–667, 685, 669–680, 686, 761–781.

33   James Kraska and Raul Pedrozo, *International Maritime Security Law*, Brill, 2013, p. 341.

34   Jaime Laude and Minnie Villanueva, "Navy Ship Scares Off Chinese Towing Boat," *Philippine Star*, October 19, 2011; "Philippines Apologizes To China Over Sea Accident," *Philippine Star*, October 19, 2011.

35   Alexis Romero, "Phl Navy: Deployment Of Warship To Spratlys Will Not Increase Tensions," *Philippine Star*, December 18, 2011.

36   Priam Nepomuceno, "PHL Navy to Stand its Ground on Scarborough Shoal Stand-Off," *Zambo Times*, April 11, 2012.

The Tribunal determined that Mischief Reef, Second Thomas Shoal and Reed Bank are low-tide elevations that form part of the Philippine EEZ and continental shelf. Accordingly, the Tribunal ruled that the Philippines has exclusive rights to explore and exploit the living and non-living resources in its EEZ and continental shelf. Initial exploration of the Reed Bank by the Philippine Department of Energy in 2005 revealed that the area contains about 3.4 trillion cubic feet of natural gas and 440 million barrels of oil.[37] If confirmed, these oil and gas fields could provide ing the Philippines.[39] Article IV of the U.S.-Philippines Mutual Defense Treaty (MDT) provides that "[e]ach Party recognizes that an armed attack in the Pacific area on either of the Parties would be dangerous to its own peace and safety and declares that it would act to meet the common dangers in accordance with its constitutional processes."[40] An armed attack includes "an armed attack on ... its armed forces, public vessels or aircraft in the Pacific."[41] Therefore, although the U.S. does not recognize Philippines territorial claims in the South China Sea, an attack by Chi-

> The Tribunal's decision could embolden the Philippines to reinvigorate its resource exploration and exploitation efforts in the vicinity of these features, and based on past practice it is not inconceivable that Manila will deploy naval ships and aircraft to support these efforts.

much needed energy resources to fuel the Philippine economy.[38] The Tribunal also found that China had violated its duty to respect Filipino traditional fishing rights at Scarborough Shoal. The Tribunal's decision regarding these matters could embolden the Philippines to reinvigorate its resource exploration and exploitation efforts in the vicinity of these features, and based on past practice it is not inconceivable that Manila will deploy naval ships and aircraft to support these efforts.

Although the U.S. does not recognize the Philippines' claims to the Kalayaan Island Group (KIG) in the Spratlys, U.S. officials have repeatedly stated that the U.S. will honor its security commitments to allies and partners in the region, includ-

nese forces against the BRP Sierra Madre (LT-57) at Second Thomas Shoal or other Filipino military units enforcing Philippine resource rights in the KIG or Scarborough Shoal, could trigger U.S. defense commitments under the MDT.

Policy Options

Although the U.S. does not take a position with regard to the legal merits of the competing claims to sovereignty over the various land features in the South China Sea, the Tribunal's de-

---

37 Jaime Laude, "Spratlys: Chinese Jets Buzzed PAF Patrol Planes/Noy – No Hurry to Protest," *Philippine Star*, May 21, 2011.

38 Al Labita, "Philippines Embraces U.S., Repels China," *Asia Times*, March 22, 2011; Alena Mae S. Flores, "UK Oil Firm Completes South China Sea Survey," *Manila Standard*, March 23, 2011.

39 Daniel Russel, SFRC Testimony; Daniel Russel, "Remarks at the Fifth Annual South China Sea Conference," Center for Strategic and International Studies / Bureau of East Asian and Pacific Affairs, July 21, 2015, <http://www.state.gov/p/eap/rls/rm/2015/07/245142.htm>; Tarra Quismundo, "US: We stand by our allies," *Philippine Daily Inquirer*, April 5, 2014, <http://globalnation.inquirer.net/101672/us-we-stand-by-our-allies>.

40 The Mutual Defense Treaty between the Philippines and the United States of America, 1951, 3 UST 3947, TIAS 2529, 177 UNTS 77, Art. IV.

41 The Mutual Defense Treaty between the Philippines and the United States of America, 1951, 3 UST 3947, TIAS 2529, 177 UNTS 77, Art. V.

cision affects U.S. security and economic interests in the region. It is therefore incumbent on the U.S. to explore the possibility of raising a number of legal, diplomatic and security policy options in response to the Award.

Legal Policy Options

The landmark decision is clearly viewed by the U.S. as a resounding victory for freedom of the seas and the rules-based legal order that it has championed since the end of the Second World War. However, the Tribunal went too far in holding that none of the features in the South China Sea are entitled to an EEZ and continental shelf because they are incapable of sustaining a stable community of people or economic activity that is not dependent on outside resources

The Tribunal went too far in holding that none of the features in the South China Sea are entitled to an EEZ and continental shelf. The U.S. should therefore temper its public support for the Award to those portions of the Tribunal's decision that have a sound basis in international law, including UNCLOS.

or purely extractive in nature. The U.S. should therefore temper its public support for the Award to those portions of the Tribunal's decision that have a sound basis in international law, including UNCLOS, and accentuate the regional and bilateral aspect of the ruling—*i.e.*, the South China Sea.

The Tribunal correctly found that the artificial islands constructed by China on barren rocks and low-tide elevations are not entitled to the full range of maritime zones. Nonetheless, other features in the Spratlys have been occupied, albeit sporadically, since the 1800s, first by Great Britain, then France, Japan, Vietnam and finally Taiwan.[42] Some of these features, particularly Itu Aba Island, could qualify as islands under UNCLOS, Article 121. It is understandable why the Tribunal reached such a conclusion—an EEZ/continental

---

42   Raul (Pete) Pedrozo, "China versus Vietnam: An Analysis of the Competing Claims in the South China Sea," CNA Occasional Paper, Center for Naval Analyses, August 2014, <https://www.cna.org/cna_files/pdf/IOP-2014-U-008433. pdf>.

shelf extension from Itu Aba would overlap Philippine claims in the South China Sea, which could lead to further confrontations with the other claimants. The United States should nevertheless distance itself from the Tribunal's analysis regarding the status of features, emphasizing that the Tribunal, while well-intended, erred in making such a sweeping determination.

Diplomatic Policy Options

Diplomatically, the United States must do a better job of rallying international support for the Award, particularly from its regional allies, ASEAN and other maritime nations. The Award also presents the U.S. with the opportunity to subtly abandon its position of neutrality with regard to the underlying sovereignty claims to some of the South China Sea land features and Scarborough Shoal.

> The United States should distance itself from the Tribunal's analysis regarding the status of features, emphasizing that the Tribunal, while well-intended, erred in making such a sweeping determination.

Historically, the U.S. has not taken a position on the underlying sovereignty claims in the South China Sea. However, it may be time for Washington to reverse course and publicly support the Philippines' claim to Scarborough Shoal, Reed Bank, Mischief Reef and Second Thomas Shoal. The latter three are low-tide elevations that clearly reside within the Philippine EEZ/continental shelf. As a matter of law, they are under the exclusive jurisdiction of the Philippines, and U.S. recognition of Philippine sovereign rights should not be viewed as taking sides in the South China Sea dispute. Additionally, there is abundant evidence to support a conclusion that the Philippines has a superior claim to Scarborough Shoal.[43] Historical Spanish and U.S. documents dating back to the 1800s, as well as U.S. and Filipino administration and control of the features during the 1900s, conclusively show that Scarborough Shoal is Philippine territory.[44]

International support for the Award has been somewhat restrained, with few nations calling on the parties to respect and comply with it.

---

43 Raul (Pete) Pedrozo, "China versus Vietnam: An Analysis of the Competing Claims in the South China Sea," August 2014; Mark Rosen, "Philippine Claims in the South China Sea: A Legal Analysis," CNA Occasional Paper, Center for Naval Analyses, August 2014, <https://www.cna.org/cna_files/pdf/IOP-2014-U-008435.pdf>.

44 Raul (Pete) Pedrozo, "China versus Vietnam: An Analysis of the Competing Claims in the South China Sea," August 2014, pp. 131-132; Mark Rosen, "Philippine Claims in the South China Sea: A Legal Analysis," August 2014, pp. 9-17.

Apart from the U.S., Japan,[45] Australia,[46] and a few other countries,[47] the international community has failed to call on the Philippines and China to abide by the ruling. India, a major force for peace and stability in the region, simply "noted" the Award and expressed its support for freedom of navigation. Singapore, Malaysia and Indonesia expressed similar lackluster support for the decision.[48] The U.S. must therefore

> The U.S. must maintain a persistent and credible presence in the region in order to deter Chinese aggression, create an atmosphere where diplomatic efforts can prevail, and respond decisively if needed.

redouble its efforts to secure public statements from other nations and regional organizations that demand Chinese and Philippine compliance with the Tribunal's Award.[49]

Security Policy Options

The United States has a fundamental interest in maintaining freedom of navigation in and over the South China Sea. Unhindered navigation and overflight by all ships and aircraft is essential for the peace and prosperity of the entire Asia-Pacific region. Any maritime claim or restriction on maritime activities in the South China Sea that is inconsistent with UNCLOS would be of serious concern to the U.S. Accordingly, U.S. forces will continue to "fly, sail, and operate wherever international

45 Fumio Kishida, "Arbitration between the Republic of the Philippines and the People's Republic of China regarding the South China Sea (Final Award by the Arbitral Tribunal)," Statement, Ministry of Foreign Affairs of Japan, July 12, 2016, <http://www.mofa.go.jp/press/release/press4e_001204.html>.

46 Julie Bishop, "Australia supports peaceful dispute resolution in the South China Sea," Media Release, Minister for Foreign Affairs, July 12, 2016, <http://foreignminister.gov.au/releases/Pages/2016/jb_mr_160712a.aspx>.

47 "Who Is Taking Sides After the South China Sea Ruling?," Asia Maritime Transparency Initiative, Center for Strategic and International Studies, August 15, 2016, <https://amti.csis.org/sides-in-south-china-sea/>.

48 "Malaysia, Singapore, Indonesia react to S. China Sea ruling," Kyodo News, July 13, 2016, <http://news.abs-cbn.com/overseas/07/13/16/malaysia-singapore-indonesia-react-to-s-china-sea-ruling>.

49 See, for example, "Joint Statement of the Japan-United States-Australia Trilateral Strategic Dialogue," Office of the Spokesperson, US Department of State, July 25, 2016, <http://www.state.gov/r/pa/prs/ps/2016/07/260442.htm>.

law allows so that others can do the same."[50]

To achieve this objective, the U.S. must maintain a persistent and credible presence in the region in order to deter Chinese aggression, create an atmosphere where diplomatic efforts can prevail, and respond decisively if needed. Increasing the number of routine patrols throughout the region, as well as the frequency and complexity of bilateral and multilateral exercises with regional partners, will help preserve navigational rights and freedoms and other lawful uses of the sea and airspace guaranteed to all nations. The Tribunal's decision additionally provides a clear legal basis for U.S. forces to conduct operations within 12 nm of China's artificial islands constructed on low-tide elevations with impunity, since these features are not entitled to a territorial sea.

The U.S. cannot and should not, however, go it alone. All nations, particularly regional states, share a responsibility in maintaining peace, stability and prosperity in the Asia-Pacific region. In this regard, the U.S. must leverage the existing regional security architecture and work with its allies and

> The Award provides an important test case for the prominence of UNCLOS as a "Constitution for the Oceans."

partners to enhance their maritime capacity and build greater interoperability through combined exercises, integrated operations, and improved maritime domain awareness. This will allow the U.S. and its partners to employ their maritime capabilities most effectively and efficiently.

Conclusion and Future Prospects

The Asia-Pacific is at a crossroads. The Award provides an important test case for the prominence of UNCLOS as a "Constitution for the Oceans," as well as highlighting the importance the Convention places on abiding by the rule of law. Faced with China's fervent repudiation of and blatant disregard for the Tribunal's decision, the international community has two choices – it can unite, stand up to Chinese aggression and exact a price for China's misbehavior, or it can do nothing and allow the South China Sea dispute to become the Sudetenland of the 21st century.

U.S. national and economic security depends, in part, on the

---

50 Abraham M. Denmark, "Testimony of Abraham M. Denmark, Deputy Assistant Secretary of Defense for East Asia," Testimony at Hearing on South China Sea Maritime Disputes, House Committee on Armed Services, Subcommittee on Seapower and Projection Forces / House Committee on Foreign Affairs, Subcommittee on Asia and the Pacific, July 7, 2016, <http://docs.house.gov/meetings/FA/FA05/20160707/105166/HHRG-114-FA05-Wstate-DenmarkA-20160707.pdf>.

maintenance of peace and stability in the South China Sea. The U.S. will therefore continue to oppose unilateral acts that it views as increasing tensions in the region (e.g., China's large-scale reclamation activities); urge claimants to exercise restraint and refrain from coercive and provocative behavior designed to change the status quo (e.g., China's

> The international community has two choices – it can unite, stand up to Chinese aggression and exact a price for China's misbehavior, or it can do nothing and allow the South China Sea dispute to become the Sudetenland of the 21st century.

militarization of its South China Sea outposts); encourage claimants to resolve their differences peacefully (e.g., through international arbitration); and maintain a credible military presence in the Asia-Pacific to deter the use or threat of force to resolve the competing claims in the South China Sea. China can also be assured that U.S. forces will continue to fly, sail, and operate wherever international law allows.

Captain Raul (Pete) Pedrozo (Ret.) is a non-resident fellow in the Stockton Center for the Study of International Law at the Naval War College. He previously served as Staff Judge Advocate, US Pacific Command, and Special Assistant to the Under Secretary of Defense for Policy. The views expressed herein do not necessarily represent the position of the US Government or the US Department of Defense.

Part IV:
Conclusion

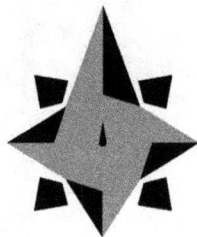

Post-Arbitration South China Sea:

International Legal Perspectives on the South China Sea Dispute after the Tribunal's Award on the Merits

Chris Whomersley

Abstract

This chapter aims to consider what implications there are for international law, and particularly the rules on settlement of disputes, in the light of the Award on Merits in the South China Sea. It addresses the issues of sovereignty over land territory, the nine-dash line, maritime delimitation, legal interpretations of rocks and islands, offshore archipelagos, fishing rights, dispute aggravation, implementation, and relevant issues. In particular, it considers what issues the Award could not deal with, how cogent its views are on the issues it did deal with and what the possible implications for the future are.

Introduction

The Award on the Merits issued by the Tribunal in the Philippines v. China arbitration case, apart from being highly controversial, is a lengthy and complex decision, amounting to 479 pages and 1202 paragraphs. No doubt there will be academic discussion of the decision, as well as, in due course, judicial consideration. This concluding chapter discusses some of the immediate implications of the Award for international law.

Sovereignty over Land Territory

The first point to note is that the Award could not, and did not, decide questions of sovereignty over land territory. Its jurisdiction was limited to "disputes concerning the interpretation or application of the Convention" (i.e., the United Nations Convention on the Law of the Sea, or UNCLOS) by virtue of Article 286 of UNCLOS. The Tribunal itself emphasised this point at both stages of the proceedings. It thus follows that the underlying sovereignty dispute between the Philippines and China, and indeed the disputes between China and the other States claiming sovereignty over features in the South China Sea, remain unresolved. There is no current mechanism whereby these disputes can be compulsorily submitted to judicial settlement without the agreement of all the parties. Moreover, given the extreme sensitivity of all States about sovereignty disputes, there is realistically no possibility that such disputes might become subject to such a compulsory regime in the foreseeable future. The fact that the fundamental dispute between the Philippines and China remains unresolved strengthens the view that the Tribunal should have thought carefully before proceeding to exercise jurisdiction when the Philippines initiated arbitration.

The Nine-Dash Line

A related point concerns the so-called nine-dash line. There has been much media comment on how the Tribunal dealt with this point. For example, the BBC reported that "an international tribunal has ruled against Chinese claims to rights in the South China Sea, backing a case brought by the Philippines."[1] However, properly, on the basis of the decisions and preconditions which the Tribunal itself made – and as indeed is inherent in its position as a body deciding disputes about the interpretation or application of UNCLOS – the Tribunal could not decide upon the sovereignty over any land territory within the nine-dash line, but only whether or not, in relation to claims to maritime zones generated by land territory in the South China Sea, UNCLOS would be the basis upon which those claims could be made. In other words, the only question which the Tribunal could consider was whether by acceding to UNCLOS China could thereafter claim solely those maritime zones provided for by UNCLOS. It was on this limited issue that the Tribunal made a decision about the nine-dash line, but even then the Tribunal said, perhaps rather defensively, that "in ratifying [UNCLOS], China has, in fact, relinquished far less in terms of its claim to historic

> The Tribunal could not decide upon the sovereignty over any land territory within the nine-dash line, but only whether or not, in relation to claims to maritime zones generated by land territory in the South China Sea, UNCLOS would be the basis upon which those claims could be made.

---

1   "South China Sea: Tribunal backs case against China brought by Philippines," BBC, July 12, 2016, <http://www.bbc.com/news/world-asia-china-36771749>.

rights than the foregoing conclusion might initially suggest,"[2] because China could still claim the maritime zones provided for in UNCLOS from any land territory in the South China Sea over which it does have sovereignty. In other words, it was inaccurate for the BBC to say that the Tribunal had "ruled against Chinese claims to rights in the South China Sea"; on the contrary, it ruled that China did have such rights to the extent that it has sovereignty over land territory in the South China Sea.

Maritime Delimitation

It is important to note that one of the optional exclusions from compulsory jurisdiction exercised by China is often described as "maritime (or sea) boundary delimitation", and the Tribunal in its latest Award uses this phrase.[3] However, more properly the exclusion is of any dispute concerning the interpretation or application of the provisions in UNCLOS concerning maritime delimitation.[4] This is important because there may be a dispute about whether those articles apply at all, and not just about the actual drawing of a line on a map. Thus, the articles only apply where States have opposite or adjacent coasts, and there could be a dispute about whether two States do have indeed such coasts. For example, in the Award on the Merits the Tribunal finds that Scarborough Shoal is a "rock"[5] and therefore generates a twelve nautical mile territorial sea, but not an exclusive economic zone or a continental shelf. However, the necessary implication of the Tribunal's finding is that the Philippines and China do not have opposite coasts in that area for the purpose of delimiting their exclusive economic zones and continental shelf; but this raises a question concerning the application of the UNCLOS articles on delimitation of the exclusive economic zone and the continental shelf, a question which is of course hotly disputed. It is submitted therefore that the questions relating to the status of the various features in the South China Sea involve "disputes concerning the interpretation or application of articles 15, 74 and 83" of UNCLOS and thus fall within the

> The only question which the Tribunal could consider was whether by acceding to UNCLOS China could thereafter claim solely those maritime zones provided for by UNCLOS.

---

2   Award, para. 263.

3   Award, paras. 6 and 204; see also Award on Jurisdiction and Admissibility, para. 155.

4   Article 298(1)(a)(i) of UNCLOS, the relevant part of which reads: "disputes concerning the interpretation or application of articles 15, 74 and 83 relating to sea boundary delimitation"; Articles 15, 74 and 83 deal, respectively, with the delimitation of the territorial sea, the exclusive economic zone and the continental shelf.

5   Award, para. 554.

optional exclusion of jurisdiction which China has exercised; it follows that the Tribunal had no jurisdiction to consider these questions.

Rocks and Islands

Turning now from these procedural questions to the substantive issues discussed in the Award, for

> The necessary implication of the Tribunal's finding is that the Philippines and China do not have opposite coasts in that area for the purpose of delimiting their exclusive economic zones and continental shelf; but this raises a question concerning the application of the UNCLOS articles on delimitation of the exclusive economic zone and the continental shelf, a question which is of course hotly disputed.

the purposes of this paper, the writer will confine his comments to four significant issues. The first is that the Tribunal devotes considerable space to a question which is one of the thorniest in the international law of the sea, namely, when is an island to be treated as a "rock" not being capable of sustaining human habitation or economic life of its own and thus as not being capable of generating an exclusive economic zone or a continental shelf. On two occasions, the International Court of Justice has passed up an opportunity to elucidate this question;[6] the Tribunal, however, engages in a very lengthy textual analysis of

the relevant provision in UNCLOS. Having done so, it says that it will then consider the relevant State practice but signally fails to do so.[7] This is disappointing because there is extensive practice, and at the least, an analysis of this practice would have shed light upon how States believe that the relevant provisions of UNCLOS should be interpreted. As it is, it would seem at first glance that the Tribunal's interpretation is a very narrow one which does not reflect State practice. In particular, the Tribunal finds that Itu Aba (or Taiping in Chinese), which has been occupied by several hundred members of the Taiwanese armed forces for around sixty years, is a "rock" which cannot sustain human habitation. This is a surprising conclusion and one which could have serious implications for the claims to maritime zones made by a number of other States.

Offshore Archipelagos

Second, the Tribunal takes a statement by the Chinese Government as meaning that it might draw straight baselines around the Spratly Islands and goes on to consider whether this would be legitimate; it does so even though the question is as at present hypothetical since straight baselines have not been drawn around the Spratly Islands[8]. In fact, a number of major maritime nations, including Denmark, France, Norway, Portugal, Spain and the United Kingdom, have drawn straight baselines around offshore archipelagos, like the Spratlys, but it appears that this practice is not accepted by the United States (who are of course not a party to UNCLOS). Leaving aside whether it was appropriate for the Tribunal to make a general pronouncement of an international legal position on the basis of a hypothetical situation, it seems difficult to accept

---

6 *Romania v. Ukraine*, ICJ Reports 2009, para. 187; *Nicaragua v. Colombia*, ICJ Reports 2012, para. 180.

7 Award, paras. 552–3.

8 Award, paras. 573–6.

that the Tribunal should have stated baldly that it would not be compatible with UNCLOS to draw straight baselines around archipelagos, without having fully explored the significant State practice to the contrary.

A "Vested Right" to Fish

Third, the Tribunal states that Filipino fishermen have a "vested right" to fish in the territorial waters of Scarborough Shoal, apparently because they have traditionally done so. The Tribunal cites no precedent for this view nor any relevant State practice, and it seems highly dubious. There is nothing in UNCLOS to support it, and it would mean oddly that foreign fishermen would have

is the first time that an international judicial body has applied this principle *ex post facto* so as to find a breach of international law. Furthermore, since China maintains that it has sovereignty over the features where these activities took place and, as indicated above, the Tribunal accepted that it had no jurisdiction to decide on the sovereignty of those features, the effect of the Tribunal's decision in this respect could be seen as a serious inhibition of the activities of a sovereign State over its own territory.

The Future

As has been stated, the Tribunal leaves unresolved the fundamental issue of the sovereignty

The questions relating to the status of the various features in the South China Sea involve "disputes concerning the interpretation or application of articles 15, 74 and 83" of UNCLOS and thus fall within the optional exclusion of jurisdiction which China has exercised; it follows that the Tribunal had no jurisdiction to consider these questions.

greater rights in a coastal State's territorial waters than in that State's exclusive economic zone, where Article 62 of UNCLOS makes clear that foreign fishermen have no right to fish.

Aggravating the Dispute

The final substantive issue to be mentioned here is the finding of the Tribunal that China has aggravated the dispute through its dredging and construction activities in the South China Sea. This is problematic in a number of respects. First, the legal precedents relied upon by the Tribunal all relate to the situation where a judicial body has been seized of a dispute and has been asked to indicate provisional measures as to the conduct of the parties pending the body's resolution of the dispute. As far as the author is aware, this

over the land features in the South China Sea. It follows therefore that sooner or later the Philippines and China, and indeed the other States bordering the South China Sea, will have to reopen discussions with a view to reaching an accommodation between them, which will enable cooperation to take place in the South China Sea. Ultimately, cooperation between the various States must of course be the way forward, a course which indeed UNCLOS encourages upon the States surrounding a semi-enclosed sea, like the South China Sea. Given this, it is questionable how helpful the existence of these proceedings has been in furthering this aim. Nevertheless, it is heartening to note that according to media reports both China and the Philippines have indicated a willingness to begin discussions about cooperation in the South China Sea.

Joint Statement of July 25, 2016

In particular, on July 25, 2016, only thirteen days after the Award was published, the Foreign Ministers of China and the ASEAN States signed a Joint Statement on the Full and Effective Implementation of the Declaration on the Conduct of Parties in the South China Sea, in which they recommitted themselves to the same undertakings

> The Tribunal's interpretation is a very narrow one which does not reflect State practice. In particular, the Tribunal finds that Itu Aba (or Taiping in Chinese), which has been occupied by several hundred members of the Taiwanese armed forces for around sixty years, is a "rock" which cannot sustain human habitation. This is a surprising conclusion and one which could have serious implications for the claims to maritime zones made by a number of other States.

as were made in that declaration (DOC) signed in 2002,[9] including "working substantively towards the early adoption of a Code of Conduct in the South China Sea (COC) based on consensus."[10] On the day of the meeting at which the Joint Statement was signed, ASEAN was reported as saying that it "believes that the full and effective implementation of the DOC is vital to maintaining

peace and stability in the region, and encourages countries concerned to handle the differences peacefully in constructive ways and through dialogue and consultation."[11]

It is very interesting that the Chinese and ASEAN Foreign Ministers recommitted themselves to the terms of the DOC in this way so shortly after the Award had been made by the Tribunal. This is particularly so since, in the Award on Jurisdiction and Admissibility, the Tribunal seemed in effect to deny the DOC any efficacy and in doing so made a number of comments on the DOC which seem questionable. In particular, when applying international law rules concerning estoppel, under which a State cannot resile from a representation if it has been relied upon by another State, the Tribunal said that the Philippines did not make a representation when signing the DOC,[12] a view which seems difficult to understand. One wonders whether an international judicial body would take the same view when the undertakings in the DOC have been repeated so shortly after the Tribunal's final Award.

Possible Implementation of Award

In particular, it is relevant that, under Article 12 of Annex VII of UNCLOS, it is the Tribunal which has the competence to decide "any controversy ... as regards the interpretation or manner of implementation of the award". This would seem to encompass, for example, a possible application by the Philippines to seek compensation for

9 "Declaration on the Conduct of Parties in the South China Sea," Foreign Ministers of ASEAN and the People's Republic of China, November 4, 2002, <https://cil.nus.edu.sg/rp/pdf/2002%20Declaration%20on%20the%20Conduct%20of%20Parties%20in%20the%20South%20China%20Sea-pdf.pdf>.

10 "Joint Statement of the Foreign Ministers of ASEAN Member States and China on the Full and Effective Implementation of the Declaration on the Conduct of Parties in the South China Sea," Association of Southeast Asian Nations, July 25, 2016, <http://asean.org/storage/2016/07/Joint-Statement-on-the-full-and-effective-implementation-of-the-DOC-FINAL.pdf>.

11 Wang Yi, "Step Towards a Closer China-ASEAN Community of Common Destiny," Ministry of Foreign Affairs, People's Republic of China, July 26, 2016, <http://www.fmprc.gov.cn/mfa_eng/zxxx_662805/t1384891.shtml>.

12 Award on Jurisdiction and Admissibility, para. 251.

the breaches of international law which the Tribunal has alleged. However, it must be questioned whether the signature of this Joint Statement, reiterating the undertaking to resolve disputes by bilateral means, would bar any such application by the Philippines.

The Permanent Members

Finally, it is noteworthy that the most recent three cases under Annex VII of UNCLOS have all involved permanent members of the United Nations Security Council, and in two of those cases, the defendant State did not participate in the proceedings, namely, China in these proceedings and Russia in the *Arctic Sunrise* case. In the third, the Chagos Marine Protected Area arbitration case brought against the United Kingdom by Mauritius, the United Kingdom did appear, even though the true aim of Mauritius in instituting

It seems difficult to accept that the Tribunal should have stated baldly that it would not be compatible with UNCLOS to draw straight baselines around archipelagos, without having fully explored the significant State practice to the contrary.

the arbitration was to challenge the United Kingdom's sovereignty over British Indian Ocean Territory, a device which the Tribunal saw through.[13] In an earlier period, the other two permanent members refused to appear in cases brought against them before the International Court of Justice, namely, the United States in the 1986 Nicaragua v. United States arbitration case regarding military and paramilitary activities and France in the New Zealand v. France arbitration case regarding nuclear tests. Neither of them has since then accepted the compulsory jurisdiction of the ICJ. The lack of confidence of the permanent members in international judicial dispute settlement procedures is quite striking and may be an issue which those who seek to promote the wider use of such procedures need to consider.

Conclusion

The Tribunal's Award will no doubt be much debated both by politicians as well as by international lawyers. Much of the difficulty with the Award lies in the fact that the key, underlying issue, sov-

---

13 Award in the Matter of the Chagos Marine Protected Area Arbitration, Permanent Court of Arbitration, March 18, 2015, paras. 212 and 221, <http://www.pcacases.com/pcadocs/MU-UK%2020150318%20Award.pdf>.

ereignty over the land features in the South China Sea, was outside the Tribunal's jurisdiction. Furthermore, doubts about whether decisions on the status of the features in the South China Sea lay within the jurisdiction of the Tribunal were only enhanced by the manner in which the Tribunal dealt with this question. In addition, at least three of the key legal conclusions reached by the Tribunal do not reflect State practice and may therefore be of concern to other States. For the future it seems inevitable that there will have to be negotiations between the

This is the first time that an international judicial body has applied this principle *ex post facto* so as to find a breach of international law.

relevant parties and one hopes that this might prove possible. Finally, the case represents a further example of a Permanent Member of the Security Council declining to appear before an international court or tribunal.

Chris Whomersley, CMG, has recently retired as Deputy Legal Adviser in the United Kingdom's Foreign & Commonwealth Office after a career spanning thirty-six years and covering many areas of international law. He spent a number of years dealing with aviation issues, and he has been involved in the Channel Tunnel project since its inception. For the last ten years, he was responsible for policy on international law of the sea. This included dealing with these issues both multilaterally and bilaterally, as well as in the European Union. He led the United Kingdom delegations in a number of bilateral negotiations on maritime delimitation. He was also the leader of the UK delegation to the International Seabed Authority, and was a member of its Finance Committee. Recently, he was responsible for the arrangements relating to the declaration of an Exclusive Economic Zone around the United Kingdom, as well as for the law updating UK legislation on deep sea mining. In June 2014 he was honoured by HM The Queen for his services to international law.

www.ingramcontent.com/pod-product-compliance
Lightning Source LLC
Chambersburg PA
CBHW051334200326
41519CB00026B/7427